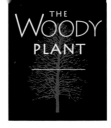

THE
WOODY
PLANT

Trees and Shrubs for Foliage

Glyn Church

Photographs Pat Greenfield

FIREFLY BOOKS

A FIREFLY BOOK

Published by Firefly Books Ltd. 2002

Originated in 2002 by David Bateman Ltd.,
30 Tarndale Grove, Albany, Auckland, New Zealand

First Printing

National Library of Canada Cataloguing in Publication Data

Church, Glyn
    Trees and shrubs for foliage
(Woody plant series)
Includes bibliographical references and index.
ISBN 1-55297-629-7 (bound)
ISBN 1-55297-628-9 (pbk.)
1. Ornamental trees. 2. Ornamental shrubs. 3. Foliage.
I. Greenfield, Pat II. Title. III. Title: Foliage. IV. Series: Church, Glyn. Woody plant series.

SB435.C483 2002   635.9'771   C2001-903295-1

Publisher Cataloging-in-Publication Data (U.S.)

Church, Glyn.
    Trees and shrubs for foliage / Glyn Church ; photographs by Pat Greenfield. – 1ˢᵗ ed.
[160] p. : col. photos., maps ; cm. (Woody Plants)
Includes bibliographic references and index.
Summary: An illustrated gardening guide to over 100 trees and shrubs selected for their foliage.
ISBN: 1-55297-629-7
ISBN: 1-55297-628-9 (pbk.)
1. Woody plants. 2. Ornamental shrubs. 3. Ornamental trees.
I. Greenfield, Pat. II. Title. III. Series.
635.976 21   CIP SB435.5.C58   2002

Published in Canada in 2002 by
Firefly Books Ltd.
3680 Victoria Park Avenue
Willowdale, Ontario
M2H 3K1

Published in the United States in 2002 by
Firefly Books (U.S.) Inc.
P.O. Box 1338, Ellicott Station
Buffalo, New York
14205

Printed in Hong Kong through Colorcraft Ltd.

Above: *Nyssa sinensis*

Opposite top right: *Daphniphyllum macropodum*

Opposite bottom: *Liriodendron tulipifera* fall color

Page 1: *Quercus palustris*

Pages 2 and 3: Eastwoodhill Arboretum, New Zealand

Contents

Introduction

If you think foliage is "just there" and unimportant, then close your eyes and imagine a garden, any garden—it may be yours or a friend's or perhaps the local park. Now imagine that same garden with every plant having the same leaf. I think most of us would give up gardening if that were the case. We somehow imagine that a garden is based on colorful flowers, and certainly they are the highlights, but they are for the most part very short-lived and we are left with the foliage for the remainder of the season.

Foliage gives us shape and texture as well as color. It is the vital contrast we need to make a garden the vibrant place that it is. In fact, it is possible to have a beautiful garden based entirely on leaves and foliage alone, but you would be hard-pressed to make an attractive garden if all your flowering plants had identical leaves.

The leaves are often the backdrop for the flowers and although the foliage sometimes masks them, the greenery usually helps to highlight them.

Foliage grows on you. When you start gardening you are impressed with big, colorful flowers and, as time goes on, you become more intrigued by smaller and more subtle blooms. Finally, you become fascinated by leaf shape and form. You know you have become a plant fanatic when you get excited about branches and trunks and the sunlight on bark and stems.

A woody plant is one with a permanent woody structure. Some woody plants die back to some extent in the winter but there is always some woody part visible throughout the year. My own garden has well over 2,000 different woody plants, and many of the photographs in this book were taken there. I have used this garden and also my experience of growing plants in windy, dry or cold climates to explain the likes and dislikes of the plants. Zones are given to show how cold a climate a plant will cope with, but they are only a guide. When a plant does not like warm or hot regions, as is the case with many *Abies*, I have included an upper as well as a lower limit, for example, zones 5 to 8. If there is no upper zone given, the plant will grow to zone 10. Its habit, however, may be slightly different in these regions, e.g. lack of fall color.

Left: *Lindera obtusiloba* fall color. Opposite: Cornus florida 'Rainbow'. Below left: *Acer palmatum*

It is very hard to generalize about the climate a plant needs in order to thrive. Within any region and even within a garden there are microclimates—places that are warmer or colder than the surrounding area. Even planting a shrub next to a wall where it gets the reflected heat can make the difference between success and failure. Similarly with soil, we can improve it and irrigate if necessary. The type of soil is critical to the well-being of some plants and irrelevant to others. Over the years I have gardened on heavy clay soils with a pH of 7.0, on rocky soil with a pH of 6.0, and currently a free-draining acidic loam of pH 5–6, so I have used my experience regarding soil types when writing the plant descriptions.

When you see how many times the English botanist Ernest Wilson (1876–1930) is mentioned, you will think I set out to write this as a tribute to him. That was not my intention: I simply chose plants I thought were great foliage plants and it just so happens he introduced most of them. In terms of bringing new plants into cultivation, he was the most successful plant hunter in history.

Because space is restricted, I tried to find my favorite genera for foliage and, as they say, "one man's meat is another man's poison," so some of your favorites may have been omitted. I genuinely like all the plants in this book. Although the book is primarily about foliage, if the plant has fabulous berries or bark then I have described them, too.

I have also included plants that may have naturalized in your region. The more I travel the more I find that what is regarded in one district as a weed is a treasure somewhere else. Sometimes this is based on the plant actually self-perpetuating in that region and sometimes it is just plain bias against a certain plant or group of plants.

I hope the selection of plants presented provides interest and variety, and that the ones you choose grow well for you.

Pat Greenfield's photographs will, I am sure, inspire you and may persuade you to look at foliage in a new light. My mission is to introduce you to some new plants and look at some familiar plants in a new way. Pat's mission is to show leaves and foliage using light—you could say in a new light.

How to use this book

The plants presented in this book are organised alphabetically by genus. If you know the common name only, you can find the botanical name entry through the index, where both botanical and common names are listed.

Each entry has a variety of information laid out in the format illustrated below, so you can quickly find what you need to know about a particular plant. The text includes not only notes on cultivation, but anecdotes and historical information, making this a fascinating book to browse through.

The table at the back of the book will help you to find plants by hardiness zone, fall color and size, as well as those native to North America. An extensive glossary covers the botanical terms used.

Genus

Common name

Family
Taxonomic grouping of genera to which this genus belongs.

Elaeagnus

THORNY ELAEAGNUS
Elaeagnaceae

*E*laeagnus is a large genus of plants with a widespread distribution from southern Europe through to Asia and over to North America. Some are deciduous while others are super-hardy evergreens, though few of them have enough merit to be brought into our gardens.

The most useful aspect of these plants is the wind-hardiness of *E. pungens* and *E. macrophylla* and the dazzling variegated leaf forms of *E. pungens* and *E.* x *ebbingei*.

Elaeagnus = wild olive (from Greek *elaeagnos*, in reference to the fruits).

Species name

Common name
These names vary from place to place. To be sure of what you are buying, always check the species name.

Elaeagnus angustifolia
OLEASTER OR RUSSIAN OLIVE
Oleaster makes a large deciduous shrub or small tree with a billowy habit, reddish stems and hidden spines. The tiny, fragrant, creamy yellow flowers appear in summertime. However, the prime reason for growing this is the silvery willow-like leaves, and it is often confused with a *Pyrus salicifolia*. It is found native in southern Europe to central Asia. Height x width 20 ft (6 m). ZONE 3.

'**Quicksilver**' is an excellent silvery leaf form grown for its consistency. Height x width 12 ft (4 m).

Angustifolia = narrow leaf.

Cultivar or form
Cultivated variety, usually bred but can be natural variety, then often called "sport." Can only be propagated true from cuttings.

Leaf shape
Gives a general indication only of the leaf shape of the genus. For more detail see the description notes in the text.

Description of genus

Meaning of botanical name

Species description and cultivation notes

Hardiness zone
These zones are guides only (see page 9). The zone range is given at the end of each species entry. If no upper limit is given, the plants will grow to zone 10, though possibly with some change to habit, e.g., some deciduous trees can become semi-evergreen. Unless otherwise stated, cultivars grow in the same zone range as the species.

Approximation of size
Height and width can be an approximation only as it varies enormously depending on your climate. If you are concerned about something growing too big, check with a local garden center to find out how they grow in your area.

Leaf shapes

Lance-shaped, lanceolate   Oval   Ovate   Rounded   Heart-shaped   Palmate lobed   Trifoliate

Hardiness zone map

This map has been prepared to agree with a system of plant hardiness zones that has been accepted as an international standard and range from 1 to 11. It shows the minimum winter temperatures that can be expected on average in different regions. Where a zone number has been given, the number corresponds with a zone shown here. That number indicates the coldest areas in which the particular plant is likely to survive through an average winter. Note that these are not necessarily the areas in which it will grow best. Because the zone number refers to the minimum temperatures, a plant given zone 7, for example, will obviously grow perfectly well in zone 8, but not in zone 6. Plants grown in a zone considerably higher than the zone with the minimum winter temperature in which they will survive might well grow but they are likely to behave differently. Note also that some readers may find the numbers a little conservative; we felt it best to err on the side of caution.

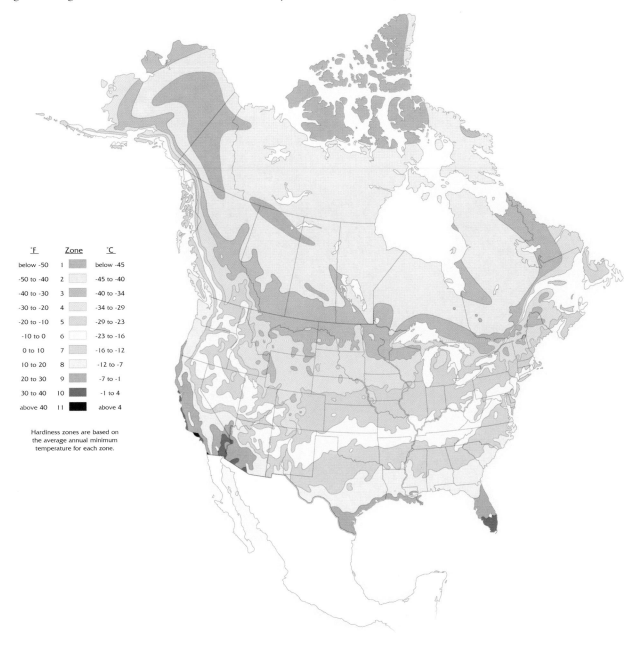

°F	Zone	°C
below -50	1	below -45
-50 to -40	2	-45 to -40
-40 to -30	3	-40 to -34
-30 to -20	4	-34 to -29
-20 to -10	5	-29 to -23
-10 to 0	6	-23 to -16
0 to 10	7	-16 to -12
10 to 20	8	-12 to -7
20 to 30	9	-7 to -1
30 to 40	10	-1 to 4
above 40	11	above 4

Hardiness zones are based on the average annual minimum temperature for each zone.

5-palmate, digitate   Pinnatified   Pinnate   Bipinnate   Conifer: comb-like   Conifer: needle-like   Conifer: scale-like

Abies

FIR
Pinaceae

The noble *Abies* are one of the most familiar plants of the Northern Hemisphere. Also known as fir trees, they love the cold climates found nearer the Arctic Circle or high up on mountainsides.

Even if you have never seen *Abies*, you have almost certainly smelled them. The sticky sap or gum from the trees is frequently used in toiletries and pharmaceutical products. It is used to create a fresh, tangy pungence and remind us of cool, natural forests.

The trees detest pollution, and acidic rain is devastating *Abies* forests in northeastern U.S.A., Europe and China. There are vast areas on the tops of the Appalachians where all the *Abies* forests have died, leaving a bleak, deserted landscape.

Like many mountain-dwellers, *Abies* are used to cold and battering winds: they thrive in cooler areas. In warmer areas they are attacked by root rot, aphids and other bugs to such an extent that it is difficult to keep them alive.

If you live in a warm climate, try *Abies firma* or the *Abies* from Central America and Mexico, such as *A. vejari*. These are more suited to warmer zones.

In a garden setting, *Abies* thrive in good, deep soil but in the wild seem to cope with tough, rocky, mountainous conditions. Avoid crowding them, as the joy of an *Abies* is its symmetrical shape. Best in an open, sunny situation, they tend to look sparse and unloved in a shady place. It is their neat, conical appearance that makes them so appealing. They have the classic Christmas tree shape, with the horizontal branches arranged in whorls or circles around the trunk.

Even the stems are tidy, as they remain smooth when the needles drop—this is one of the two easy ways to tell *Abies* from *Picea* or spruces. *Abies* have smooth stems while *Picea* have little pegs left where the needles were attached. It is easy to remember as piceas have "pegs," therefore "p" for pegs and "p" for piceas. Also, on older plants, *Abies* cones sit upright on top of the branches while *Picea* cones hang down or are pendulous. Thus "p" for pendulous and "p" for piceas. Some *Abies* have fantastically colored cones in shades of blue and purple. These cones break up or disintegrate on the tree rather than fall intact, as do the cones of pines and piceas.

Abies = pine trees.

Abies alba
EUROPEAN SILVER FIR

Abies alba is a common tree in the mountains of Europe, becoming a very large tree in time, but fairly slow-growing in gardens. It has a neat, pyramid shape when young, and smooth, gray bark. Although hardy to zone 5 in cold regions, it is often tempted into growth too soon in mild climates and then hit by late frosts. The tree enjoys a moist climate and also tolerates shade. Height 80–100 ft (25–30 m) x width 12–20 ft (4–6 m). ZONES 5 TO 8.

Alba = white (refers to the silver reverse on the dark leaves).

Abies balsamea
BALSAM FIR OR BALM OF GILEAD

A tough, cold-hardy, conical tree from eastern Canada and U.S.A., but it is not happy growing in mild regions. It tolerates cold, damp and even swampy places. The dark green leaves emit a

Above: *Abies concolor* 'Candicans'
Left: *Abies concolor* 'Candicans' with *Carya illinoinensis*.

greens, and the amazing purple cones sitting upright on the branches. It was found in China by Père Paul Farges (1844–1912), and successfully introduced to Western gardens by E. H. Wilson (1876–1930) at the beginning of the 20th century. Height 30–50 ft (10–15 m) x width 10–12 ft (3–4 m). ZONE 5 OR 6.

Abies firma
JAPANESE FIR

This tree may not be as neat or as formal as most *Abies*, but it does have one thing in its favor, namely its willingness to grow in warmer, moist climates. Most firs hate humidity, but this one will cope with warm, wet summers. Dark green, long needles give it the characteristic Christmas tree look. Height 30–50 ft (10–15 m) x width 10–12 ft (3–4 m). ZONE 7.

Firma = firm, stout or durable.

Abies grandis
GRAND FIR OR GIANT FIR

This fir from western U.S.A. is appropriately named, as it is one of the largest and most beautiful of all trees. *Abies grandis* is a typical, upright Christmas tree shape with upswept branch tips when young. Older trees have a more billowy shape and smooth trunks with interesting crack patterns. In a garden setting it prefers a deep soil, high rainfall and plenty of shelter, though in the wild it puts up with less than ideal conditions. Shiny, dark green leaves are nicely scented and the contrast between the older dark leaves and the bright, soft green new growth is stunning. Height 80–200 ft (25–60 m) x width 15–25 ft (5–8 m). ZONE 5 OR 6.

Grandis = grand or magnificent.

Abies holophylla
MANCHURIAN FIR

Abies holophylla forms a huge, imposing tree in the mountains of Korea and northern China. The long, dark green leaves seem to sit on top of the stems. In a garden situation it is one of the most desirable firs, with a tidy structure and slow growth habit. It tends to keep the older leaves longer than many *Abies*, as the name *holophylla* suggests. Height 30–60 ft (10–20 m) x width 15–20 ft (5–6 m). ZONE 5.

Holophylla = totally covered in leaves (*holo* = all, whole or covered; *phylla* = leaf).

strong balsam scent that is extracted for cosmetics and fragrances. Height 50 ft (15 m) x width 15 ft (5 m). ZONES 3 TO 9.

There are several dwarf forms ideal for rockery gardens, including **'Nana'** and **'Hudsonia'**. Both height 2 ft (60 cm) x width 3 ft (90 cm).

Abies concolor
WHITE FIR

This is a striking tree with vivid, blue-gray foliage, especially on the form known as **'Candicans'**. Very long needles can be dark green on some clones, while the blue-gray forms are worthy of a place in any garden. The blue-gray effect is created by a white luster that rubs off in your hand. Being a native of southwestern U.S.A. and Mexico it thrives on heat and drought, and resents wet summers. Height 80–130 ft (25–40 m) x width 15–22 ft (5–7 m). ZONES 3 TO 8.

Abies concolor lowiana is much hardier, growing to ZONE 3. Same height and width as *A. concolor*.

Concolor = one color.

Abies fargesii, syn A. sutchuenensis
FARGES FIR

Abies fargesii is a huge, upright tree in the wild, but in cultivation it forms a medium-sized tree with a very formal shape. The highlights are the lovely, soft, new growth in spring in lush, rich

Far right: *Abies fargesii* with spring growth and purple cone.

Above left: *Abies koreana*
Above right: *Abies nordmanniana*

acidic soil and a cool, moist climate. Height 80–120 ft (25–35 m) x width 15–20 ft (5–6 m). ZONES 6 TO 8.

Magnifica = magnificent.

Above: *Abies vejari,* with *Pinus koraiensis* at front right.

Abies koreana
KOREAN FIR

This is an ideal garden plant because of its neat habit and slow growth rate. Leaves appear dark green from above, but a slight breeze or different angle enhances the bluish white effect found by viewing from below. Stunning, purple cones appear on quite young plants. It seems to endure pollution better than most. Height 30 ft (10 m) x width 20 ft (6 m). ZONE 5 OR 6.

Koreana = Korea.

Abies lasiocarpa
SUBALPINE FIR

Abies lasiocarpa forms a narrow, upright tree with distinct gray-green leaves. As the common name suggests, it needs cold climates to perform well. It tolerates dry as well as cold but is not easy to grow in warm, moist climes. This plant grows naturally from Alaska down to Mexico. Height 90 ft (25 m) x width 10–12 ft (3–4 m). ZONES 5 TO 6.

Lasiocarpa = hairy or woolly fruits.

Abies lasiocarpa var arizonica 'Compacta'
Lovely bluish gray leaves. Better suited to gardens with its slower growth rate. Height 10–15 ft (3–5 m) x width 6–10 ft (2–3 m).

Abies magnifica
CALIFORNIA RED FIR

A tall, slender tree from the mountains of northern California and Oregon. The long, curved, blue-gray leaves make this one of the most attractive of the genus and the way they sit on top of the stems is an unusual trait shared by *Abies procera*. The tree needs an

Abies nordmanniana
CAUCASIAN FIR

This is a very ornamental tree at any age. Young trees are tidy and dense with shiny green leaves. Older trees are stately, with drooping tips to the horizontal branches. It grows best in regions with cool winters and appears to cope well with dry summers. It is a good first-choice *Abies* for gardeners, being easier to grow than most species. The tree is from Turkey, and named after its discoverer, Alexander von Nordmann (1843–1866), a professor of zoology. Height 130 ft (40 m) x width 20 ft (6 m). ZONES 4 TO 8.

Abies procera, syn A. nobilis
NOBLE FIR

Abies procera has a similar leaf pattern to *A. magnifica*, with the leaves sitting on top of the stems, but the tree has a more spreading habit. It has a typical, upswept, Christmas tree shape with very big cones, and the stems packed with bluish gray leaves. It likes a cool, moist climate and good, deep soil. *Abies procera* is found naturally in Oregon and Washington and is one of the many fine conifers discovered by David Douglas (1799–1834) on his travels through the U.S.A. Douglas was an intrepid Scottish explorer who spent the last ten years of his life scouring the "new continent" for useful plants. Height 80–150 ft (25–45 m) x width 20–28 ft (6–9 m). ZONE 5 OR 6.

Procera = tall or slender.

Abies procera 'Glauca'
This has attractive, bright blue leaves. Height 50 ft (15 m) x width 20 ft (6 m). There is also a prostrate form, **'Glauca Prostrata'**, which is grown as a novelty.

Abies veitchii
VEITCH FIR

A small Japanese fir, its densely packed leaves turn up to reveal the white undersides. Like *Abies koreana*, it is more willing to grow in a polluted atmosphere than most of its cousins. It was discovered on Mount Fuji, Japan, by John Gould Veitch (1839–1870) in 1860. A member of the famous Veitch Nursery in England, he traveled to Japan in search of new garden plants. Height 50–70 ft (15–20 m) x width 12–20 ft (4–6 m). ZONES 3 TO 8.

Abies vejari
VEJAR FIR

This Mexican species is valuable for gardeners in warmer climates who fancy an *Abies* but have trouble growing the cooler-climate versions. The tree has a structured, open habit with whorls of branches and large gaps between each tier. The dark green leaves are held tightly to the stems, adding to the tidy, open look of the tree. It is happy in wet or dry conditions and tolerates alkaline and extremely acidic soils. Height 30–70 ft (10–20 m) x width 10–15 ft (3–5 m). ZONE 7 OR 8.

Vejari = place in Mexico.

Left: *Abies veitchii* (top) with *Juniperus taxifolia*.
Below: *Abies procera* 'Glauca Prostrata'

Acer

MAPLE
Aceraceae

Maples—it would be impossible to have a collection of plants grown for their leaves without including them. They are the epitome of garden-worthy trees and shrubs grown for their foliage.

Maples vary from small, bushy, Japanese varieties with soft, ferny foliage, through to forest giants like sycamore and red maple. One characteristic of maples is that their leaves are all opposite. We tend to think of maples as hardy, deciduous trees and shrubs, and most of them do fit into this category. However, there are numerous evergreen maples from the warmer parts of Asia. These evergreen types are mostly tender, needing warmer zones.

It is difficult to generalize about such a large and diverse genus, but the following should be a good guide to these trees. A sheltered site is a prerequisite, as few maples will thrive in a constantly windy situation. A sunny site is essential for good health and general well-being. Maples are not too fussy about soil as long as it is well-drained and, while most prefer acidic or neutral soils, many will cope with alkaline clays.

Maples are ideal landscape trees as you can shift them at virtually any size or age without too much of a setback in growth. They are grown primarily for their ornate leaves and in many cases for their scintillating fall colors. Maples have become a standby for parks and gardens around the world, and are now a part of our lives to such an extent it is hard to imagine our gardens without them.

Pests and diseases are limited to the occasional attack by aphids and perhaps some root rot in humid regions. There is a new black stem fungus, a form of *Verticillium* wilt, which can kill or deform the smaller species.

Acer = hard or sharp (referring to the Roman use of maple wood for lances and spears).

Acer buergerianum, syn *A. trifidum*
TRIDENT MAPLE

When you see this plant in gardens it is a small, rounded tree. In the wild it is much taller, but its slow-growing nature means that we can accommodate it in a home setting. Move close and you will see the unusual hammered bark and knobbly, grooved stems. The tree almost looks as if it is made of stone rather than wood, and the timber is rock-hard and heavy. The small, shiny leaves have three points like a trident and they seem to cling tightly to the branches. This is borne out come fall time when the yellow, gold and orange leaves seem reluctant to drop. The new spring leaves, by contrast, are very pale green—even yellow—creating a very exciting seasonal effect. It is a good choice for windier places than you would normally choose for a maple. *Acer buergerianum* is

Below: *Acer henryi*

A. *davidii* is named after Père Armand David (1826–1900), who went to China as a missionary in 1862 and spent the next 12 years cataloging new plants and animals. Height and width 50 ft (15 m). ZONES 5 TO 7.

There are several named forms. **'Ernest Wilson'** has pale green leaves that are orange in the fall. Height 25 ft (8 m) x width 30 ft (10 m). **'George Forrest'** has an attractive trunk and dark leaves with red petioles, but the fall color is not the best. Height 40 ft (12 m) x width 15 ft (5 m).

A. morrisonense from Taiwan and **A. pensylvanicum** from eastern U.S.A. are similar.

Acer griseum
PAPERBARK MAPLE

Mention *Acer griseum* to any keen gardener and they picture shiny, mahogany trunks with reels of paper-thin bark peeling prettily away from the smooth, round branches. Some portions of young stems are dark purple, almost black. These trunks are fabulous on any day of the year but excel themselves when wet with rain or backlit with sunlight. You simply have to have one. Like *A. davidii*, the trunks are not the only reason for possessing one. The trifoliate, slightly hairy leaves are pretty through the summer. They astonish by arriving so late in spring, but it is in fall when they bless us with a fantastic display of color. Warm orange and tan with a sprinkling of red contrasting with the dark brown trunks makes it an essential plant for any sheltered garden. Other attractive features are that it is a small tree, slow-growing, and a strong contender for a place in a suburban garden. It is easy to grow from cold zone 4 to warm zone 10. *A. griseum* was collected in central China in 1901 by Ernest Wilson. Height x width 30 ft (10 m). ZONES 4 TO 9.

Griseum = gray (referring to the soft, gray hairs on the surface of the leaves).

Acer henryi, syn A. cissifolium subsp henryi

This is a small tree with a "Boston Ivy" look about it. The leaf is divided into three leaflets (trifoliate). Soft, bronzy new growth develops into a subtle gray-green. The leaves are strongly serrated (sawtooth-edged), and have a prominent red petiole or leaf stalk. They can be 6 in (15 cm) long and yet give the impression of being a small, delicate leaf. Leaves are opposite along distinctive green stems turning soft brown.

This species forms an upright tree with a series of closely packed, vertical branches. Trees with narrow angles where the branches and trunk meet are prone to splitting in strong winds. The wider the angle, the stronger it will be. Upright, multi-trunked trees are more likely to split when the branches expand and push each other apart.

The fall colors can be sizzling reds and golds. *Acer henryi* is one of the many trees neglected by the nursery industry around the world and so rarely available, yet it will easily fit into most suburban gardens.

This species was named after Augustine Henry who first discovered the plant in central China in 1889. Henry was an Irish doctor whose passion was plant collecting. Based in China for nearly twenty years from 1880, he sent thousands of dried plant specimens as well as seeds to Kew Gardens, London. Many of his plant discoveries were later introduced into cultivation by E. H. Wilson, including *Acer henryi* in 1903. Height 25 ft (8 m) x width 30 ft (10 m). It is perfectly hardy and capable of growing in most conditions. ZONE 4.

Acer cissifolium is a very similar species from Japan.

Above: *Acer griseum*

named after Heinrich Burger (1806–1858), a German naturalist who spent time collecting in Japan. The tree is from Korea and eastern China. Height 30 ft (10 m) x width 25 ft (8 m). ZONES 5 TO 9.

Acer davidii
SNAKEBARK MAPLE

Acer davidii is grown primarily for the striated, "snakeskin-bark" trunks, usually seen as gray streaks on a green background but sometimes as red on gray. However, do not overlook the glorious foliage: large, glossy, oval leaves are rich green all summer, often with obvious red petioles. Expect some fine scarlet-reds in the fall. The tree has a narrow, upright habit when young and spreads with age, and it is pruned to emphasize the trunk. It was collected in central China in 1879 by Charles Maries.

Acer negundo

ASH-LEAVED MAPLE, BOX ELDER, MANITOBA MAPLE

This is a very easily grown maple that is exceedingly wind-hardy (most maples hate wind). It is magnanimous in the range of conditions it will abide, including wet clay or rocky and dry soils. Some of the wild forms of this North American plant grow in California and Mexico and so it is able to cope with heat and drought much better than its fellow maples, and yet it is equally at home in a high rainfall area. The yellow fall color is passable, but not as spectacular as most maples.

Although *Acer negundo* grows across an incredible range compared to other maples, it may not thrive everywhere. Check with your local garden supplier or parks department to see whether it flourishes in your region. It does not mind regular or severe pruning should the need ever arise.

It is one of the few maples easily grown from cuttings. No serious pests or diseases are known, but it is prone to dieback if not happy with the given climate.

A very fast-growing tree, it quickly forms a dense mop-top, and is a candidate for anyone needing an "instant tree."

This species was so named by Carl Linnaeus (1707–1778), as the leaf is similar to *Vitex negundo*, a widespread Asiatic plant. Height 50 ft (15 m) x width 30 ft (10 m). ZONE 5.

Negundo = an Indian name for the *Vitex*.

Acer negundo 'Flamingo'

Bright pink new growth opening to green with a white border. Like so many variegated plants, it appreciates a little shade in a hot or dry climate, as it is prone to sun scorch. Height 50 ft (15 m) x width 30 ft (10 m).

Acer negundo 'Kelly's Gold'

This dashing, pure golden-yellow leaf variety is a beacon in any garden. It keeps its color well through summer and does not fade or scorch. Height 50 ft (15 m) x width 30 ft (10 m).

Acer negundo var violaceum

This is a naturally occurring variety, so it is described as var (variety) *violaceum*, rather than the way a cultivar or clone that is found or created in gardens is given a capital letter, as in 'Flamingo'. It has glorious, long, pink tassle flowers in early spring before the leaves, so this is a flowering tree, attractive from quite some distance and very appealing at close quarters. When in flower the whole tree is abuzz with bees. The new growth has a purplish tinge. Height 50 ft (15 m) x width 30 ft (10 m).

Acer palmatum

JAPANESE MAPLE

This small, good-looking mop-headed tree would fit into almost any garden and be deserving of its place, yet we hardly ever see it in species form. There are myriad forms with lacy foliage, ranging in color from soft green through to red and on to deep purple and bronze. These cultivars are propagated by grafting, a time-consuming and highly skilled operation. Because of the slow growth rate and the cost of grafting they are usually expensive plants to buy.

Acer palmatum is easily grown in any soil as long as the drainage is good. It is grown primarily for its delicate leafy mound in summer and scintillating fall colors in combinations of rich reds, purple and orange. It demands adequate shelter and cannot abide wind. Height 25 ft (8 m) x width 30 ft (10 m). Cold winters are not a problem. ZONES 6 TO 9.

Palmatum = hand-like, as in hand or palm.

Acer palmatum 'Bloodgood'

This comes from the Bloodgood Nursery in New York. It has probably the darkest leaves of any *palmatum* cultivar—they are dark, blood-red leaves and so 'Bloodgood' is, ironically, an appropriate name. The strong color remains through summer, although there is no fall color of any distinction. One of the finest cultivars and justifiably popular. Height x width 15 ft (5 m).

Acer palmatum 'Butterfly'

This has pale gray-green leaves margined and splashed with creamy white, turning pink or red in the fall. The leaves have a bubbled and twisted look about them, appealing to those gardeners who like variegation. Height 10 ft (3 m) x width 5 ft (1.5 m).

Far left:
Acer negundo
'Kelly's Gold'

Left: *Acer negundo*
var *violaceum*

Above and right:
Acer palmatum

Acer palmatum 'Crimson Queen'

'Crimson Queen' is a small, dense shrub with a weeping habit and fine crimson to purple-red leaves. It grows to about half its attainable height unless grafted up high to give a taller bush. Height 10 ft (3 m) x width 12 ft (4 m). A very popular maple and ideal for small gardens.

'**Red Dragon**' is a darker version of 'Crimson Queen'.

Acer palmatum 'Dissectum', syn *A. p.* var *dissectum*

This maple is usually seen as a wide-spreading mound of a plant. It is grown for the feathery dissected leaves, but choose a protected site as any strong wind will destroy the fragile foliage. Height 6 ft (2 m) x width 10 ft (3 m).

There are several named color forms from the original green. '**Atropurpureum**' has purple leaves and '**Nigrum**' is even darker with blackish purple leaves. '**Filigree**' has very finely cut leaves taking on orange colors in the fall.

Acer palmatum 'Seiryu'

This terrific tree with lacy, dissected foliage is ideal for small, sheltered gardens. If you have room for only one small tree, then this should be on your list of possible species. The bright green leaves turn orange and yellow in the fall and even to dark purple in some districts. It has green stems and still looks attractive in winter. Height 9–15 ft (3–5 m) x width 6–10 ft (2–3 m).

Acer palmatum 'Senkaki'

CORAL BARK MAPLE

Coral bark maple is a stunning small tree with bright red stems highlighting new pale green spring growth and beautiful yellow fall foliage. In winter these red stems have the scene to themselves, so it is an exciting tree in any season of the year. Height 20 ft (6 m) x width 15 ft (5 m).

Acer palmatum 'Shishigashira', syn *A. p.* 'Ribesifolium'

This forms a small, upright tree or more likely a large shrub. Its tiny green leaves are curled at the edges. The inner leaves tend to be bigger and the curled leaves almost give a variegated appearance. Even the fall color looks variegated, with hues of orange and purple. It is a fascinating plant, always attracting attention. Sometimes grown as *A. p.* 'Ribesifolium'. Height 12 ft (4 m) x width 10 ft (3 m).

Acer palmatum 'Trompenburg'

Bold purple leaves, where the margins of the leaf roll under, give the plant an attractive clean look. Fall color is scarlet and quite stunning. Forms a wide-spreading shrub. Height 6 ft (2 m) x width 10 ft (3 m).

Acer palmatum 'Villa Taranto'

A fine feathery-foliaged plant with long, wispy leaves. The spring leaves seem multi-colored with hints of red and orange changing to green for summer and then yellow in fall. Named after a famous garden in northern Italy. Height 10 ft (3 m) x width 10 ft (3 m).

Above: *Acer pentaphyllum*

Acer pentaphyllum

Acer pentaphyllum forms a rounded tree, with slightly striated or striped, almost peeling, light brown bark. The palmate leaves are pale yellow-green with a hint of red and have prominent red petioles or leaf stalks, creating an almost multi-colored effect. It is a charming plant.

Cultivated trees are reluctant to set viable seed and grafting is difficult. Thankfully it will grow from cuttings, although the success rate is not high. *Acer pentaphyllum* has a fragile, delicate look about it and is certainly not a tree for an open, windswept site. It needs sanctuary, looking radiant in a sheltered dell.

This species was discovered in western China by Joseph Rock (1884–1962) as recently as 1929, and is still very rare in cultivation. There is a famous specimen in the Strybing Arboretum of the Golden Gate Park in San Francisco, from which most of the trees in the world have been propagated. Height 30 ft (10 m) x width 25 ft (8 m). ZONE 7 OR 8.

Pent = five; *phyllum* = leaf.

Acer platanoides

NORWAY MAPLE

The Norway maple is a fast-growing tree with a big, rounded crown and dense foliage. There are several clones that are ideal for large gardens. The Norway maple is similar in some ways to the sugar maple but differs in that it has a milky sap when you remove a leaf. *Acer platanoides* is a good street tree in cool climates because of its resistance to smoke, dust and insect pests. One drawback in a garden situation is that the tree can be too dominant, robbing all the soil nutrients and casting too much shade, making it difficult to grow other plants in the vicinity. Height 80 ft (25 m) x width 50 ft (15 m). ZONES 3 TO 7.

Platanoides = leaf like a *Platanus* or plane tree. (The London plane returns the compliment as it is called *Platanus acerifolia* = leaf like a maple.)

Acer platanoides 'Crimson King'

This provides a large, fast-growing tree for immediate impact. The large, glossy leaves are a stunning crimson-purple. The flowers are exciting, too, which is unusual for a maple. They are bright yellow with red bracts. Height x width 50 ft (15 m).

Acer platanoides 'Drummondii'

HARLEQUIN MAPLE

A selected form with a creamy-white band surrounding the green center of the leaf. This conspicuous variegation fades to create a pleasing, soft creamy-green tree from a distance. Height x width 30–40 ft (10–12 m).

Acer pseudoplatanus

PLANETREE MAPLE, SYCAMORE MAPLE

While the common sycamore is far too big a tree for most gardens, some of the colorful leaf clones will fit easily into a small space as they grow very slowly. The common sycamore was introduced to Britain from Europe by the Romans and has since become naturalized because it germinates so readily, and grows in a wide range of soils. Height 100 ft (30 m) x width 80 ft (25 m). ZONES 4 TO 8.

The following dwarf forms of sycamore are ideal for small, sheltered gardens in cool climates. They usually form bushes 6–12 ft (2–4 m) high and 6–10 ft (2–3 m) wide. Pink to pale orange

Above: *Acer platanoides* with fall color.

Right: *Acer platanoides* 'Crimson King', with a rhododendron.

spring growth gradually converts to cream and then green as summer progresses. Unfortunately, the colors are not so intense in warmer climates. Although they will grow from zone 3 through to zone 10, both 'Brilliantissimum' and 'Prinz Handjery' seem to perform best in cold winter regions.

'Brilliantissimum' is a super plant, a delicious shade of shrimp pink. **'Esk Sunset'** is bright pink with a purple reverse. It seems to tolerate strong sunlight better than 'Brilliantissimum' and 'Prinz Handjery'. **'Prinz Handjery'** has a purple hue and prominent veins.

Pseudo = false; *platanus* = plane tree.

Acer rubrum
RED MAPLE, SCARLET MAPLE, SWAMP MAPLE

An outstanding tree, *Acer rubrum* grows naturally along the length of the Appalachians from Canada southwards. While in the wild it changes to brilliant orange and scarlets in the fall, it is very variable and unreliable for fall color, so selected forms are best for parks and gardens. Called red maple for the red fall color, it could just as easily earn the name for the red buds in spring, which open to display red flowers followed by red seeds. Height 70 ft (20 m) x width 30 ft (10 m). ZONES 3 TO 9.

Rubrum = red.

Acer rubrum 'October Glory'
A first-class tree with a neat, narrow, upright habit in gardens, soon forming a good medium-sized tree with smooth bark. Height 40 ft (12 m) x width 20 ft (6 m).

Acer rubrum 'Red Sunset'
A large-leaf variety and one of the first to color up in fall with stunning reds and scarlet. Height 40 ft (12 m) x width 20 ft (6 m).

Acer rubrum 'Scanlon'
This is a well-known cultivar with more orange in the fall color and a narrower columnar habit, which is useful in a confined space. Height 50 ft (15 m) x width 15 ft (5 m).

Above: *Acer rubrum* 'Scanlon' (left) and a seedling of *A. rubrum* (right).

Acer saccharinum
SILVER MAPLE

Silver maple is a fast-growing tree from the forests of eastern North America. The big sycamore-sized leaves have five lobes and are instantly recognizable with their silvery white reverse; any breeze will ruffle the leaves to flash the silver side. Fall colors are reds, oranges and yellows. It is suitable only for large woodland gardens because it is prone to wind damage and grows very tall. Height 80 ft (25 m) x width 50 ft (15 m). ZONES 4 TO 9.

Saccharinum = sugar.

Below: *Acer pseudoplatanus* 'Brilliantissimum'

Above: *Acer saccharum* (right), with *Taiwania cryptomerioides* (left).

Acer saccharum
SUGAR MAPLE

You will recognize this one as the tree providing maple syrup from the sap of the tree in spring. It is also a large ornamental tree with robust trifoliate leaves coloring to a mix of radiant reds, orange and scarlet in the fall. It is not a good choice for city gardens, as it is too big for most and it does not like pollution. Height 70 ft (20 m) x width 40 ft (12 m). ZONES 4 TO 9.

Saccharum = sugar.

Acer saccharum 'Newton Sentry'

This clone exhibits a columnar habit with a slow-growing nature and is the best choice for gardens. Height 30 ft (10 m) x width 8 ft (2.5 m).

Acer saccharum 'Temple's Upright'

This is as it sounds: a narrow, columnar form with a pleasing salmon-orange fall color. Height 70 ft (20 m) x width 15 ft (5 m).

Acer shirasawanum, syn A. japonicum

A large shrub or small tree, *Acer shirasawanum* is ideal for court-yards and patio planting. It prefers a cool, windless environment or at least protection from hot sun. Sometimes called the full-moon maple because of the orb-like green leaves, which turn red and orange in the later part of the year. ZONES 5 TO 9.

Two forms worth cultivating are **'Vitifolium'** and the smaller, yellow-leafed **'Aureum'**, which is prone to sunburn. Height x width for all 20 ft (6 m).

Shirasawanum = after Japanese name Shirasawa; *aureum* = yellow; *vitifolium* = leaf like a grape.

Actinidia

Actinidia kolomikta
VARIEGATED KIWI VINE
Actinidiaceae

This is a very unusual plant. Some of the leaves of this vigorous climber are spattered with creamy white markings and others have bright, shrimp-pink splashed across them. It is almost as if a painter has emptied paint pots over your climbing vine. Only the male plant has these bright tricolor leaves, while the female plant is less gaudy and therefore not seen in cultivation. Fragrant, white, "apple blossom" flowers in spring are interesting rather than showy.

Actinidia kolomikta is quite hardy, which is a surprise for such an exotic-looking species. Not only are the leaves psychedelic, they are tropical-sized (6 in/15 cm wide and long) and heart-shaped. Despite its appearance, it is not really happy in hot climates. Being deciduous, it has a bright new coat of colors every spring. The vivid coloration is diminished by hot weather and excess soil fertility. Heavy shade will also reduce the bright colors, so to gain the most from this plant you need to site it carefully. It definitely needs some shelter from cold winds. Acidic to neutral, well-drained soil will reduce the risk of root rot, which attacks in humid conditions or if the soil is overly wet for any length of time. It has no pests or diseases apart from dieback and root rot when young. Once the plant is established it seems quite robust.

This plant is a sister of the edible kiwifruit or 'Zespri', *Actinidia chinensis*. Both are deciduous vines, though the kiwifruit is much more vigorous, needing monthly pruning to contain it. The species comes from north China, Korea, Manchuria and Japan. In its natural setting, it climbs by twining around stems of trees and shrubs. When grown next to a wall it needs wires or some means of vertical support. Height 15 ft (5 m). ZONES 5 TO 8.

Actinidia = ray, referring to the radiating male stamens, like outstretched fingers; *kolomikta* = a local common name.

Above:
Actinidia kolomikta

Below:
Acer shirasawanum 'Aureum'

Alangium

VARIABLE

Alangium platanifolium
Alangiaceae

This is an unusual and rare small tree with a near-perfect structure. A thin central leader trunk supports a whorl of branches followed by clean, clear stem and another whorl of branches, creating a series of tiers and a pleasing, open habit. Even the branches are at a perfect 45-degree angle to the trunk, and the clean, smooth, light brown stems enhance this symmetrical effect.

The leaves of this deciduous plant are sumptuous. Each unique, lopsided leaf will have a different lobe pattern, with three, five or seven lobes. Leaves on healthy juvenile plants are often 6 in (15 cm) across in every direction. Sometimes you will look at the bush and think every leaf has been positioned carefully, as they all appear in twin planes, almost like a staircase climbing the stem. In fall the tree loses leaves one at a time from inside the bush, each leaf changing to rich butter-gold before falling, although it does not have a fall display as such.

Alangiums will grow in sun or part-shade, though the structure is much more pleasing when grown in the open. It is not wind-tolerant and so needs a sheltered site, as the plant is prone to breakages. Any reasonable soil is acceptable and occasionally the plant may sucker if grown on a slope.

Hanging bunches of tiny, white, fragrant bell flowers appear in summer followed by aqua-blue berries. It seems to like moisture—it grows naturally in Korean forests very close to streams. It is not prone to any pests or diseases. Height 10 ft (3 m) x width 6 ft (2 m). It is reasonably hardy, but the tree can be cut back by very cold weather. ZONES 6 TO 9.

Above: *Alangium platanifolium*

There is a bigger-leafed form called **A. p. macrophyllum**, and a similar Chinese species called ***Alangium chinensis***.

Alangium = a Tamil word; *platanifolium* = foliage like a plane tree.

Albizia, syn Paraserianthes

Mimosaceae or Fabaceae

When you first see an *Albizia*, you will think it is an *Acacia*. They are very similar, but the beautiful feathery foliage of the *Albizia* is more graceful. Albizias have fluffy flowers and are in the mimosa section of the Fabaceae or Pea family and are a mix of evergreen and deciduous trees. They are named for an Italian naturalist called Filippo degli Albizzi.

Albizia julibrissin
MIMOSA, SILK TREE
This deciduous plant becomes a very wide, flat-topped tree. It has a horizontal appearance, making it prone to wind damage, therefore it needs a sheltered site. The foliage folds at night like mimosa (sensitive plant).

Lush climates encourage soft, sappy growth that is even more prone to wind damage. Although this is a deciduous species and seemingly more hardy, it needs a hot baking in summer to thrive. Hot and preferably dry summers suit it just fine and result in a

huge crop of fluffy, pink, pompom flowers. Pink-flushed stamens are like the fuzz or strands of silk. Mimosa is an excellent shade tree and a common garden and street tree in the warmer parts of Europe and California. Any free-draining soil will suffice, and it is easy to transplant at virtually any age. Sometimes it is attacked by a wilt disease in hot, wet climates. The plant originates from China. Height 20 ft (6 m) x width 12–20 ft (4–6 m). ZONE 6.

Julibrissin = old Persian word for silken.

Albizia julibrissin 'Rosea'

A selected form with balls of bright pink, crimson-tipped stamens. This extra-hardy form was first noticed growing in Seoul, South Korea.

Albizia lophantha, syn *A. distachya*

CAPE WATTLE, PLUME ALBIZIA, SWAMP WATTLE

Albizia lophantha is a very fast-growing tree, reaching 12 ft (4 m) high in just two years, with a trunk some 8 in (20 cm) thick. It produces a huge crop of brown pods laden with large, shiny, black seeds, which ensure its continuance. The flowers are a narrow cylinder of bright yellow-green fluff like a bottlebrush, which demands to be touched in the same way as does velvet. Despite the dazzling flowers the leaves are the highlight, as the arched leaves are simply luscious, and of a much-divided, doubly pinnate type. This sun-loving, evergreen shrub or small tree is difficult to transplant and it is best to sow two or three seeds where you want to grow one. It is reasonably wind-tolerant and yet just as likely to topple over at ground level in strong winds. In a cooler climate this fine foliage plant will grow in a sheltered site and is not likely to spread by seed, so you can have all the benefits and none of the drawbacks. Wet or dry climates and any soil types are fine. Height 6–30 ft (2–10 m) x width 3–10 ft (1–3 m). ZONE 8.

Lophantha = crest-flowered.

Alniphyllum

Alniphyllum fortunei

Styracaceae

Unlike the previous *Alangium*, this plant is just beginning to escape the obscurity of life in botanical gardens. It looks like being a worthy addition to a large shrub collection, for its glossy, hand-sized leaves and mass of white *Styrax*-like bell flowers in spring or early summer. The flower display gets better and better year after year and the foliage is always top-notch.

Alniphyllum fortunei forms a neat, upright shrub with a tapering, pyramid shape. The plant has an open habit and so the reddish stems and smooth brown trunk are a special feature. It goes on to form a small tree in just a few years. The shiny new leaves become matt as they age and are almost a lime green with a hint of red. They are large and luscious with something of a tropical air about them. They seem reluctant to drop in the fall, and change color to red before dropping one at a time, so the bush never has an overall splash of color, just a leaf here and a leaf there. It tolerates most soils and is proving hardy in colder regions. It is also happy in high rainfall areas and equally content in a tough summer-drought climate. The only pest noted to date is stem borer. This species comes from western China in the Yunnan and Szechwan provinces. Height 30 ft (10 m) x width 20 ft (6 m). ZONE 6.

Alniphyllum = leaf like an alnus; *fortunei* = Robert Fortune (1812–1880) (the man responsible for bringing tea plants out of China).

Alniphyllum fortunei var *macrophyllum*

This has bigger leaves that are darker green and glossier. They are convex and arched as opposed to the valley-shape of the straight species. Shiny, pale-green new growth appears throughout summer, contrasting with the darker green, older leaves. It is semi-evergreen in mild climates and tends to be more open and gangly than the species. Like the species plant it tolerates most soils and is hardy in colder regions. Not a plant for a windy site, which would almost certainly disfigure the bush. Happy in high rainfall areas and equally content in a tough summer-drought climate. The only pest noted so far is stem borer. Height 30 ft (10 m) x width 20 ft (6 m). ZONE 7 OR 8.

Macro = big; *phyllum* = leaf.

Amelanchier

SHADBUSH, SNOWY MESPILUS
Rosaceae

A melanchiers are a confused group of plants. They have at times been cataloged as *Mespilus*, *Aronia*, *Pyrus* or *Crataegus* and even botanists have difficulty telling species apart. They are beautiful plants and you should select named forms in order to get the bush you need.

They are all hardy deciduous shrubs or small trees and have similar flowers and leaves. The leaves are round or oval, looking like coins attached to stems. They have a tidy, wholesome appearance, keeping a slightly shiny, clean surface intact all summer, and turning to reds and golds in the fall. Some have a bluish cast to the leaves, enhancing the neat appearance. Although the individual flowers are small, when they are massed together the overall effect is stunning. To see vast areas of mountain tops smothered in a white haze of *Amelanchier* flowers is one of the highlights of an Appalachian spring. The flowers are very tough, surviving frost, snow and biting cold winds. Then at the end of summer the plants oblige us with stupendous fall colors.

Amelanchiers are easy to grow in any soil that is not too dry or poor. Most of them need an acidic or neutral soil. They are supremely cold and wind hardy. Full sun is ideal and they take on a thin and unloved appearance in shade. With an upright brush habit they are an ideal plant for the back of a perennial or shrub border. Some form small trees and can be used as lawn specimens. Even big specimens can be moved successfully, and they can be transplanted at any time during the dormant winter

Above: *Alniphyllum fortunei*

Above: *Alniphyllum fortunei* var *macrophyllum* in flower.

period. They also do not mind being pruned either for outline shape or more drastically if your plant gets too big for its allotted space.

Amelanchiers are prone to cankers and fireblight. They grow naturally all across the cooler regions of the Northern Hemisphere.

Amelanchier = adaptation of amelancier, an old name for *Amelanchier ovalis* in Europe.

Amelanchier alnifolia

ALDER-LEAVED SERVICEBERRY

Amelanchier alnifolia is a big, bushy plant from northwest U.S.A. and Canada, with clusters of white flowers in the spring. It does not spread wildly, but tends to sucker a little, gradually forming a thicket from the base. This species will grow in alkaline or acidic soil. Height x width 12 ft (4 m). ZONE 4 OR 5.

'Regent' is a compact form that grows as a small suckering plant. Height x width 4–6 ft (1.2–2 m).

Alnifolia = leaves like an *Alnus* or alder.

Amelanchier arborea
DOWNY SERVICEBERRY

This species may need pruning in a garden situation to make it into a tidy, rounded, small tree. The oval leaves are slightly hairy or downy and have colorful fall tints. Its arching racemes of white flowers are sweetly scented and are followed by red berries. This species originates from the eastern U.S.A. and Canada. Height 25 ft (8 m) x width 30 ft (10 m). ZONES 4 TO 9.

Arborea = tree.

Amelanchier asiatica
ASIAN SERVICEBERRY

A large, upright shrub with bronzy new growth and attractive smooth stems. In the spring it has racemes of large, white, scented flowers. It copes with lime soil. This species occurs naturally in China, Korea and Japan. Height 25 ft (8 m) x width 30 ft (10 m). ZONES 5 TO 9.

Asiatica = from Asia.

Amelanchier canadensis
SHADBUSH

Amelanchier canadensis forms a handsome upright shrub with a tendency to sucker. The white flowers on erect racemes in the spring are followed by black berries. The smooth green leaves turn fiery reds and orange in the fall. This species originates from the eastern U.S.A. and Canada. Height 20 ft (6 m) x width 10 ft (3 m). ZONES 3 TO 9.

Canadensis = from Canada.

Amelanchier x grandiflora
(A. arborea x A. laevis)
APPLE SERVICEBERRY

This is appropriately named as it has the best flowers of all the amelanchiers. Big clusters of large white flowers are dazzling in the spring. The new spring growth that follows is initially bronze, changing to green for the summer and on to a stunning mix of scarlet, orange and yellow in the fall. Most forms have a tidy upright shape and they can be trained as a single leader bush, thus making them more amenable to planting as a lawn specimen. Height 25 ft (8 m) x width 30 ft (10 m). ZONES 5 TO 8.

Above: *Amelanchier laevis*

'Ballerina' is a Dutch selection renowned for its terrific flower display and fine fall colors of reds and purple, and has the added attraction of being resistant to fireblight. **'Fall Brilliance'** has particularly good red fall color. **'Robin Hill'** is compact and broadly upright, with pink-tinged flowers. Height 25 ft (8 m) x width 15 ft (5 m). **'Rubescens'** has dark pink buds and paler pink-tinged flowers.

Grandi = grand or big; *flora* = flower.

Above: *Amelanchier canadensis*

Amelanchier laevis
ALLEGHENY SERVICEBERRY

Amelanchier laevis forms a large shrub or small tree covered in fragrant white flowers in spring. The new leaves are often bronzy red, changing to green for the summer and rich fall colors. One of the best amelanchiers for flowers and leaf color, it originates from U.S.A and Canada. Height x width 25 ft (8 m). ZONES 5 TO 9.

'Cumulus' is bigger and more disease-resistant than the straight species. It occurs naturally in northern U.S.A. and Canada. Height x width 25 ft (8 m). ZONES 5 TO 9.

Laevis = smooth.

Amelanchier lamarckii
This lovely plant has confused gardeners and botanists alike for many years. Firstly it was called *Crataegus racemosa* by Jean-Baptiste Lamarck (1744–1829) as long ago as 1783. At times people have thought it a European species, then a hybrid and then perhaps an

Above: *Amelanchier lamarckii*, with *Fraxinus chinensis* on the right.

Right: *Amelanchier lamarckii*

obscure American species. At times it has been lumped in with *A. canadensis* and *A. laevis*. Now it is thought to be a minor species from North America. Whatever the complexities of its origin, it is a fabulous plant with neat foliage, great fall color and attractive flowers. The new growth in spring is bronzy, quickly followed by a mass of dainty white flowers. During summer the leaves always look clean and presentable and turn fiery oranges and reds in fall. It is a bush with a very tidy habit and can be trained into a small tree or standard shape. Height 30 ft (10 m) x width 40 ft (12 m). ZONES 5 TO 9.

Ampelopsis

Vitaceae

*A*mpelopsis are related to grapes and Boston ivy. They have the same kind of tendrils for climbing in trees and, given a convenient prop to climb, will hasten to the top to be in the sunlight. Most vines naturally have their roots in shade while the uppermost part reaches for the sun. This is why you often hear people talk about rampant climbers taking over a fence, trellis or tree. They are only doing what comes naturally, trying to reach the sun. Give a climber a 6 ft (2 m) fence to climb, it will grow

just over 6 ft and then flower. But give it a 60 ft (20 m) tree to climb and generally it will not flower until it has reached the topmost branches. The flowering is often triggered by sunlight and in the case of *Ampelopsis* it needs the heat from the sun to set a good crop of fruits, some of which are stunning blue or purple berries. It is the same with grapes, the only difference being that the viticulturist thins the leaves of a grapevine to allow more sunlight onto the grapes. This extra heat and sun makes the grapes sweeter with a higher sugar content. Like grapes, *Ampelopsis* can be pruned according to the space given.

They are not fussy about the soil as long as it is well-drained. Being deciduous means they are hardy and some have spectacular fall colors, but the flowers are insignificant. Like most climbers they prefer a sheltered site, but they are quite hardy to cold.

Ampelopsis = like a vine.

Ampelopsis brevipedunculata 'Elegans'
PORCELAIN BERRY, PORCELAIN VINE
A three-lobed, grape-like vine from Korea and northern China, this has scintillating aqua-blue berries. The leaves on the straight species are fairly dull but 'Elegans' has unusual variegation. Its leaves are splashed with white and pink in a very distinctive way. Because of the variegation (i.e. less green leaf area), the plant is less vigorous and therefore ideal for small spaces and patios. Give it some shade to prevent sun scorch, as many plants with white on the leaves are prone to sunburn. It has the same beautiful blue berries and surprisingly it comes true from seed (exactly like the parent). The surprise here is a variegated plant sending up identical seedlings, as most multi-colored plants would have seedlings reverting to the ordinary green.

Originating from northeast Asia, it was introduced by Philipp von Siebold (1796–1866), an eye surgeon who made Japan his home. Height 15 ft (5 m). ZONES 5 TO 8.

Brevipedunculata = short peduncles, or flower stalks.

Ampelopsis megalophylla
This climber has huge leaves, divided into oval leaflets up to 6 in (15 cm) long, which provide good fall color. The tiny, insignificant flowers result in purple to black, shiny berries. The plant is originally from western China. Height 30 ft (10 m). ZONES 5 TO 8.

Megalo = enormous; *phylla* = leaf.

Above: *Ampelopsis brevipedunculata* 'Elegans'

Above: *Aphananthe aspera*

Aphananthe

Aphananthe aspera
Ulmaceae

*A*phananthe is very similar to *Zelkova*, with rough-surfaced, hairy leaves. The serrated leaves can easily be mistaken for an elm or *Zelkova*, although they are a lighter, paler green and more consistent color. The crowded stems have a sweeping habit, making the overall appearance very attractive, almost pendulous. The plant originates from Japan, Korea and China. Height 60 ft (18 m) x width 60 ft (18 m). ZONE 5.

Aphanthe = inconspicuous; *anthe* = flowers; *aspera* = rough
(referring to the very rough surface of the leaves).

Aralia

Araliaceae

*A*ralias are luxuriant, tropical-looking and elegant. An ideal setting is a city backyard garden where soil space is limited, perhaps a narrow bed next to a wall where the bold leaves will soften the harsh concrete backdrop. They seem happier when hemmed in with poor soil than when given rich soil which generates lush, pithy growth liable to frost and wind damage.

They are not at all demanding about soil or situation as long as it is reasonably sheltered. High or low rainfall is okay and hot sun or partial shade is fine. Bitter, cold winters and frosts hold no threat to these deciduous shrubs, and they have no significant pests or diseases.

Some aralias sucker and so spread around the garden. Because the berries are popular with birds, aralias can also naturalize easily in warmer climates. Watch out for the thorns on the stems.

Aralia = adaptation of a local Japanese name.

Aralia chinensis
CHINESE ANGELICA
Chinese angelica is very similar to *Aralia elata* and they are often confused in cultivation. *Aralia chinensis* has a huge head of flowers coming off a central core, while the flowers of *A. elata* have flower stalks of equal length branching out in a radiating, explosive pattern. *A. chinensis* has a less prickly stem, lower growth habit or stature and very short stalks on the leaflets. Native to China. Height x width 30 ft (10 m). ZONES 4 TO 9.

Chinensis = from China.

Left: *Aralia chinensis*
Far left: *Aralia spinosa* with *Hydrangea arborescens* 'Annabelle' in flower below.

Aralia continentalis
This herbaceous species has soft leaves up to 3 ft (1 m) long and no spines. It is a native of Korea, where it dies down to a crown in the winter. Height x width 10 ft (3 m). ZONE 6.

Continentalis = continental.

Aralia elata
JAPANESE ANGELICA TREE
Aralia elata forms a large, open shrub that is seen at its best when grown as an isolated specimen. It is a magnificent structural plant with enormous lacy leaves. Hidden away in a shrubbery, all of this is lost. The huge, double-pinnate leaves can be 3–4 ft (1–1.2 m) or more long and tend to be clustered around the tip of the stem.

Right and far right:
Araucaria araucana

The bare stems beneath are usually covered in sharp spines. Prominent scars result where old leaves have fallen off. The overall effect is a sparse, architectural plant. Huge panicles of tiny white flowers in fall are more like a froth of flowers. *A. elata* originates from Japan, northern China and Korea. This species can eventually form a 30 ft (10 m) tree but is more often seen as a 6–10 ft (2–3 m) x 6–10 ft (2–3 m) shrub. ZONES 4 TO 9.

There are several named and variegated forms one of which, **'Aureovariegata'**, has leaf margins splashed with yellow. Height x width 15 ft (5 m). **'Variegata'** is similar to 'Aureovariegata', but has creamy white variegations.

Elata = tall or beautiful.

Aralia spinosa
HERCULES' CLUB, DEVIL'S WALKING STICK
This species has tremendous architectural leaves—up to 2 ft (70 cm) long and wide, with ovate leaflets that are dark green above and paler green underneath. The huge plumes of white, frothy flowers appear in midsummer and are 12–18 in (30–50 cm) long. It suckers vigorously and produces lots of seeds eagerly spread by birds. It is very spiny. A native of eastern U.S.A., growing in moist sites. Height 30 ft (10 m) x width 15 ft (5 m). ZONES 4 TO 9.

Spinosa = spiny.

Araucaria

Araucaria araucana, syn *A. imbricata*
CHILEAN PINE, MONKEY PUZZLE
Araucariaceae

Araucaria araucana caused a sensation in Britain when first introduced from Chile in the 1800s. The perfect and yet quirky shape really took the fancy of the landed gentry and whole avenues of this fine tree were planted. It thrives in wetter regions and the best specimens seen today are in cool, wet climates similar to its Chilean homeland. This *Araucaria* is one of the few Southern Hemisphere conifers to thrive in the Northern Hemisphere.

British gardeners coined the name "monkey puzzle" because it would be so hard for a monkey to fathom how to climb it. In fact the sharp points to the scale-like leaves would put off any but the most determined climber. The leaves are a really dark, rich green and are waxy and hard.

It is a slow-growing, stately tree, best seen as a single specimen. It is reasonably wind-tolerant, and not too fussy about soil or ground conditions. Height 50–80 ft (15–25 m) x width 22–30 ft (7–10 m). ZONE 7.

Araucaria araucana = derived from a tribe of Chilean Indians called Araucanos.

Aronia

CHOKEBERRY
Rosaceae

This genus is an easily overlooked group of plants from the Appalachian Mountains in eastern U.S.A. Initially you may think they have not much to commend them, but slowly they reveal their qualities. These deciduous shrubs are grown for their spring flowers and wonderful fall colors. They are related to *Sorbus* and have similar heads of off-white flowers from the tops of the stems in late spring.

All through summer aronias fade into the background, simply providing more greenery, but you will notice them again come fall when the leaves turn scintillating shades of orange, reds and scarlets.

These North American natives grow in full sun or part shade. They cope with wet or dry soil and are often found growing in swamps in the wild. Plant them in acidic or neutral soil as they do not like lime. *Aronia* are easy-care shrubs ideal for borders or in woodland gardens. They have a reasonably tidy, upright shape and can be pruned to keep them neat. They are easy to transplant in winter.

Aronia = an old name for one of the *Sorbus* species.

Aronia arbutifolia
RED CHOKEBERRY

An upright hardy shrub, the simple dark green leaves of this *Aronia* turn to dazzling reds and orange in the fall. The leaves are hairy on the lower surface. Clusters of white flowers appear in late spring and are followed by attractive red berries. This species originates from eastern North America. Height 10 ft (3 m) x width 5 ft (1.5 m). ZONES 5 TO 9.

'Brilliantissima' is a selected form with more flowers and stunning fall colors. Height 6–8 ft (2–2.5 m) x width 4–6 ft (1.2–2 m).

Arbutifolia = leaf like an *Arbutus*.

Aronia melanocarpa
BLACK CHOKEBERRY

A shoulder-high shrub with glossy leaves and fabulous fall color. Clusters of off-white flowers are followed by shiny black berries. Sometimes the bush suckers and becomes a thicket. **'Fall Magic'** has consistently good fall color and bigger berries. For both, height 6 ft (2 m) x width 10 ft (3 m). ZONES 4 TO 9.

Melanocarpa = dark or black fruits.

Aucuba

Aucuba japonica
JAPANESE LAUREL
Cornaceae

Above: *Aronia arbutifolia*

Aucuba japonica, like other aucubas, has big glossy leaves 8 in (20 cm) long, and despite being hardy the plant has an almost tropical look. I think this is one of those shrubs you plant when you first start gardening. Then, because it is so easy and robust, you forget it for years until you eventually realize how valuable a plant it is.

Aucuba was used initially as an indoor plant for poorly lit Victorian parlors and was sold from stallholders' barrows in London. Japanese laurel was perhaps overused in Victorian gardens because it is so tough, growing as it does in dense shade and often without a drop of rain for months on end.

Plant an *Aucuba* on those poor, dry sites on the shady side of the house where nothing wants to grow. It will thrive there and claim the space as its own. It does not matter whether the soil is alkaline or acidic, dry, rocky or virtually non-existent. *A. japonica* will even grow at the base of growth-inhibiting trees like beech, which rob the site of nutrients and light.

Its virtues do not end there, because it is also capable of growing in windy sites and coastal places, and it is seemingly immune to pests and diseases. Moreover, it is cold-hardy and one of the toughest, hardiest plants on the planet.

Such easy-care plants are hard to come by. You can even grow it in pots and tubs, and neglect to water it as often as you had planned. It is easy to transplant at any stage and you can prune it drastically, should you feel the need.

The flowers are relatively unattractive. Tiny male and female flowers are on separate plants and just one male plant will

fertilize a host of females to produce their sumptuous red berries. The berries are untouched by birds and make good winter indoor decorations. Height x width 10 ft (3 m). ZONE 6.

You are more likely to be familiar with one or more of the multitudinous variegated forms than the straight green species. **'Crotonifolia'** (female) is named after the tropical croton plant with splashes of leaf color. This leaf is spotted with gold as if a painter flicked a brush at it. **'Gold Dust'** is a male version of 'Crotonifolia'.

'Mr Goldstrike' is similar to 'Gold Dust' and is male. Height x width 4–6 ft (1.2–2 m). The leaves of **'Picturata'** (female) have a big splash of yellow through the middle of the leaf. **'Sulfurea Marginata'** (female) has a pale yellow margin around the green leaf.

Aucuba = a Japanese name; *japonica* = from Japan.

Left: *Aucuba omeiensis*

Above: *Aucuba japonica* 'Crotonifolia'

Aucuba omeiensis

First discovered on the sacred mountain Emei Shan in central China. It is more tree-like than other species, with a big, bold, upright habit. Leaves are a dull gray-green, but quite exciting despite this seemingly dim color. They are large leaves, bigger than a hand, with bold serrations. Height 15 ft (5 m) x width 10 ft (3 m). Hardy and happy in ZONE 9, but as yet it is uncertain how it will perform in cooler climates.

Omeiensis = from Mt Emei in China.

Berberis

BARBERRY
Berberidaceae

*B*erberis are a mix of evergreen and deciduous shrubs called upon to fill the difficult roles in parks and gardens. They are often employed to direct foot traffic because of their spines, deterring anyone from taking a shortcut. They can fill the same role in your garden, but it does pay to plant them away from the path so that you do not get stabbed every time you pass by.

Berberis form a huge group of plants from Europe, Asia, and North and South America. They have managed to colonize more of the world than most woody plants and now gardeners are helping them conquer new lands. They are even becoming naturalized in warmer countries and so you should be careful not to let them seed freely and spread around.

They are obviously tough survivors and will grow just about anywhere, and are not fussy about site or soil, hot sun or cold winds.

Berberis = an old Arabic name.

Berberis darwinii

This species is teeming with golden-yellow blossoms in spring followed by a large crop of bluish berries in fall. Hungry birds spread the seeds, having devoured the fleshy berries, so ideally cut off the flower heads before they set fruit.

Usually *Berberis darwinii* forms an upright bush, and its rich, glossy green leaves are like miniature holly. It is hard to imagine a shrub with tiny, holly-like leaves can be so stunning, but the glistening leaves are the greenest green you have ever seen.

The bell-like flowers are quite charming, a bit like an orange *Pieris*, and highlight the foliage. This species is surprisingly wind-hardy, even growing in sight of the sea. It is a great shrub for cool

Above: *Berberis thunbergii* 'Aurea'

Above: *Berberis thunbergii* 'Rose Glow'

districts. It was first discovered by Charles Darwin (1809–1882) in Chile in 1835 during the *Beagle* voyage to South America and the Galapagos. Height x width 6–10 ft (2–3 m). ZONES 7 TO 9.

Berberis thunbergii
JAPANESE BARBERRY

This is a compact Japanese shrub ideal for those tough sites with compacted soil, poor drainage, or drafty cold winds. Its spines make it another pedestrian regulator, preventing anyone taking shortcuts across your piece of garden. It makes an ideal hedge or barrier because it is dense and does not mind constant pruning. Ideally, trim it in late winter just before the new spring growth. Beware of the spines when pruning as they are truly vicious. If the plant or hedge should get tatty, it is easily renovated by drastic pruning, quickly recovering to show off a sparkling coat of new leaves. The bark is most unusual, having corky ridges like some

ancient pine tree, and the wood of the stems and roots is bright yellow. This is an exceptionally tough plant that will grow in clay, rocky or sandy sites and will tolerate drought. It can tolerate more or less any soil except swampy or boggy ground.

Small clusters of yellow flowers decorate the bush in spring, followed by shiny red berries. Try to remove the berries before they ripen to prevent their spread. Although it is deciduous, in warm climates the bare period is brief as the leaves fall very late in the season. Red fall color can be stunning some years. It is very cold-hardy, with no pests.

The species is named after Carl Peter Thunberg (1743–1828), a Swedish plant collector who was one of the first botanists to fossick in Japan and responsible for collecting some of the first hydrangeas and viburnums. Thunberg was a student of Linnaeus, the "father of modern botany," who was responsible for giving us a two-name system for plants and animals. Height 3 ft (1 m), occasionally more x width 8 ft (2.5 m). ZONES 5 TO 8.

Berberis thunbergii 'Aurea'

'Aurea' is a brilliant yellow version of this tough shrub. It will brighten a dull or shady part of your garden, opening pale yellow, maturing to blazing yellow and turning gold in the fall. It makes a tidy, compact plant. Height x width 3–4 ft (1–1.2 m).

Berberis thunbergii 'Rose Glow'

This is an easily grown plant for beginner gardeners, best in full sun for good health and leaf color. It has purple leaves speckled with cream and pale pink. It is not a plant for the faint-hearted or those who enjoy subtlety.

Betula

BIRCH
Betulaceae

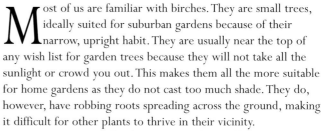

Most of us are familiar with birches. They are small trees, ideally suited for suburban gardens because of their narrow, upright habit. They are usually near the top of any wish list for garden trees because they will not take all the sunlight or crowd you out. This makes them all the more suitable for home gardens as they do not cast too much shade. They do, however, have robbing roots spreading across the ground, making it difficult for other plants to thrive in their vicinity.

Given time, some birches can get to be sizable trees, but within a gardener's lifetime they are unlikely to be a problem. When we look closely at the leaves it is not for the beauty of any one leaf or group of leaves that we enjoy them, but rather the delicate patterns they create and the overall elegance of the tree. Being open and airy allows birches to show off their fine trunks and this is where we find the most variation. There is not much variation in the leaf shapes or in the sizes of birch trees.

Birches handle poor soil, and some even tolerate wet and boggy ground. Some gardeners imagine all birches cope with wet soils, but this is not true. Choose carefully if you want a birch to grow in wet, boggy ground. They all grow in extremely acidic or alkaline soil, and most tolerate cold, sometimes even severe cold conditions. Most also cope with city pollution and windy sites. Nearly all prefer an open, sunny site and you usually see them as isolated trees or small groups in suburban gardens.

Sometimes they can be difficult to grow, as not all of them enjoy warm climates or extremely dry places. They transplant easily in winter, though buying a large specimen is often a false economy as younger plants soon catch up to the slowly acclimatizing older plant.

Birches are prone to rust diseases, which can defoliate them, and borer can be a problem, too. While we regard them as deciduous there are a few obscure evergreen species. Birches are notoriously difficult to tell apart as the leaf shape and size is so similar in many of the species and even the bark color can vary from white to pink to purple in the same species. Seedling variation only adds to the confusion, so for gardens choose grafted plants consistent with the parent tree.

Betula = old Latin name for birch tree.

Betula albo-sinensis
CHINESE PAPER BIRCH

A beautiful tree in cool climates, *Betula albo-sinensis* has smooth pink or even orangish trunks, peeling with large slivers of older bark. Its glossy leaves are deep green above, lighter beneath, turning yellow in fall. It needs a cool or cold climate. It was first introduced from northern China by Ernest Wilson (1876–1930). Height 80 ft (25 m) x width 30 ft (10 m). ZONES 5 TO 8.

Albo = white; *sinensis* = Chinese.

Betula albo-sinensis var septentrionalis

The northernmost form has smaller, rough, elm-like leaves with orangish or even dark brown bark. The leaves are paler and dull.

Below: *Betula lenta*

It needs a cool or cold climate. It was first introduced from northern China by Ernest Wilson (1876–1930). ZONES 5 TO 8.

Septentrionalis = northern.

Betula alleghaniensis, syn *B. lutea*
YELLOW BIRCH

Yellow birch is a superb tree, but for reasons I cannot fathom it has never been popular with gardeners. Perhaps grafting a good named form for consistency would solve the problem. It becomes a tidy columnar tree with an even outline, and the fairly large, ovate, hairy leaves turn gold in fall. The best trunks are olive to gold and shiny smooth with horizontal markings. It is very tolerant of wet ground. It originates from the Appalachians and is named for the Allegheny Mountains. Height 80 ft (25 m) x width 30 ft (10 m). ZONES 4 TO 9.

Lutea = yellow.

Betula ermanii
ERMAN'S BIRCH

Betula ermanii is a big tall tree, but specimens do vary in attractiveness. The good selections have a pure white glistening trunk or perhaps a hint of pink or salmon. Its dull, dark green leaves turn yellow in fall. This species originates from Siberia, Japan and Korea. G. A. Erman (1806–1877) was a German traveler and collector. Height 70 ft (20 m) x width 40 ft (12 m). ZONES 5 TO 9.

Betula ermanii 'Grayswood Hill', syn *B. costata* 'Grayswood Hill'

This is an outstanding version of *B. ermanii*, with pure white bark.

Betula lenta
CHERRY BIRCH, SWEET BIRCH

Cherry birch has very attractive, rich green, cherry-like leaves. Many birches look fine with their new spring growth but start looking tatty from midsummer onward, but cherry birch leaves look good all summer and are possibly the best foliage of any *Betula* species, with a lovely golden yellow fall color. The young trunks are smooth and shiny in a beautiful mahogany color. It originates from eastern U.S.A. Height 50 ft (15 m) x width 40 ft (12 m). ZONES 3 TO 9.

Lenta = spotted or having lenticels or breathing holes on the trunks.

Betula maximowicziana
MONARCH BIRCH

Worth growing for the wonderful leaves, this is the largest of the genus. The rounded, serrated leaves can be up to 6 in (15 cm) long, turning rich yellow gold in fall. The trunks are smooth and olive brown, peeling in horizontal fashion, and quietly pleasing. It is a native of Japan. Carl Maximowicz (1827–1891) was an authority on Siberian and Japanese plants and collected many himself. Height 80 ft (25 m) x width 40 ft (12 m). ZONES 6 TO 9.

Betula nigra
BLACK BIRCH, RIVER BIRCH

A good black birch can stop a group of gardeners in their tracks. Warm brown and pink new trunks are revealed by the pages of peeling bark. The overall effect is fascinating, with great wads of rough bark peeling this way and that. The younger stems are almost smooth and black while the mid-age trunks have enchanting beauty. Much older trunks are rugged but have ceased to peel.

Look to replace a number of trees every few years to keep the most attractive mid-age range. The leaves are exciting, being very dark and diamond shape, turning gold in the fall. It is possible to grow the trees in a swamp but they are equally at home in a much drier site. Very easy in warmer zones. From Canada and eastern U.S.A. Height 60 ft (18 m) x width 40 ft (12 m). ZONES 4 TO 9.

Betula davurica from northern China is very similar.

Nigra = black.

Betula nigra 'Heritage'

This is an excellent named clone with consistently good bark, shaggy and red-brown, becoming blackish or gray-white on older trees. The leaves are larger and glossier than the species. For this species most seedlings forms are good too. ZONES 4 TO 9.

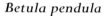

Betula papyrifera
PAPER BIRCH

A big, bold, conical tree with beautiful white trunks, paper birch's fall foliage is a good clean yellow. This cold-hardy tree is native to North America from Alaska downward. It grows in cold climates but is surprisingly hardy in warm climates too. Height 70 ft (20 m) or more x width 30 ft (10 m). ZONES 2 TO 9.

Papyrifera = paper.

Betula pendula
COMMON SILVER BIRCH

You will see this upright tree in many gardens. Young trees have white trunks while older trees have rough corrugated bark and trunks. Some forms have outstanding white trunks but many seedling forms are lackluster. The newer branches have a weeping habit, creating a beautiful tumbling effect. The fall color is a clear yellow in the cool climates it prefers. It originates from Europe through to Siberia. Height 80 ft (25 m) x width 30 ft (10 m). ZONES 2 TO 8.

B. p. 'Dalecarlica' (Swedish birch) is an upright, slender version with very finely cut leaves. Height 70 ft (20 m) x width 20 ft (6 m). Definitely needs a cold climate. **'Laciniata'** is similar to 'Dalecarlica'. **'Tristis'** is an outstanding airy form with beautiful white trunks. ZONES 2 TO 8. **'Youngii'** (Young's weeping birch) is

Left: *Betula pendula*

Above: *Betula nigra*

Above: *Betula platyphylla* var *japonica*

Above: *Betula utilis* var *prattii*

a lovely weeping version. Make sure you train it up to the height you want before allowing it to weep or it will become a short dome. Height x width 25 ft (8 m). ZONES 2 TO 8.

    B. pubescens is similar to *B. pendula* only it is less weeping.

Pendula = referring to the weeping habit.

Betula platyphylla **var** *japonica*
JAPANESE BIRCH

This is similar to *Betula pendula* but with larger leaves and white trunks. Leaves are diamond shaped and yellowish green. It grows in warm climates but often defoliates early without any of the yellow fall color. Originates from Japan. Height 70 ft (20 m) x width 40 ft (12 m). ZONES 4 TO 9.

Platyphylla = broad leaf; *japonica* = from Japan.

Betula platyphylla **var** *japonica* **'Whitespire'**

A worthy named form with fabulous white trunks and dark green leaves. It also seems resistant to many insect pests.

Betula utilis
HIMALAYAN BIRCH

Himalayan birch is a very variable and sometimes wonderful birch, its trunks varying from chalky white to pink to mahogany and even purples and black. Its dark green leaves turn yellow in fall. A native of China and the Himalayas. Height 60 ft (18 m) x width 30 ft (10 m). ZONES 5 TO 9.

Utilis = useful, as in utilize.

Betula utilis jacquemontii
WHITE-BARKED HIMALAYAN BIRCH

This used to be a species in its own right. The good forms have fabulous bright white bark, the form **'Silver Shadow'** being a fine example. **'Jermyns'**, named after the Hilliers Gardens in Eng-

land, is another excellent white. Although used to cold, it grows very well in warm zones too. Victor Jacquemont (1801–1832) was a French botanist who worked in India and the Himalayas. Height 60 ft (18 m) x width 30 ft (10 m).

Betula utilis **var** *prattii*

This has purplish brown trunks as good as *Prunus serrula* or *Acer griseum*. It grows well in cold and warm zones. Height 60 ft (18 m) x width 30 ft (10 m).

Buxus

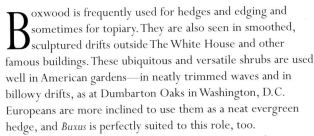

BOXWOOD, COMMON BOX
Buxaceae

Boxwood is frequently used for hedges and edging and sometimes for topiary. They are also seen in smoothed, sculptured drifts outside The White House and other famous buildings. These ubiquitous and versatile shrubs are used well in American gardens—in neatly trimmed waves and in billowy drifts, as at Dumbarton Oaks in Washington, D.C. Europeans are more inclined to use them as a neat evergreen hedge, and *Buxus* is perfectly suited to this role, too.

    Reliably hardy, the plants always remain dense and evergreen, with no tendency to die out or have dead branches as do lavenders and *Santolina*. The dark green foliage is permanently lush, healthy looking, and resplendent in the hot midday sun.

    Boxwood timber is used for making ornate boxes and for wood engraving. Its slow-growing nature is an advantage for clipping or topiary. Having reached the desired height they do

Right: *Buxus sempervirens*

not try to outgrow the situation. If they do, they can be pruned severely and recover well.

Boxwood are fine in full sun or semi-shade, and do not mind frosts. Poor, dry, sandy soil or hard clays are all the same to these tough plants, and they are easy to transplant. Often *Buxus* are grown in pots for shaping and topiary and if allowed to dry out and wilt they can easily be revived. They are virtually free of pests and diseases, which is why they are so long-lived. If you have ever seen the flowers then consider yourself observant, as most people have never noticed the tiny yellow flowers in spring. Even though the flowers are miniscule, the plants do have a lovely fragrance. Next time you are walking past a boxwood hedge, run your hands over the top and you will notice a pleasant tangy scent wafting in the air.

Buxus = Greek word referring to the hardness of the wood.

Buxus microphylla
SMALL-LEAVED BOXWOOD
This is a tougher, more cold-hardy smaller version than *Buxus sempervirens*, ideal for smaller hedges. From Korea and Japan. Height 30 in (75 cm) x width 5 ft (1.5 m). ZONES 6 TO 9.

Micro = small; *phylla* = leaf.

Buxus microphylla **var** *japonica*
The Japanese version has two advantages over other boxwoods. It is seemingly tougher and more shade-tolerant than other *Buxus*, but is not as tidy or as ornamental. Mid to deep-green leaves. Height 5 ft (1.5 m) x width 4 ft (1.2 m). ZONE 6.

Buxus microphylla **var** *koreana,* **syn** *B. sinica* **var** *insularis*
This is a smaller, slower-growing version, which may be advantageous in your situation and will cope with more winter cold than other *Buxus*. Height 24 in (60 cm) x width 30 in (75 cm). ZONE 5.

Buxus sempervirens
BOXWOOD
Familiar to us all, with its glossy, dark green leaves, this plant has a multitude of uses as a hedge, screen, topiary or in Japanese-style gardens, but somehow we never grow it just for itself. It has a certain charm and a pleasing scent, making it an excellent corner-

stone plant where paths meet. *Buxus sempervirens* is ideal for taller hedges. It can be pruned to a stump and will regenerate, which is presumably why it has lasted for generations in some gardens. It originates from Europe, North Africa and Turkey. Height x width 15 ft (5 m). ZONES 6 TO 8.

Sempervirens = full of life or evergreen.

Buxus sempervirens 'Aureomarginata'
Creamy yellow and green leaves make this a true variegated plant, but somehow it always looks one color from a distance and so it appears a pale shade of green. Height 8 ft (2.5 m) x width 10 ft (3 m). ZONE 6.

Buxus sempervirens 'Suffruticosa'
EDGING BOXWOOD
This is a low, dense shrub, ideal for small, neat hedges. It is commonly used as an edging to paths and flowerbeds. Small, ovate leaves are bright, shiny green. Height 6 ft (2 m) x width 9 ft (2.5 m). ZONE 6.

Camptotheca

Camptotheca acuminata
Nyssaceae

Camptotheca acuminata is a wonderful plant that is new to Western gardeners, one that shows great potential as a garden or avenue tree. The big leaves are scooped down the middle, forming a perfect valley. The leaves are dark green above with prominent red veins and the new leaves are a lovely rich red. These beautiful new leaves are produced all through summer and give the impression a flock of dark red butterflies has just landed. It is deciduous and has no fall color, but this is more than compensated for by the new leaves at the tips of the stems all through summer.

The wide-spreading, horizontal branches eventually give in to gravity, weeping down with the weight of the foliage. The new growth then turns up toward the light to give a beautiful

Below left: *Buxus sempervirens* 'Aureomarginata' Below right: *Buxus sempervirens* as billowy shrubs.

Above left and right:
Camptotheca acuminata

sweeping effect. The stems are smooth pale gray with unusual bulges, making it look like elephant hide. Clusters of greenish white flowers in late spring are intriguing rather than beautiful. The plant is seemingly tolerant of hot climates and quite dry conditions and yet is very happy in warm conditions. Plant it in a sheltered site. To date, it is known to do well in very acidic, well-drained soil. There are no obvious pests. It transplants easily from pots, and probably would not like to be shifted from an open ground nursery. It has been known to survive heavy frosts. Native to China, where it is grown as a street tree. Height 60 ft (20 m) x width 40 ft (12 m). ZONES 7 OR 8.

Campto = bent (from the Greek *campilo*); *theca* = case or envelope; *acuminatas* = tapered point to the leaf.

Carpinus

HORNBEAM
Carpinaceae

*C*arpinus are unsung heroes. They get on and do the job, but hardly ever get noticed or crowned with awards. They earn merit by growing in difficult sites and then sticking doggedly to the task. The simple leaves have prominent veins and are toothed around the edge. The leaf surface is often puckered or rough. But the best thing about the leaves is they look as good at the end of summer as they did in the spring. They do not fade, or burn or get eaten by pests or wind-blasted.

Carpinus betulus

HORNBEAM
Carpinus betulus is frequently used as a street tree in difficult sites in among city paving where the soil conditions are less than wonderful. Amsterdam and other European cities have many fine spec-

Far right:
Carpinus betulus

imens lining the streets. The form **'Fastigiata'** is the upright clone most often seen in urban settings.

Its tidy, upright habit provides an ideal shape for city streets with tall buildings but they can look just as good in a garden situation. Like other hornbeams, it grows easily in any soil, including heavy or alkaline conditions. It looks good all summer—consistently green and lush. The fall color of hornbeam is yellow and, if made into a hedge, will often keep its leaves all winter like a beech. It is very cold-hardy, reasonably wind-hardy and generally an easy-care tree.

Above: *Carpinus turczaninowii*

Hornbeam has zigzag twigs and a very even leaf pattern with leaves arranged alternately. It is as if every leaf has been made in the same mold. They are furrowed with prominent veins and have highly serrated edges. Often the new foliage hangs down in a pendulous fashion, like a curtain of foliage. In the fall they have quite pretty hop-like seed structures; it is like a lantern made up of overlapping greenish white petals. The seed cases are more exciting than the thin catkin flowers that appear in the spring. Originates from Europe, Turkey and the Ukraine. Height 80 ft (25 m) x width 70 ft (20 m). ZONES 4 TO 8.

Betulus = birch, for the similarity to birches (*Betula* spp.).

Carpinus caroliniana
AMERICAN HORNBEAM, BLUE BEECH, IRONWOOD
American hornbeam has blue-green leaves with excellent red and yellow fall color if the climate suits. It is a very hardy, handsome tree, willing to grow in poor soil and tolerating extremes of heat and cold. Native to the Carolinas and other parts of eastern U.S.A., and Mexico. Height 40 ft (12 m) x width 50 ft (15 m). ZONES 3 TO 9.

Caroliniana = from Carolina.

Carpinus turczaninowii
This species has lovely, large, puckered leaves with reddish bronze new growth. It forms a wall of foliage over the interlacing black stems. It often stays a shrubby size and is more easily accommodated in gardens than some other species. A native of Japan, Korea and China. Height 20–40 ft (6–12 m) x width 30 ft (10 m). ZONES 6 TO 9.

Turczaninowii = named after Nicolaus Turczaninow (1796–1864).

Carya

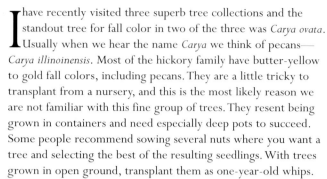

HICKORY, PECAN
Juglandaceae

I have recently visited three superb tree collections and the standout tree for fall color in two of the three was *Carya ovata*. Usually when we hear the name *Carya* we think of pecans— *Carya illinoinensis*. Most of the hickory family have butter-yellow to gold fall colors, including pecans. They are a little tricky to transplant from a nursery, and this is the most likely reason we are not familiar with this fine group of trees. They resent being grown in containers and need especially deep pots to succeed. Some people recommend sowing several nuts where you want a tree and selecting the best of the resulting seedlings. With trees grown in open ground, transplant them as one-year-old whips.

All the cultivated *Carya* are from the east coast of the U.S.A. and they are all deciduous with big, bold, ash-like leaves, and some produce delicious nuts. They demand a deep, rich soil and do not like impoverished sites. Thriving in hot summers and full sun, *Carya* will grow in cold regions as long as the summers are

Left and below:
Carya aquatica

Above: *Carya ovata*

bitter, thus the common name. The leaves are made up of seven or nine leaflets, and turn brilliant golden yellow in the fall. It is the toughest and easiest of the hickorys for mild maritime regions. Originates from eastern U.S.A. Height 80 ft (25 m) x width 50 ft (15 m). ZONES 5 TO 8.

Cordiformis = heart-shaped.

Carya illinoinensis
PECAN

Pecan forms a large, wide-spreading tree suitable only for parks and very large gardens. Its good butter-yellow fall leaf color is a bonus as it is mostly grown for its delicious nuts. It prefers a continental climate with cold winters and hot summers. Pecan is tricky to grow in maritime areas where it suffers from dieback and coral spot. It is found native in southern U.S.A. Height 100 ft (30 m) x width 70 ft (20 m). ZONES 5 TO 9.

Illinoinensis = from Illinois.

Carya ovata
SHAGBARK HICKORY

Shagbark hickory offers big, bold, wide leaflets and superb butter-yellow fall color. It forms a small, upright tree, making it suitable for small gardens. I can heartily recommend this as a garden tree, while most *Carya* are too big. The bark peels in strips, thus the common name. The nuts have a sweet kernel, but they do not rival the pecan. Native to eastern U.S.A. and Canada. Height 80 ft (25 m) x width 50 ft (15 m). ZONES 4 TO 8.

Ovata = ovate leaves.

Carya tomentosa
MOCKERNUT

A medium-sized tree producing very valuable timber, mockernut is second only to *Carya ovata* for splendid fall color. This one has the added bonus of aromatic leaves. They are fragrant when crushed but often the scent lingers in the air without any need to touch the leaves. The flowers are fragrant, too, and result in a crop of sweet nuts. Height 80 ft (25 m) x width 30 ft (10 m). ZONE 5.

Tomentosa = hairy or woolly, referring to the leaves.

Cedrus

CEDAR
Pinaceae

*C*edrus is a small genus of four species, and now some botanists are saying they are regional variations of just one species. Whatever the ins and outs of the botanical discussions, from a gardener's point of view there are three or four distinct types and each has its place—though mostly it is in a park rather than a garden as they grow so big.

"Stately" is the word that comes to mind when I think of cedars. These evergreen conifers are superb park trees and ideal for school grounds and other spacious places. Cedars are easily grown given a sunny site and reasonable drainage. Any soil and virtually any climate will do, as long as it is not too windy—*Cedrus deodara* is especially prone to wind burn. Other than that they are easily pleased. Ideally they need their own space to look majestic, and will lose their elegance and grandeur if crowded by other trees. ZONES 5 TO 9.

Cedrus = from *kedros*, an old Greek word for cedar.

warm. Keep them away from windy sites. The male flowers are on triple-spike catkins on last year's wood, while the female flowers are at the tip of the new growth.

Carya = walnut. (The Greek word for walnut is *karya* and somehow these related trees got the name. Karya was the daughter of Dion, King of Laconia. Bacchus, the god of wine, turned this Spartan maiden into a walnut tree.)

Carya aquatica
WATER HICKORY

This magnificent tree likes to grow near water, which is only natural as it comes from the swamps and riverbanks of southeastern U.S.A. The long, narrow leaflets distinguish it from fellow *Carya* with their fat, wide leaflets. It has good golden-yellow fall color lasting for several weeks. The light brown, peeling bark is an appealing feature. Suitable for moist regions. Height 80 ft (25 m) x width 30 ft (10 m). ZONE 6.

Aquatica = living in or near water.

Carya cordiformis
BITTERNUT, BITTERNUT HICKORY, SWAMP HICKORY

A big, fast-growing tree, bitternut grows naturally in deep, silty river soils and seems to cope with wettish ground. The fruit is

Cedrus atlantica, syn *C. libani* subsp *atlantica*
ATLAS CEDAR

Atlas cedar forms a huge conical tree with upturned branches in a gray-green, intermediate color. There are numerous colored forms. It is a native of the Atlas Mountains of Morocco and Algeria, hence the name *atlantica*. It copes well with hotter, drier climates. Height 130 ft (40 m) x width 30 ft (10 m). ZONES 6 TO 9.

Atlantica = from the Atlantic.

Cedrus atlantica 'Glauca'
BLUE ATLAS CEDAR

This is a very exciting gray-blue foliage tree and, because it is relatively slow-growing, it can be planted in suburban gardens with a view to replacing it after 10 to 15 years. Height 130 ft (40 m) x width 30 ft (10 m).

Cedrus atlantica 'Glauca Pendula'

The pendent habit of this variety creates an illusion of a curtain of foliage. It stays compact enough to grow in small gardens. Plant this stylish cultivar at the top of a bank and let it weep down like a waterfall. Height x width 30 ft (10 m).

Above: *Cedrus atlantica* 'Glauca Pendula' (center), with *Chamaecyparis lawsoniana* 'Blue Weeper' and the ground cover *Juniperus* x *media* 'Pftizeriana Glauca'.

Cedrus deodara
DEODAR CEDAR, HIMALAYAN CEDAR

The Deodar cedar is a graceful, large tree with pendulous tips to the branches. The usual form seen in cultivation has glaucous leaves but the tree appears a consistent green color from a distance. The cultivated form has longer leaves than other species. Probably the best species for cool, wet climates. It is native to the Himalayan region. Height 130 ft (40 m) x width 30 ft (10 m). ZONES 7 TO 9.

'Aurea' has golden yellow leaves in the spring, gradually greening through summer. Height 50 ft (15 m) x width 25 ft (8 m). 'Pendula' is a spreading bush with tumbling, pendulous growth. It makes a fine ground cover for large gardens. Height 3 ft (1 m) x width 10 ft (3 m). 'Prostrata' is truly ground hugging and can be grown in rockeries. Height 4 in (10 cm) x width 3 ft (1 m). 'Vink's Golden' provides an improvement on the gold color. Height 50 ft (15 m) x width 25 ft (8 m).

Above and left:
Cedrus deodara

Cedrus libani
CEDAR OF LEBANON

Cedar of Lebanon is the classical park tree. Its dark green to gray-green leaves are borne on layers of tiered branches. It forms a dense tree when young but as it ages the tiered effect becomes ever more pronounced, as if it has been pruned for this "oriental" shape. It is much too big for most gardens, but there are numerous small varieties, such as **'Golden Dwarf'** and **'Nana'**. For both, height 4 ft (1.2 m) x width 5 ft (1.5 m). ZONES 7 TO 9.

'Sargentii' is probably the most striking clone, being a weeping dwarf. Height x width 3–6 ft (1–2 m).

Cercidiphyllum

Cercidiphyllaceae

Cercidiphyllums are all alone in a family of their own, one that has confused botanists for years and is somehow thought to be related to magnolias.

Cercidiphyllum = leaf like a *Cercis*.
(Most people seeing one for the first time think it is a *Cercis*.)

Cercidiphyllum japonicum
KATSURA TREE

As a young plant it is very upright with multiple stems or leaders. These young stems are black and smooth and as the tree ages the trunks slowly separate to form a wide, spreading tree. It is not the sort of tree to push you out of house and home so you can enjoy it as a bushy shrub for quite some time. The attractive flaky bark on older trees is somewhat similar to elms.

Leaves are rounded or oval with a crinkle-cut, serrated edge, and are arranged in opposite fashion and have pretty red stalks or petioles. It looks as if a designer has been busy with the neat, almost perfect, placement of the leaves.

The katsura tree is rather tricky to establish, which is possibly why you do not see it more often. Transplant as young as possible, because bigger specimens resent being moved. Ideally it requires good, deep, rich soil, or even clay, as long as it stays moist in summer; it does not like to dry out. Shelter from cold or fierce

winds is essential. It is very winter-hardy, but new growth can be hit by frost in a fluctuating spring climate.

There are no pests, but the trees do seem prone to root rot and perhaps the new *Trichoderma* fungi are the answer. *Trichoderma* are naturally occurring fungi that fill up space and thus keep deadly fungi at bay. Different forms of this "friendly fungi" can now be purchased to protect grapes and peaches against diseases.

It is deciduous and has tiny red flowers at the time the new leaves emerge. Male and female flowers are on separate trees. Height 70 ft (20 m) x width 50 ft (15 m). ZONES 4 TO 8.

Japonica = from Japan.

Cercidiphyllum japonicum var sinense
This form usually has a single trunk and in the wilds of China is the largest of all deciduous trees. If, like me, you have only seen modestly sized trees in cultivation, it is hard to imagine them growing so big. The fall color is usually shades of red, orange and salmon and the tree gives off a spicy odor of cotton candy at leaf fall. Height 70 ft (21 m) x width 50 ft (15 m).

Sinense = Chinese.

Cercidiphyllum japonicum 'Pendulum'
The weeping form is a magnificent sight but unfortunately very rare. Washington Arboretum has a splendid specimen in its Asian garden. Height 20 ft (6 m) x width 25 ft (8 m).

Cercidiphyllum japonicum var magnificum, syn C. magnificum
This is considered by some to be a separate species, and by others to be a form of C. *japonicum*. The leaves are larger and paler and more wavy at the edges. It is appropriately named as it is magnificent with these crinkle-cut leaf edges like a cookie, and has lovely yellow fall tints. Usually it forms a single-trunked shrub with smooth, light brown stems. It is happy in a continental climate, with very cold winters and hot, hot summers. Native to Japan. Height 30 ft (10 m) x width 25 ft (8 m). ZONE 6.

Magnificum = magnificent.

Below right: *Cercidiphyllum japonicum* var *magnificum* with *Azalea* 'Red Poppy'. Below left: *Cercidiphyllum japonicum*

Cercis

Fabaceae

how me a *Cercis* that is not desirable. We have eight in our garden and I still want more of them, namely *C. texensis* 'Oklahoma', which I saw in North Carolina. Why are they so lovely? Well, their shiny, heart-shaped leaves are irresistible and most have a total froth of flowers on the bare stems in early spring. They are a true herald of spring, trumpeting the pageant of flowers to come in the warmer months. This sort of flowering display can be seen from miles away—well, at least from a passing bus, and that is saying something for a deciduous tree. These magnificent flowering trees can rival cherry blossom and yet they are rarely given that status.

Happy in acidic or alkaline soil, *Cercis* prefer moist, well-drained sites but are quite tolerant of heavy clays and dry soils. They are genuine sun lovers and are quite at home in any warm summer climate. Tolerant of cold winters, provided they have enough summer heat to ripen the wood, they will even cope with hot inland climates with periods of drought.

Sometimes they are ungainly and multi-branched when young and you may need to give them some pruning and training to achieve the desired shape. They resent transplanting and so take care at this stage. Occasionally they are attacked by borer or thrips in a warm climate but in general can be thought of as pest-free. Coral spot fungus may attack them in cool climates.

So why would you include a *Cercis* in your garden? For the sheer mass display of flowers in the spring; because it is one of the earliest trees or shrubs to flower; and last, but not least, for their bold, heart-shaped leaves, undamaged by wind and weather and looking as good near fall as they did in the spring.

Cercis = from the Greek work *kerkis*, meaning shuttlecock.

Cercis canadensis
EASTERN REDBUD
Eastern redbud sets North American hills and campuses alight in April with masses of rose-pink, pea-like flowers. It grows all through eastern U.S.A. and Canada and could more accurately be called *Cercis appalachianensis*. Occasionally growing in some shade but flowering best in full sun, like most *Cercis* it needs summer

Above: *Cercis* leaf.

heat to ripen the wood to survive cold winters, and this is why it does not thrive in cool summer regions. The fall color is usually pale yellow and not spectacular, although some years it seems a stronger canary yellow. Height x width 30 ft (10 m). ZONES 5 TO 9.

'**Oklahoma**' and '**Forest Pansy**' are the two best *Cercis* for leaf color and texture. '**Appalachian Red**' is the best red-flowered form available.

Canadensis = from Canada.

Cercis canadensis 'Forest Pansy'
If one plant epitomizes fabulous foliage, then this is it. It probably attracts more attention in my garden than any other plant. The new leaves are almost black when they first unfurl, turning to burgundy wine. It retains this stunning color in climates with cool summers, but lightens to shades of green in the hot summers of Texas.

Fall can bring an intensity of purple colors or it can be a simple curl and drop of dull leaves depending on the season. The lovely black, shiny bark has a "touch me" quality about it. Height x width 15 ft (5 m). ZONE 6.

Cercis canadensis var texensis 'Oklahoma'
This top selection of *Cercis canadensis* offers rich, rosy magenta flowers followed by thick, glossy leaves with a very rich, dark green color. It tends to keep a smaller compact shape and fits comfortably into suburban gardens. Originates from the southern U.S.A. Best in a hot or warm climate although quite hardy. Height x width 15 ft (5 m). ZONES 6 TO 9.

Cercis chinensis
CHINESE REDBUD
Chinese redbud usually forms a small, wide-spreading tree, typically three times as wide as it is high. It has a very dense, twiggy nature and so does not have the simple clean structure of some

Above: *Cercis canadensis*

Cercis siliquastrum
JUDAS TREE

Judas tree forms a small, deciduous tree with an arching habit and often as wide or wider than it is high. The pretty rosy purple flowers appear on the bare stems in spring, followed by smooth, heart-shaped leaves. It is a southern European tree flourishing in hot, dry conditions. Height x width 30 ft (10 m). ZONES 6 TO 9.

Siliquastrum = having pods.

Chamaecyparis

FALSE CYPRESS
Cupressaceae

This small group of conifers has probably given rise to more cultivars than any other genus. Multitudinous twisted, curly and contorted mutations, not to mention gray, yellow, blue and green varieties, are available. Even a fanatic could not wish to own every cultivar in the huge selection.

Chamaecyparis foliage is more feathery than the thinner, coarser *Cupressus*. Most have flattened foliage as if it has been ironed into one plane but numerous cultivars have a more fluffy, puffed up appearance. Some can be clipped and used for hedges. They are easily transplanted, even at a late stage, because of their mass of fibrous roots. They do need careful preparation by root pruning over a period of weeks during winter before you attempt to shift them to their new home. They are not as tough or as hardy in coastal conditions as *Cupressus* but they are more cold-tolerant. Plant them in open, sunny places. Shade from overhanging trees or competition for light with neighboring shrubs will cause them to lose their shape and their luster.

They do like shelter from cold or salt-laden winds, though they will tolerate less than ideal conditions. Most are such easy-

other *Cercis*. Bold, heart-shaped leaves are glossy above and have a distinct point. The gray stems have prominent black buds.

It is sometimes believed that this plant does not like cold winters but as it hails from the Beijing region this does not make sense. Like most *Cercis* it thrives in climates with warm to hot summers and so will tolerate any sort of winter cold. It is probably typical of plants from northern China and Korea in needing a distinct winter followed by a rapid, almost instant spring, rather than a fluctuating weather pattern.

My own three seedling plants from Beijing Botanical Gardens are 6 ft (2 m) high after ten years and are a beacon in the spring with their masses of rosy cerise to purple flowers. It tends to flower early and is thus more vulnerable to late spring frosts. Height 20 ft (6 m) x width 15–30 ft (5–10 m). ZONES 6 TO 9.

'Avondale' is a selected prolific flower form with vivid purple blooms and a compact habit. Height x width 10 ft (3 m).

Chinensis = from China.

Left: *Chamaecyparis lawsoniana* 'Pembury Blue'

Above: *Chamaecyparis lawsoniana* 'Lane'

care shrubs, you will not need to tend them for ten years or more.

Chamaecyparis are prone to canker, a disease that can ringbark and kill branches or even whole trees. Thankfully it is not common, or as devastating as it sounds. The plants like good drainage and are prone to disease if the soil is poorly drained. Having said that, they do need access to moisture all year round, and are not good plants for drought-prone regions.

This is a valuable group of evergreens for providing structure in the garden or to hide certain views. Conifers and other evergreens are the essential "flesh on the bones" of the winter garden—a time when you need some enticement to go outside. Achieve this effect by using evergreens to divide different areas and add mystery.

Chamai = dwarf; *cyparis* = like *Cupressus* (cypress).

Chamaecyparis lawsoniana, syn *Cupressus lawsoniana*

LAWSON FALSE CYPRESS

This is a tough, wind and cold-hardy conifer with flattened strands of foliage. The color varies considerably and this is best seen in hedges of seedling plants where they vary from shades of gray through to dark blackish green. In a garden setting you are more likely to grow one of the named cultivars that tend to be smaller and have brighter colors. The small rounded cones are green at first, becoming brown when mature. Lawson false cypress was named after the Lawson Nursery in Edinburgh, Scotland. Seeds sent to them in 1854 from northwestern California by plant collector William Murray were the first in Europe. Charles Lawson (1794–1873) wrote the definitive book on conifers for that time and grew every conifer species then known in cultivation. Height 50–130 ft (15–40 m) x width 6–15 ft (2–5 m). ZONES 5 TO 9.

There are numerous cultivars for smaller gardens.

'Columnaris'

This has a very narrow, columnar habit with upright branches. The foliage is green on top and bluish green beneath. It is ideal for confined spaces. Height 30 ft (10 m) x width 3 ft (1 m).

'Lane'

'Lane' has brilliant golden foliage and is one of the best for bright color. When you look closely the foliage is green within the bush and a whitish yellow on the outside of the shrub. It has an upright, neat, tidy habit. Height x width 9 ft (3 m).

'Pembury Blue'

A beautiful conifer with pendent blue-gray foliage in a very upright conical shape. Height 50 ft (15 m) x width 25 ft (8 m).

'Triomphe de Boskoop'

This is a reliable blue cultivar, eventually forming a large, upright tree. Height 30 ft (10 m) x width 20 ft (6 m).

Chamaecyparis obtusa

Chamaecyparis obtusa has dark green, blunt, round-ended leaves. Naturally a tall forest giant from Japan, it is rarely seen in its natural form in gardens. There is a magnificent giant specimen at the Killerton Gardens in Devon, England.

Normally we only see fancy cultivars like those below. Height 70 ft (20 m) x width 20 ft (6 m). ZONES 4 TO 8.

Obtusa = blunt, referring to the leaves.

'Caespitosa'

One of the smallest conifers and therefore ideal for rockeries, 'Caespitosa' has very tight, nuggety growth in rich, dark green. Height x width 6–12 in (15–30 cm).

'Crippsii'

This is a big, bold, golden conifer in a tidy pyramidal shape. It makes an ideal specimen plant for large gardens. Height 50 ft (15 m) x width 25 ft (8 m).

'Minima'

One of the smallest conifers you are likely to see, this is a slow-growing dwarf. It makes a dense little mound of bright green. Height x width 16 in (40 cm).

'Nana Aurea'

Bright golden-yellow in summer, this tends to go a muddy bronze with patches of white in winter. It has tight scallops of foliage, and is a flat-topped dwarf. Height 6 ft (2 m) x width 4–6 ft (1.2–2 m).

Nana = small.

'Nana Gracilis'

This looks like some ocean-dwelling "brain" coral with its tight swirls of rich green growth. It has a dense, pyramidal habit. Height 10 ft (3 m) x width 6 ft (2 m).

'Nana Lutea'

A more true yellow than 'Aurea' and it keeps its color. It is even a good color in semi-shade, which it prefers. This is a conical dwarf. Height 12 in (30 cm) x width 10 in (25 cm). ZONES 5 TO 8.

Chamaecyparis pisifera

Another forest tree from Japan, but seen in our gardens in the miniature forms, usually with gray-blue, frothy foliage. There is an amazing specimen of this at Killerton Gardens, Devon, England. Height 70 ft (20 m) x width 15 ft (5 m). ZONES 4 TO 8.

Pisifera = pea-bearing, referring to the pea-sized cones.

Above: *Chamaecyparis obtusa* 'Minima' is the very small plant, with *C. o.* 'Nana Lutea' (back left) and *C. o.* 'Raraflora' (right).

Above: *Chamaecyparis pisifera* 'Boulevard'

'Boulevard'

'Boulevard' forms a very small and compact, upright, conical bush with fluffy blue foliage. Somehow the soft appearance invites you to touch or stroke it. It will cope with some shade and still do well, but it does need a moist climate. Height 3–30 ft (1–10 m) x width 3–15 ft (1–5 m).

'Filifera Aurea'

This unique conifer, a "love it or hate it" plant, has long, thin strands of foliage like golden yellow spaghetti. You will not confuse this with any other plant. It performs best in full sun and needs to be the center of attention. Height 40 ft (12 m) x width 30 ft (10 m).

'Gold Spangle'

Brilliant yellow shooting stars leap out of a dense conical bush, which can be clipped to any shape. The soft tips of the new growth are pendulous, adding to the charm of this shrub. Height 10 ft (3 m) x width 6 ft (2 m).

Above: *Cornus alternifolia* 'Argentea' with *C. chinensis* (left).

Cornus

DOGWOOD
Cornaceae

*C*ornus is a diverse group of plants including everything from the ground-hugging *Cornus canadensis* to the thicket-forming shrub with shiny, colored stems, *C. stolonifera*. Then there is the European *C. mas* with its froth of tiny yellow flowers in early spring, and the more familiar *C. florida* with big white bracts in the spring, and finally the evergreen Himalayan strawberry tree, *C. capitata*. They hail from virtually every part of the globe, though mostly Asia and the U.S.A. Some have been moved into a separate genus and then have been brought back again into the *Cornus* fold. They are mostly deciduous trees, with just a few evergreen types to add spice.

With such a diversity of form it is not surprising they have been grown for flower, foliage, fruit and ornamental stems. *Cornus* is a happy group of plants found growing in most soils and is generally drought-tolerant. Some, like *C. stolonifera*, will cope with wet and boggy ground. In a garden situation, keep the roots cool with a mulch of bark or woodchips.

Full sun and shelter from cold winds are the requirements for the ornamental flowering *Cornus*. Actually, the sumptuous flowers are made up of bracts, rather than petals. These flowering *Cornus* grow best in a continental climate: hot summers, cold winters and a long, hot, dry fall to ripen the wood and encourage flowering. Even the so-called tender *C. capitata* will thrive in these conditions, as long as the winters are not too cruel.

Cornus = from Latin *cornu*, referring to the hard wood used for spears. (Dogwood is from an old custom of bathing mangy dogs using the bark of *C. sanguinea*.)

Cornus alternifolia
PAGODA DOGWOOD
Often seen as a multi-stemmed shrub, pagoda dogwood eventually becomes a wide deciduous tree. The spreading branch network laid out in tiers gives it an oriental look. The leaves are alternate, hence the name, and are mid-green becoming red and purple in the fall. The small white flowers are of no great merit. It needs a moist soil and a sheltered site. It originates from Canada and eastern U.S.A. Height x width 20 ft (6 m). ZONES 4 TO 8.

Alternifolia = alternate leaves.

Cornus alternifolia 'Argentea', syn *C. a.* 'Variegata'
'Argentea' has slightly smaller white-edged leaves. The tree has a misty, ephemeral appearance when seen from a distance, with the "bones" of the bush visible through the light and lacy foliage. Height 10 ft (3 m) x width 8 ft (2.5 m).

Cornus capitata
HIMALAYAN STRAWBERRY TREE
Cornus capitata is a big, bold, evergreen tree covered in a mass of creamy yellow flowers in early summer. The large, strawberry-like fruits are popular with birds, but generally not with people, as they are very smelly. Although it is regarded as tender, given a hot summer climate, it will survive cool winters. Height x width 40 ft (12 m). ZONE 8 OR 9.

Capitata = dense cluster or head.

Cornus controversa
GIANT DOGWOOD
Aptly called the "wedding cake tree" with its layers of branches decorated with creamy white, frothy flowers in the spring—the icing on the cake. Flowers appear in early summer, followed by small, black fruits. There are no showy bracts and yet the floral display is still worthy of the name. Each flower head is a mass of white flowers in flat clusters at the end of the stems. With the horizontal branches as well, it looks similar to *Viburnum* 'Lanarth'.

It is easily distinguished from other *Cornus*, being one of the few species with alternate leaves, which possibly gives it its name, being different to other species. The slightly scented large leaves are folded down the middle like a valley. If you bend a leaf in half and gently tear it apart, the sticky sap in the veins will hold the two halves together. This unusual trait is true of most dogwoods.

Cornus controversa forms a wide-spreading shrub or small tree with whorls of branches. Each tier of three or four branches emerges from the trunk at the same level and then there is a gap of 3 ft (1 m) or so and then another layer of branches.

It is easy to enhance the Japanese style by pruning to augment that effect. It also shows off the attractive, smooth, gray trunks. It makes an architectural plant in winter after the final show of purple-red fall leaves.

Below: *Cornus controversa* with *Rhododendron elliottii* (left) and *Disanthus cercidifolius* (front right).

Right: *Cornus florida*

To grow well, the plant needs full sun, protection from wind and good drainage to prevent root rot diseases. Originates from China, the Himalayas and Japan. Height x width 50 ft (15 m). ZONES 6 TO 9.

Controversa = different (to other *Cornus* species).

Cornus controversa 'Variegata'

This is a splendid form with silver-edged leaves shown off to perfection by the tiered horizontal habit. The plant was a chance find in a French nursery in the 1890s. It is common in France and Italy and only becoming available elsewhere as nurseries graft plants onto green seedlings. If you are ever in Ireland, visit Dunloe Castle to see the best one in the world. Height x width 25 ft (8 m). ZONE 6.

Cornus 'Eddie's White Wonder' (*C. florida* x *C. nuttallii*)

A hybrid between two fine species, this makes a tidy, upright bush with gaudy white flowers. It is a hardy, reliable performer with mid-green leaves and good fall color as a bonus. Height 20 ft (6 m) x width 15 ft (5 m). ZONES 5 TO 8.

Cornus florida

FLOWERING DOGWOOD

For me, nothing beats the thrill seeing a plant in the wild or its natural state. Not a new plant which has yet to be cataloged (this is most unlikely) but rather a plant we are all familiar with in our gardens. I still remember the thrill of seeing *Cornus florida* in flower, growing on the edge of the woods on John Palmer's farm in the Appalachians. No matter how many times you have seen it in cultivation, somehow the wild plant is more vivid and brings more joy.

Cornus florida has a clean, pleasing, tiered habit visible in winter, with smooth, gray-brown stems. Leaves are a smooth gray-green and given the right conditions the fall color is a scintillating palette of reds, gold and orange. It enjoys cold winters and baking summer heat followed by a hot, dry fall. Hot summers ripen the wood to withstand winter cold and "sets" a good crop of flower buds as well as enhancing the gorgeous fall color.

In a mild climate or fluctuating winter temperatures this *Cornus* is susceptible to late spring frost damage. Also the fall color does not "sing the same song." In a mild climate they struggle to survive, taking three steps forward and then two back. Even when unmolested by stem borer and root rot they give the appearance of being unhappy.

There is a devastating new disease called *Anthracnose* for which there seems no cure. First noticed as spots or blotches on the new leaves, the next stage is severe dieback of the branches. *C. florida* and *C. nuttallii* are particularly susceptible, while *C. sanguinea* and *C. alba* are also affected.

Cornus florida prefers a neutral or acidic soil, and needs to be free-draining to keep root rot at bay. Shelter from wind is essential, too. Given the right conditions this is the ultimate woodland shrub, with good structure, great fall color and wonderful flowers. The flowers perch along the branches like a transient flock of butterflies. The wild forms are pure white, although many pink

and red cultivars are available. Height 20 ft (6 m) x width 25 ft (8 m). ZONES 5 TO 8.

There are numerous cultivars available, including: **'Apple Blossom'**, with soft pink and white flowers; **'Cherokee Chief'**, which has deep rose red flowers; **'White Cloud'** is a particularly good white form.

Florida = rich in flowers, not the state.
(Plants from Florida are called *floridana*.)

Cornus florida **'Rainbow'**

There are a few variegated forms, and this is one of the better ones. Compact and upright in habit, it has rich tri-colored yellow and green leaves with a hint of red turning to rich scarlet. Height 10 ft (3 m) x width 8 ft (2.5 m).

Cornus kousa **var** *chinensis*
KOUSA DOGWOOD

Kousa dogwood makes a tiered bush, covered in large white flowers in summer, similar to *Cornus florida* except each bract is pointed at the tip, rather than being rounded. It has lovely wavy-margined, dark green leaves similar to *C. florida* and superb fall color. The variety usually found in cultivation is the Chinese form introduced by E. H. Wilson (1876–1930) from central China in 1907. Height 8 ft (2.5 m) x width 6 ft (2 m). ZONES 5 TO 8.

Kousa = the Japanese name for their native tree.

Cornus nuttallii
PACIFIC DOGWOOD

Pacific dogwood is a big, broad, deciduous tree suitable for large gardens and often seen in parks and public gardens. Gorgeous rich green, glossy leaves 5 in (13 cm) long provide fall colors of reds, purple and yellow. In spring the foliage is a superb backdrop to the large creamy white bract "flowers," sometimes with a hint of pink. It prefers deep acidic soil and a moist climate, sheltered from strong winds. Named for Thomas Nuttall (1786–1859) an early pioneer and botanist traveling through America and Canada. It originates from western North America. Height 40 ft (12 m) x width 25 ft (8 m). ZONE 7 OR 8.

Cornus walteri

Although rarely seen in gardens, this hardy tree is easy to please. It has terminal clusters of white flowers in the summer, and superb gray-green leaves all in one plane. Generally seen as a small upright tree in gardens, often with appealing bark. Another E. H. Wilson introduction. Height 20–30 ft (6–10 m) x width 10–15 ft (3–5 m). ZONE 6.

Walteri = origin unknown.

Cotinus

SMOKE TREE
Anacardiaceae

*C*otinus are what I call students' plants. When you first begin learning plants, you have to learn to recognize key features. Well, the *Cotinus* genus is easy, as the leaves are unmistakable and unique. Once you have seen their spherical leaves, you will recognize the plants anywhere.

There are only two species, one growing in hot, dry places from eastern Europe through to the Great Wall of China, and the other from Tennessee and north to Texas. Both are deciduous and very cold-hardy, growing to zone 4, and yet they are equally at home in moist zones 9 and 10 locations. While they will cope with wind, they are showier in a sheltered garden. They positively "sing" in the sun but look drab and jaded in the shade. Any soil will suffice; in fact they thrive and give of their best in poor soils. *Cotinus* are very drought-tolerant. No pest or disease would dare touch them, possibly because of the poisons within. Have a care and beware when pruning as some are allergic to the sticky stem juice. Avoid getting it on your clothes or it will stain the fabric.

The flowers are a froth of creamy gray and this gives rise to the common name of smoke bush, as it appears the bush is on fire when covered in plumes of "gray smoke" in summer. They are some of the very best garden shrubs for fall color, ranging from red to orange to scintillating "Papal purple." Some books claim they need cold climates for stunning fall color, and yet I have seen stupendous fall colors in frost-free regions. Even the summer leaf color is outstanding on cultivars such as *Cotinus* x 'Grace'.

A ruthless pruning in winter will revitalize the plants, resulting in bigger leaves and better fall color, and one technique is to cut the bushes back to stumps 3 ft (1 m) high every winter.

They are the perfect plants to site at the end of a lawn vista, with positive "wow appeal" all summer. Definitely one of my favorite shrubs, the only difficulty is choosing which variety to grow.

Cotinus = from Greek *kotinus*, wild oilve.

Cotinus coggygria, syn *Rhus cotinus*
SMOKE BUSH, VENETIAN SUMAC

This is rarely seen in gardens in the seedling or wild form as the cultivars are more reliable for leaf color. Left to its own devices it is a small tree with plumes of fluffy flowers in midsummer. It looks very appealing in the rain, when it becomes almost pendulous with the weight of the water droplets. The rounded leaves are often quite small, while the cultivars tend to have bigger, bolder leaves. Height x width 15 ft (5 m). ZONE 5.

Coggygria = Greek name for smoke tree, *koggugia*.

Below: *Cotinus coggygria*

Above: *Cotinus coggygria* 'Royal Purple'

'Daydream'
The fluffy, creamy white flowers take on a pink tinge to create a dreamy effect. It has a reasonably tidy, dense habit compared to more rangy varieties, and it has neat green foliage. Height x width 15 ft (5 m).

'Nordine Red'
A terrific red wine leaf color. Two characteristics worth noting are that it is more cold-hardy than most clones and it colors up well in regions with hot summers. Height x width 15 ft (5 m). ZONE 4.

'Royal Purple'
Rich, dark purple leaves through summer change to reds and scarlets before leaf fall. 'Royal Purple' is justifiably one of the most popular clones. **Velvet Cloak** is very similar.

Cotinus obovatus, syn *C. americanus*, *Rhus cotinoides*
AMERICAN SMOKE TREE, CHITTAMWOOD

More tree-like than *Cotinus coggygria*, American smoke tree is often grown as a pollarded tree. It has stunning fall color in bright orange, reds and golds. The leaves are much larger than *C. coggygria*, and this trait is imparted to the hybrids. It is happy in acidic or alkaline soil and again this tolerance is imparted to the hybrids. Height 30 ft (10 m) x width 25 ft (8 m). ZONES 4 TO 9.

Obovatus = egg-shaped.

Cotinus x 'Grace'
The perfect orbs that grace the stems on this plant seem like some new interplanetary import. The leaves are large, luscious and purple-red and it often has a second flush of red growth just after midsummer, providing an exciting contrast with the older leaves. These plum-colored leaves turn scintillating scarlet in fall. Even the flower heads are more vibrant in purplish-mauve pink. Raised by Peter Dummer at Hilliers Nursery in England in 1978, *C.* x 'Grace' is a hybrid between the two species. Height x width 15 ft (5 m). ZONES 4 TO 9.

Cotinus x 'Flame', syn C. coggygria 'Flame'

This is another hybrid with oval, light green leaves, turning bright orange-red in fall. The fruiting panicles are purple pink. Height 20 ft (6 m) x width 15 ft (5 m). ZONES 5 TO 9.

Cotoneaster

Rosaceae

It is difficult to imagine *Cotoneaster* being related to apples and pears, but when you look closely at the five-petaled white flowers it is not so hard to believe. The clusters of creamy white flowers are popular with bees. Cotoneasters come in a variety of shapes and guises. Most are deciduous, but there are many evergreen ones too. They vary in size from tiny, ground-hugging shrubs up to small trees. Most are grown for a combination of bright red berries and foliage, meaning fall color on the deciduous ones and rough, tough leaves on the evergreens.

I think of them as being useful shrubs, rather than glorious ones. Birds spread the seeds and so stray plants can emerge. But there is certainly no denying their hardiness and robust nature. They will grow in any soil, no matter how poor or thin, and often fruit best when on hard, dry banks.

Most are extremely wind-tolerant and while they prefer full sun, they will also grow in shade. Fireblight disease is the only major drawback, other than the crop of seedlings in some climates.

Cotone = quince; *aster* = likeness.

Cotoneaster bullatus

This has the best leaf of the genus, with rich red fall colors, although it is semi-evergreen in warmer places. The red berries hang out over the leaves looking very attractive to us and to the local bird population. The bigger-leaf form, which was known as *C. bullatus* var *macrophyllus* is now known as *C. rehderi*. *C. bullatus* originates from China. Height x width 9 ft (3 m). ZONES 6 TO 8.

Bullatus = bullate (corrugated with ridges between the veins).

Cotoneaster congestus, syn C. pyrenaicus

This evergreen forms a neat little mound of a plant, ideal for rockeries, and has dull, pale green leaves. It has red buds, pink flowers and a crop of red berries. Its leaves are congested (close together), hence the name. It comes from the Himalayan region. Height 28 in (70 cm) x width 36 in (90 cm). ZONE 7 OR 8.

Congestus = referring to the close together leaves.

Cotoneaster franchetii

A big, arching shrub, *Cotoneaster franchetti* is ideal as a backdrop or shelter. This very tough evergreen or semi-evergreen plant will withstand strong winds and grow in poor soils. Like most cotoneasters it can be trained to any shape you want and can be clipped round or opened up Asian-style. The dark green leaves are attractive and the clusters of off-white flowers are followed by orange-red berries. Seedlings can be a pest in warmer regions. It loses a portion of the leaves in cooler climates. Adrien René Franchet was the Director of the Natural History Museum in France during the late 19th century. He had the mammoth task of collating all the specimens sent home by David and Delavay, two

Above: *Cotoneaster franchetii*

Left: *Cotoneaster horizontalis* 'Variegatus'

missionaries who collected plants by the thousand. Height x width 10 ft (3 m). ZONES 7 TO 9.

Cotoneaster horizontalis
ROCKSPRAY

While this is a great ground cover, it looks best when planted against a wall, where it sits up vertically, displaying its neat herringbone stem patterns. It forms a hardy, deciduous shrub with glossy dark green leaves, purple-red fall leaf color and masses of red berries. It is ideal for sun or shady places. Rockspray is semi-evergreen in warmer climates. Height 3 ft (1 m) x width 5 ft (1.5 m). ZONES 5 TO 9.

Horizontalis = horizontally growing.

Cotoneaster x watereri 'John Waterer'

This makes a tall semi-evergreen shrub with long, dark, handsome leaves. The arching branches help keep a tidy, pleasing shape.

While it looks good as a foliage plant all year, the highlight is fall, when it is laden with hot orange-red berries. It is named after the famous Waterer Nursery in Surrey, England. Height x width 15 ft (5 m). ZONES 6 TO 8.

Cryptomeria

Cryptomeria japonica
JAPANESE CEDAR
Taxodiaceae

In the forests of Japan lives a tremendously tall tree dominating the surrounding forest. It starts life as a typical conifer with a conical, Christmas tree shape and dark evergreen leaves. The foliage is quite different from other conifers in that it is like some strange undersea coral or maybe blackish green fingers searching for the light. Along the fingers are whorls of spiky, pointed leaves that are sharp—take care.

The trunks have a marvelous, warm brown appearance and peeling vertical strips of bark are shed throughout the year. The branches start out growing upward toward the light, but as the tree ages and the branches lengthen, the weight of the greenery tends to make the branch swoop down and then up again at the sunny end where the tips still seek the light. The shade cast by the branches is so dense that no plants can survive beneath the tree and the mat of dead leaves is all the ground cover one would desire.

When planted in a garden this evergreen tree grows rapidly

Above: A very old specimen of *Cryptomeria japonica* 'Compacta Nana'.

(up to 3 ft [1 m] a year in a warm climate), keeping the narrow columnar habit in the early years and eventually becoming more space-consuming as the tree expands. All Cryptomerias transplant easily from pots or from open ground if carefully root-pruned in advance. Once planted in your garden, do not be tempted to shift one as it will end in tears.

Easy to grow in any free-draining soil, and any climate to zone 6, although it does not like prolonged droughts. *Cryptomeria japonica* is extremely wind-hardy and is used for windbreaks and

Right: *Cryptomeria japonica* 'Vilmoriniana

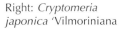

Above: *Cryptomeria japonica* 'Sekkan-Sugi'

farm hedges, where it is valued for speed of growth as well as its tolerance to wind. It also has the ability to regenerate when cut with hedge trimmers and is resistant to pests and diseases. I have seen it survive cyclonic winds when other so-called wind-hardy *Cupressus* and coastal pines have been decimated by the storms. On top of all these attributes it is very attractive. The tips of each stem are vertical while the foliage beneath is almost pendulous. This twin "up and down" pattern is very pleasing to the eye.

Plants grown from seed vary considerably and can be quite ragged and slow-growing. Named forms are best if you want lush, healthy growth. A wind-hardy clone called **'Egmont'** has rich green foliage; **'Benjamin Franklin'** has a hint of blue in the foliage, and was selected for tolerance to strong winds and salt spray. **'Yoshino'** is a rapid grower, keeping a good pyramid shape and is very cold-hardy.

All parts of the flower are hidden. This must be one of those botanical puzzles, because while we do not usually think of conifers as having flowers, at least not visible ones, the flowers on *Cryptomeria* are quite prominent in springtime. Just touch a branch in flower and you will be showered in a cloud of pollen dust. The long, thin, male flowers the size of a rice grain produce all this pollen. The pea-sized female flowers at the tips of last season's growth are green with a hint of purple-blue. After pollination the resulting round, brown cones release their seeds in the spring, ready for germination.

While there is only one species of *Cryptomeria* (there is a Chinese species which most botanists consider identical to the Japanese species) there are umpteen cultivars, many of which will fit into any suburban garden. Height 80 ft (25 m) x width 20 ft (6 m). ZONES 6 TO 9.

There are numerous dwarf forms of the adult type with finger-like foliage including *C. j.* **'Araucarioides'**, which looks as if it belongs under water rather than in a garden with its long,

whippy stems clothed in dark green leaves. This is a form of the adult foliage so the stems and leaves are dark green. Height x width 6 ft (2 m). **'Bandai-sugi'** is a dome of foliage like a mossy log and a very tight, compact plant. It is a great rockery plant that can be clipped to shape. Height x width 6 ft (2 m).

While some cultivars put up with a little shade, they do not shine when planted in such a position.

Crypto = hidden (as in crypt);
meria = part (all parts of the flower are hidden); *japonica* = from Japan.

Cryptomeria japonica 'Elegans'

This juvenile form of the species looks very different to its parent. It is lovely and soft to touch and has a feathery appearance. It is bright green all through summer, turning a lovely burnished bronze in the winter months. It is an ideal garden shrub as it is very slow-growing in the early years, but will eventually form a tree. As the branches elongate they have a tendency to lean at extreme angles or even fall over without appearing to suffer any harm. It is quite common to see trees with distorted branches as they find a new sense of direction. Although this is the juvenile form, I have yet to see a tree changing from this into adult foliage, and yet some of the juveniles must be around 80 years old. How long does it have to be juvenile before it matures? In other juvenile conifers, like *Chamaecyparis*, it is quite common to see the fluffy juveniles changing to adult form when the bush gets older. Height 20–30 ft (6–10 m) x width 20 ft (6 m).

'Elegans Compacta' is an even slower, more compact form of the above, with soft, dark green, glossy juvenile foliage. Height x width 6–12 ft (2–4 m).

Below: *Cryptomeria japonica* 'Elegans' with bronze winter foliage.

Cunninghamia

Cunninghamia lanceolata, syn *C. sinensis*
CHINA FIR
Taxodiaceae

China fir is an elegant plant, worthy of a space in every large garden. I say "large garden" because it does eventually become a tree and by that time you will be so in love with it you will not have the heart to cut it out. It is vaguely reminiscent of the monkey puzzle, with very spiky, pale green stems completely enclosed in long, sharp, pointed leaves with a distinct gray-green streak underneath. The leaves have a shiny, lustrous, polished finish that adds considerably to their appeal. The bush has an upright, conical habit. In its juvenile stage it will be clothed to the ground, suppressing any weeds. Older trees gradually lose their lower branches, revealing the peeling red-brown bark. While the trunks are attractive, keep the greenery to ground level if possible.

It is a typical conifer in that it is evergreen, a dense pyramid when young, and produces cones. Like most conifers it prefers a well-drained soil but otherwise is not fussy. It seems to prefer a wettish climate, but I have seen it thrive in drought-prone regions, and it is easily transplanted from pots or open ground. It must be grown in full sun to be at its best, as it tends to get ragged and rather open when in too much shade. The tree is reasonably cold-hardy, but for a plant with seemingly impregnable defenses it does not like strong or frequent winds.

No pest or disease seems brave enough to tackle it. Even gardeners should beware when working close to their *Cunninghamia* as any quick move on your part may receive a "sharp" rebuke.

It was named after James Cunningham, who discovered *C. lanceolata* on Chusan Island off the coast of China in 1701 while working for the East India Company. Cunningham was the first westerner to write a description of the cultivation of tea and introduced the first camellias to the west. The plant was later introduced to cultivation by William Kerr (as in *Kerria*), a Kew Gardens collector, in 1804. Height 70 ft (20 m) or more x width 20 ft (6 m). ZONES 6 OR 7.

'Chason's Gift' has dark green leaves and a neat pyramidal shape. **'Glauca'** has bright gray-blue foliage and tends to be more open in habit. Both height 50 ft (15 m) x width 15 ft (5 m).

When the above cultivars are grown from cuttings they may not want to form a proper tree initially. If the cuttings are taken from horizontal or side growths, the resulting plant also wants to grow sideways. These plants are best unstaked and left to lie prostrate until eventually the plant will put up a new, strong leader from ground level. Cuttings from terminal growths do not suffer from this problem, but it is often difficult to find terminal growths for cuttings, especially if the tree has a single leader.

Lanceolata = spear or lance-shaped (leaves).

Cunninghamia konishii
This is a similar species from Taiwan and is slightly less hardy than *Cunninghamia lanceolata*. The foliage is softer to the touch and is a useful method of identification, while *C. lanceolata* is too prickly to hold. It was discovered by Mr. Konishi on Mt. Randai, Taiwan, in 1908. Height 50 ft (15 m) x width 15 ft (5 m). ZONE 7.

Cupressus

CYPRESS
Cupressaceae

Most *Cupressus* are huge trees but with a bit of good fortune you can find some to fit in your garden. All have dense evergreen foliage, some with soft pendulous growth and others with fierce spiky, scaly leaves. They are popular for a variety of reasons, including having various color forms from dark green to gold to gray. Some are extremely wind tolerant and others are drought-hardy, which is a surprise in the conifer world.

Cupressus arizonica copes with semi-desert conditions and *C. macrocarpa* grows on the cliffs at Monterey in California, resisting the sea, the salt and storm winds. Most are tolerant of heavy soils with slow drainage and they seem indifferent to acidity, alkalinity and any hot or windy site. They are sometimes not as cold-hardy as we might like. The related *Chamaecyparis* are far more resilient in this respect.

Cupressus do not transplant easily from open ground. While most conifers make ideal hedges, this is not so for *Cupressus*, as they may have dead patches when trimmed. Some are prone to canker, a fungus that kills off the occasional branch, ruining the shape and appearance of the plant.

Cupressus = equal or symmetrical growth (from Greek *kuparissos*).

Below:
Cunninghamia lanceolata

Above: *Cupressus arizonica* 'Blue Ice'

Above: *Cupressus macrocarpa* yellow form.

Cupressus arizonica var *glabra*, syn *C. glabra*
SMOOTH CYPRESS

Smooth cypress forms a gray-green, tough, wiry plant that is very drought-hardy and sun-resilient. It is attractive in a rugged sort of way, and is sometimes used for hedges. A form called **'Blue Ice'** is extremely wind-hardy, coping with salt winds as well. Originates from southwestern U.S.A. Height 30–50 ft (10–15 m) x width 12–15 ft (4–5 m). ZONE 7.

Arizonica = from Arizona.

Cupressus macrocarpa
MONTEREY CYPRESS

Cupressus macrocarpa is a huge character tree from the California coast, thus the common name. It is supremely wind-hardy, as you would imagine, growing on these west-coast cliffs looking out at miles of ocean, which produces some wonderful old "character" trees shaped by the elements. The habit is somewhat like a cedar of Lebanon with its platforms of foliage. Commonly used as a windbreak, it is now gaining favor as a timber tree, producing fine-grained yellow timber, ideal for interior cladding. Height 100 ft (30 m) x width 12–40 ft (4–12 m). ZONE 8.

There are numerous cultivars for smaller gardens. **'Aurea Saligna'** has lovely weeping yellow foliage. The plant is surprisingly tough, surviving lashings of wind and salt. Height 30 ft (10 m) x width 15 ft (5 m). **'Greenstead Magnificent'** is a beautiful blue-gray, rugged ground cover. If you want to try something different, train it up a stake and then let it cascade out from the top at, say, 6 ft (2 m) for an unusual "umbrella" effect. Height 2 ft (60 cm) x width 4–5 ft (1.5 m). **'Horizontalis Aurea'** is a quick-growing, tough plant, ideal for dense ground cover. It is bright yellow in full sun, but tends to lose that color if at all shaded. Height 2 ft (60 cm) x width 6 ft (2 m). **'Lutea'** is an excellent hardy yellow form. Height 30 ft (10 m) x width 20 ft (6 m).

Macrocarpa = big seed case.

Left: *Cupressus macrocarpa* 'Lutea'

Cupressus sempervirens
ITALIAN CYPRESS, MEDITERRANEAN CYPRESS

Familiar to any traveler to the Mediterranean region, this narrow, pencil-like tree is sometimes referred to as the "Cypress of the Ancients" because of its longevity and prominence in any landscape. Two forms exist, one with a more upright, tidy, narrow habit, called **'Stricta'** or **'Fastigiata'**, and blackish green foliage. This is a great accent plant, though it can get untidy when old. Trim or tie it to maintain the perfect shape. Height 70 ft (20 m) x width 10 ft (3 m).

The other form, **'Horizontalis'**, has a wider habit and more spreading branches, though the name is confusing as we tend to think of any plant called *horizontalis* as being a flat ground cover sort of plant. Height 70 ft (20 m) x width 20 ft (6 m).

Young plants are subject to cold injury, but they are certainly tough once established. They cope with wind, poor soil and extreme drought. These plants are native to the eastern Mediterranean and Iran. Height 70 ft (20 m) x width 3–20 ft (1–6 m). ZONE 8.

'Green Pencil' is a very slender pencil form from Hilliers Gardens in England. Its foliage is bright green and the plant is hardy. It is also known as **'Green Spire'**. Height 10 ft (3 m) x width 2 ft (60 cm).

'Swane's Golden' is an Australian form with golden foliage and is probably the best upright golden conifer, in a perfect rocket shape. It is happy in full sun and is generally a pretty tough specimen, though it does not like coastal winds. Happy in dry sites. Height 20 ft (6 m) x width 3 ft (1 m).

> *Sempervirens* = evergreen or everlasting; *stricta* and *fastigiata* = erect.

Cupressus torulosa
BHUTAN CYPRESS

I like this weeping, dense, conical tree. The overall effect is a bluish green, slightly weeping pyramid. If you need a large dense conifer with a pleasing, pendulous habit, then this will fit the bill. It is quite fast-growing, say, 9 ft (3 m) in 10 years, so it is not going to dominate too quickly. It prefers a warm, moist climate. Bhutan cypress originates from the Himalayan region. Height 100 ft (30 m) x width 30 ft (10 m). ZONE 7 OR 8.

> *Torulosa* = mounded or weeping.

Below: *Cupressus torulosa* 'Cashmeriana', in the middle with blue foliage, with *Acer palmatum* 'Red Dragon' (below) and *Casurina torulosa* (left).

Above: *Cupressus sempervirens* 'Swane's Golden', with *Pinus radiata* in the background.

Cupressus torulosa 'Cashmeriana' syn C. cashmeriana
KASHMIR CYPRESS

This is, without a doubt, my most cherished evergreen conifer. The graceful waterfall of gray-blue foliage is soft and gentle. Plant one beside a body of water and let it work its magic on you. Pendulous trees give rise to the best reflections in ponds and lakes. A wet climate seems to be essential for this species, so planting by a pond always helps. I am not saying it likes wet feet, just a high and regular rainfall.

It is so slow-growing it will be a shrub for many years in your garden, and by the time you realize it is going to be a tree it will be too late and you will not be able to part with it whatever size it seeks to attain. Although the foliage is pendulous, the inner tree has upright, ascending branches with reddish-brown, peeling trunks showing themselves occasionally through the screen of foliage. The overall shape is an upright cone with a thin, pointed top. I have seen them judiciously pruned Asian-style to show off an occasional branch, and it looked magical.

It is not as hardy as one would like and can be damaged by frost. It does not like wind either, which will ruin the soft, feathery look. If you are gardening in a windy site, try **C. torulosa 'Glauca'** for a similar look from a tougher plant.

Kashmir cypress, however, is rarely attacked by canker or any pests. Transplant as a young plant from pots as it is not easy to establish. It is not the kind of plant you buy on impulse. They often look scruffy when young, and it is usually sold to those who know it and want one, rather than browsers. Originates from the Himalayan region. Height 100 ft (30 m) x width 30 ft (10 m). ZONE 8.

Above: *Daphniphyllum macropodum*

Daphniphyllum

Daphniphyllaceae

If daphniphyllums had flowers to rival a rhododendron, we would all want one. The smooth, rich, dark, blackish green leaves are reminiscent of many a hybrid rhododendron and, like them, the plants are happy to grow in shade. The tiny yellow-green female and purplish male flowers are not in the same league as a rhododendron or even a daphne. In fact they probably would not make the league at all. They are easily missed unless you know what to look for, and they are more likely to be found by scent. Clusters of these acrid-smelling flowers appear beneath the stems in spring. The fact it is an evergreen plant tends to hide the flowers even more. Male and female flowers appear on separate plants. But forget the flowers: it is as top foliage plants that daphniphyllums are known best.

Any well-drained soil will suffice as they thrive in acidic or alkaline soil. I have seen them growing out of cliff faces in Korea, so drought holds no terrors, while they are equally happy in a wet climate. Full hot sun or semi-shade is fine and they cope with a breezy to windy site. Add to this the lack of pests and diseases and you have very tough plants. Certainly they are among the best large evergreens for those difficult shady spots in the garden.

Two species are in general cultivation and the one most often encountered is *Daphniphyllum macropodum*, not that either of them is common or familiar to many gardeners.

Daphniphyllum = leaf like a daphne.

Daphniphyllum macropodum, syn *D. glaucescens*
In nature this is a small tree, but in the garden it makes a nicely rounded bush. The thick, waxy leaf is of a typical rhododendron hybrid size and about 6 in (15 cm) long, dark green above and dull gray beneath. The leaves are thick and waxy in a clean oval shape. Seedling variation means some are more dramatic than others, though they all have smooth, paddle-like leaves. Some have very striking red petioles (leaf stalks) and reddish purple stems. These good forms are quite stunning, and perhaps the best clones should

be selected and named, though they are rather tricky to propagate from cuttings. This plant is hardy and easily established in the garden.

Daphniphyllum macropodum is fairly common in the forests of Korea and Japan, and is also found on the Chinese mainland. It was introduced by Charles Maries (1851–1902) for the famous Veitch Nursery in England in 1870, and just nine years later it won a First Class Certificate award from the Royal Horticultural Society in England for its foliage. Ninety-nine years later it won another F.C.C. for foliage and fruits, which are bluish black and the size of a pea. Height 20 ft (6 m) x width 15 ft (5 m). ZONE 7.

Macropodum = stout-stalked.

Daphniphyllum humile
This is a lesser-known species, and the shrub is a brilliant, dense, evergreen ground cover for shady sites. Its wide-spreading habit makes it an ideal weed suppressor. The fact that it is free of pests and looks so healthy all year-round is a bonus. Such easy-care evergreen shrubs are a rarity. It was also collected in Japan (1879) by Charles Maries. Height 3 ft (1 m) x width 3–6 ft (1–2 m). ZONE 8.

Humile = small or dwarf.

Decaisnea

Decaisnea fargesii
Lardizabalaceae

Decaisnea is a genus of just two plants in a rather obscure family. *Decaisnea insignis* is the other species, distinguished by its yellow fruits, but otherwise is very similar to *D. fargesii*.

Why plant a *Decaisnea*? Well, they are one of the best foliage plants for a small garden. Bold leaves to 36 in (90 cm) long have a central stalk and large opposite leaflets with a bluish green sheen. The new growth has a luster that rubs off in time or in your hand. It has panicles of narrow, yellowish green Turk's caps, almost like a squid in the water with those long tentacles trailing away from the body—or in this case from the top of the flower. There is no obvious scent. It is a pity it does not have stunning flowers or fragrance because we would all want one.

The flowers are intriguing when seen close up but are easily missed and the plant is more often grown for the amazing fruits. They are in a shade of blue rarely seen in the plant world. Finger-sized pods in deep, metallic blue hang in clusters in fall and winter, becoming obvious after leaf fall. Filled with a fleshy pulp, the black seeds within germinate easily under the plant. Having established several isolated plants I now have a small group of seedlings under each one. This plant will not take over your garden as the seedlings are easily removed and each plant takes up only a small amount of space.

The plant is a narrow, upright, deciduous shrub. There is a grayish look about the bark, and the bush tends to be multi-trunked with large, prominent yellow buds on the newer stems and black buds on the older growth. It is deserving of a place in a larger garden as a foliage plant. The yellow fall color is unexceptional.

Decaisnea fargesii can be rather temperamental to grow and tends to either thrive or die out, with no half measures, so it may pay to plant more than one. It detests being grown in pots and seems prone to root diseases. No other pests or diseases

Right: *Decaisnea fargesii* in fall color with *Pieris* (front).

attack it once planted in the ground. It is an unusual deciduous shrub that is easy-care once over the establishment period. Easily accommodated in a small garden because of its upright habit, it makes a superb contrast plant because of its unique foliage. Grow it in any free-draining soil with shelter from strong winds. Sun or semi-shade is fine. And it is hardy, growing in cold regions and yet just as well in warmer climates.

Decaisnea originate from western China and were named after Joseph Decaisne (1807–1882), director of the Jardin des Plantes in Paris. The first plants were grown from seeds sent to France in 1895 by Père Paul Farges (1844–1912), who also introduced the *Davidia* tree two years later. Farges was one of many Christian missionaries sent from France to China in that era. They completed a staggering amount of botanical work and cataloging of plants. Height x width 6–20 ft (2–6 m). ZONE 6.

Dipteronia

Dipteronia sinensis
Aceraceae

You will recognize the family if not the genus, as Aceraceae is part of the maple group. This rare tree is the only other plant in the maple family, making it unique in more ways than one. Like most maples, it is deciduous and, like so many of its relatives, hails from China.

Initially you will think it is a different genus from maples because it has ash-like leaves. However, this is not quite as odd as you may think, as some maples have pinnate leaves, such as *Acer negundo*. The leaves are opposite, just like maples, and they are pinnate, like an ash tree, with five pairs and one terminal leaf. Individual leaflets are serrated in a similar fashion to *Acer henryi*. The erect panicles of tiny, greenish yellow flowers make very little impact and they are very much like maples as you might

expect. What distinguishes *Diptoneria* from *Acer* are the seed cases. The fruits are winged all the way around like an elm, rather than the typical one-sided maple wing. The winged seeds are in large attractive bunches, and are a light green color eventually turning rich burnished red.

The young growth stems are smooth and shiny and the plant tends to grow speedily in the early years. The upright structure often creates a multi-stemmed bush, forming a vase shape. Ultimately it is a small tree, but is more often seen as a shrub. Unfortunately it is prone to dieback after a few years, which is possibly why we do not see this plant more often as it cannot be relied upon to grow well. Perhaps root rots are the problem as the trees have a tendency to romp for a year or two and then go into a decline.

It is equally happy with cold or warm winters. Give it full sun, good drainage and a sheltered site and hope for the best. No pests or diseases bother it other than dieback and this may be overcome by using the new friendly *Trichoderma* fungi (see *Cercidiphyllum*). *Dipteronia* can be grown from seeds when available, or may be grown by layering or cuttings.

Dipteronia was introduced from central China by the tireless Ernest Wilson (1876–1930) for the Veitch Nursery in England around 1900. Height x width 30 ft (10 m). ZONE 7.

There is one other even more obscure species, *Dipteronia dyeriana*, which is very rarely seen.

Dipteronia = two-winged, though the wings fuse to form a circle; *sinensis* = from China (*sino* comes from the Greek *sinai* = an Oriental people).

Above: *Dipteronia sinensis*

Disanthus

Disanthus cercidifolius
Hamamelidaceae

Most people would take this for a *Cercis*, even though it is a totally different family and is in fact related to *Hamamelis* or witch hazel.

The leaf is just like a *Cercis* and gives the species name. Alternate heart-shaped leaves 4 in (10 cm) long are bluish green with a glazed or polished surface. Luckily they seem to keep this sumptuous look all summer and do not deteriorate as some leaves do. They certainly "earn their keep" in fall, changing to rich red wine colors with hints of red and orange. *Disanthus cercidifolius* needs to be planted in a prominent place as this is likely to be a highlight bush in fall. It is generally seen only in woodland gardens and grown for the glossy summer leaf and the scintillating fall colors. It is not an easy plant to blend into a suburban garden.

Even in woodland gardens it is not always easy to please, but you will think it is worth the effort when you succeed. Ideally a moist but well-drained soil is required, and it is probably best planted in full sun or semi-shade with no wind. It is very cold-hardy and happier in a cool climate. Unfortunately it is not happy in a moist, humid climate where it suffers from root rot.

The tiny, purple-maroon flowers appear on the stems in late fall, which is a most unusual time for any woody plant to flower. Thus the fruits from the previous year appear at the same time as the new flowers.

Disanthus cercidifolius makes an arching shrub with stems covered in prominent lenticels (or breathing holes), giving the stems a rough texture. It is monotypic, meaning there is only one species in the world, and was first discovered in Japan and more recently found in southeast China. Height x width 6–10 ft (2–3 m). ZONES 4–8.

Disanthus = paired flowers; *cercidifolius* = leaf like a *Cercis*.

Above: *Disanthus cercidifolius*

Elaeagnus

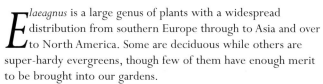

Elaeagnaceae

Right: *Elaeagnus pungens* 'Maculata'

Elaeagnus is a large genus of plants with a widespread distribution from southern Europe through to Asia and over to North America. Some are deciduous while others are super-hardy evergreens, though few of them have enough merit to be brought into our gardens.

The most useful aspect of these plants is the wind-hardiness of *Elaeagnus pungens* and *E. macrophylla* and the dazzling variegated leaf forms of *E. pungens* and *E.* x *ebbingei*.

Elaeagnus = wild olive, from Greek "elaeagnos," in reference to the fruits.

Elaeagnus angustifolia
OLEASTER OR RUSSIAN OLIVE

Oleaster makes a large deciduous shrub or small tree with a billowy habit, reddish stems and hidden spines. The tiny, fragrant, creamy yellow flowers appear in summertime. However, the prime reason for growing this plant is the silvery willow-like leaves. It is often confused with a *Pyrus salicifolia*. Native to southern Europe through to central Asia. Height x width 20 ft (6 m). ZONE 3.

'Quicksilver' is an excellent silvery leaf form, grown for its consistency of color. Height x width 12 ft (4 m).

Angustifolia = narrow leaf.

Elaeagnus x ebbingei (E. macrophylla x E. pungens)

A big, rounded, evergreen shrub with large, leathery leaves, dark green above and scaly and silvery beneath. The fragrant white flowers appear in the fall. Height x width 12 ft (4 m). ZONE 7.

'Gilt Edge' has dark green leaves with a wide, creamy yellow margin. 'Limelight' has silvery young leaves turning green, with yellow and pale green centers. For both, height x width 10 ft (3 m).

Ebbingei = named after Dutch plantsman J. W. E. Ebbinge.

Elaeagnus pungens
THORNY ELAEAGNUS

Ideally suited to coastal gardens with its tough evergreen leaves covered in bronzy brown scales, so if you need an indestructible shrub then put thorny elaeagnus on top of your list of possibilities. It makes a supremely tough plant, tolerating drought, hot sun and gale-force winds. I have seen them come through storms totally unscathed, while so-called tough plants like *Callistemon* and *Cupressus macrocarpa* were smashed to pieces.

Elaeagnus pungens forms an excellent dense hedge but needs frequent trimming, so you may want a lower maintenance plant. It can be pruned drastically with a chainsaw and regenerates quickly even from bare stems. Take care when pruning, as they have long spikes on the stems that initially do not seem especially vicious, but after pruning a large bush you will agree that they should be avoided.

Thin, white, fragrant flowers are hidden deep inside the bush and only the scent gives them away. The long fruits are reddish brown and distributed by birds, causing it to become naturalized in warmer climates. It also has a habit of throwing out long, arching stems, which put out roots when they touch the ground, thus forming a thicket. A native of Japan. Height 12 ft (4 m) x width 15 ft (5 m). ZONE 7.

'Dicksonii' is a variegated form where the leaves have a wide margin of golden yellow. 'Maculata' has leaves with a splash of

gold in the center of the leaf so it is the reverse of 'Dicksonii'. There are other variegated forms and all need any reverted green stems removed at the base or the whole plant will revert to the stronger greenish brown form and not remain variegated.

Pungens = strong smelling, pungent.

Below: *Enkianthus campanulatus*

Elaeagnus umbellata
FALL OLIVE

Fall olive is a big, wide-spreading, deciduous shrub with bright green leaves, silvery beneath. The wavy margined leaves are 4 in (10 cm) long. The fragrant yellow-white flowers appear in late spring and the resulting red speckled fruits are far more impressive. It originates from the Himalayan region, China and Japan. Height x width 15 ft (5 m). ZONE 4.

'Titan' is a good named form with an upright habit and silvery tinged, olive green leaves. Height 12 ft (4 m) x width 6 ft (2 m).

Umbellata = umbel-shaped flowers.

Enkianthus

Ericaceae

*E*nkianthus are a group of shrubs from the Himalayas, through China to Japan. They are compact, tidy shrubs, fitting easily into any suburban garden. You will not need the pruning shears on these little treasures. Mostly deciduous, they come up trumps with a breathtaking display of fall colors. So if you have a small garden or limited space and you want a splash of color in the fall, then look no further than *Enkianthus*.

They all have smooth stems and distinctive whorls of foliage at the tips, leaving regions of bare stem. So the pattern of a whorl of leaves / smooth stem, whorl of leaves / smooth stem is distinct and attractive. Simple, shiny, single leaves are rather

Left: *Enkianthus perulatus*, fall color.

plain until the "Fall Fairy" illuminates them. The fall color is stupendous, even in regions not renowned for it.

Clusters of tiny bell-shaped flowers typical of the Erica family appear in spring. They are quite cute, though being small are easily missed. They are good cut flowers for a small vase, and this is a good way to admire them. Being Ericaceae they must have acidic, well-drained soil, but they are not fussy about zones, growing from cool zone 5 through to wet and warm zone 9. They will grow in partial shade but color up best if grown in full sun. A mulch of bark or woodchip will keep them in tip-top health. It seems all the shrubs in the Erica family, such as *Rhododendron* and *Pieris*, appreciate a mulch because they have a mass of fine fibrous roots near the surface. These roots hate to be disturbed and so any digging or hand weeding is anathema to them. The mulch also keeps the roots cool and the ground moist, as they hate to dry out. It has no pests or diseases, and is easy to transplant at any age, just like rhododendrons.

Enkianthus = enlarged flower, from Greek "enkuos," meaning enlarged, and "anthos," meaning flower; referring to the fat-bellied flowers).

Enkianthus campanulatus
REDVEIN ENKIANTHUS

This has tiny opaque flowers in late spring, dashed with light pink and red. It forms a small, upright shrub, easily kept as a column shape around 6 ft (2 m). There are good fall colors in reds and orange. From Japan. Height x width 12–15 ft (4–5 m). ZONE 5.

The form called **E. c. palibini** has redder flowers.

Campanulatus = bell (referring to the flowers).

Enkianthus perulatus

Enkianthus perulatus forms a dense, compact shrub, often growing wider than it does high. It looks splendid at the front of a border as it is so tidy with its groomed, flat-topped habit. It could almost be used as a low hedge with its permanently clipped appearance.

Young stems are reddish and the small, smooth, oval leaves have a slight blue tinge but they are not riveting until fall. One of the most reliable shrubs for fall color, even in mild, moist areas, and it even performs well in hot climates. The small, white, bell-shaped flowers in spring are a bonus. Height x width 6 ft (2 m). ZONE 6.

Perulatus = with perules (bud scales).

Enkianthus quinqueflorus

Originally from Hong Kong, this is the only evergreen species in the genus. The rounded leaves have a sharp, pointed tip. They are shiny and waxy and look like they are made of plastic. The pink bell-shaped flowers are comparatively large for the genus. It is easy to imagine a plant from Hong Kong would be tender, but it is surprising how hardy the plants are from this region, such as *Rhodoleia*. Height 10 ft (3 m) x width 3–4 ft (1 m). ZONE 8.

Quinqueflorus = five flowers.

Eucalyptus

GUM, IRONBARK
Myrtaceae

Eucalyptus is a group of Australian trees rapidly colonizing the rest of the world with the help of man and his spade. Proving popular as fast-growing timber and fuel trees, they will grow in conditions most plants would abhor. Many have adapted to a life of hot sun and low rainfall. Tough, leathery leaves allow them to survive drought and even desert conditions. The unique evergreen leaves are instantly recognizable as those of a gum tree, even if you are looking at a new species. Nearly all of them have the characteristic blue-gray, leathery leaves, which tend to hang down. The thick leaves and the angle they present to the sun reduce water loss, accounting for their ability to withstand drought and thus their appeal in the drier parts of the world. This does not stop the rest of us growing good eucalyptus, as most species are just as happy in high rainfall areas. They simply grow faster if given lush conditions. Growth rates of up to 3 ft (1 m) a year makes them "instant" trees for new suburban gardens.

Many eucalyptus have two types of foliage, with juvenile leaves when young differing greatly from the adult form. Often eucalyptus species also have attractive peeling bark, shed in flakes or sometimes in long, stringy quills.

The flowers are a "brush" of brightly colored stamens, attractive to nectar-feeding birds. Most are white or cream and easily missed or passed by without notice, while a few have stunning red or pink flowers. Eucalyptus can be grown in pots from seed, but should be planted out when very young, say 12–18 in (30–50 cm) high. If they stay in a pot until they are over 3 ft (1 m) high, the roots will have twined around the base of the pot and when planted out will seem to thrive for a year or three before falling over one day in a strong wind. The circling roots will have strangled the tree. So, plant when young and make sure the roots are radiating out in "starfish" fashion.

Eucalyptus are sun lovers and are not happy in shade. They vary in cold-hardiness and seed gathered from plants in colder regions will be hardier. In general they do not like hard frosts. Drought-tolerance is their main claim to fame. Some species have adapted to growing in wet, swampy places. Most are very tolerant of strong winds, at least the leaves are. Wind poses more of a threat to the whole tree, often pushing the tree over at ground level.

Eucalyptus = well-concealed, from Greek "eu," meaning good and "kalypto," meaning conceal or a veil; refers to the calyx that covers the flower and falls off like a cap.

Eucalyptus ficifolia
RED-FLOWERING GUM

This is not only one of the best eucalyptus species for foliage, it is the best flowering gum also. In high summer, stunning red or orange flowers smother the whole tree. The color varies from tree to tree with seedling variation, some are even pink. It is possible to buy guaranteed color forms grown by grafting a colored form onto a seedling. A tree of modest proportions and dense habit, the adult leaves are similar to the juvenile leaves: broadly lance-shaped, mid to deep green above and paler below. It is wind-hardy and good in coastal regions. Originates from western Australia. Height 20–50 ft (6–15 m) x width 15–70 ft (5–20 m). ZONE 9.

Ficifolia = fig-like or *Ficus* leaf.

Eucalyptus globulus
TASMANIAN BLUE GUM

An ungainly plant in the juvenile stages with rather straggly branches and silver-blue juvenile leaves emerging straight from the stem. The adult form is far more attractive with its lance-like, blue-green leaves. It ultimately forms a big tree. Tasmanian blue gum is native to Victoria and Tasmania in Australia. Height 50–160 ft (15–50 m) x width 30–80 ft (10–25 m). ZONE 8 OR 9.

Globulus = globe-shaped (referring to the juvenile leaves).

Eucalyptus gunnii, syn E. divaricata
CIDER GUM, SILVER DOLLAR GUM

The stunning, silver juvenile leaves are popular for cut foliage in vases. *Eucalyptus gunnii* is sometimes known as silver dollar gum because of the round silver leaves. The sickle-shaped adult leaves are a rich green. The reddish-brown bark peels, revealing new white bark beneath to form interesting patterns up the trunks. Hardier than most gums, it comes from high-country Tasmania. It was named for Ronald Gunn, an amateur botanist whose day job was superintendent of convicts in Tasmania in the 1820s and 1830s. If you have never grown gums before and you live in a cold area, then this is the one to practice with. Height 30–80 ft (10–25 m) x width 20–50 ft (6–15 m). ZONE 7.

Eucalyptus nicholii
NARROW-LEAVED BLACK PEPPERMINT

Considering the huge number of gum species—over 700 at last count—this one is pretty special, as it is regarded as the best foliage plant of the lot. It is most attractive as a young plant, forming a graceful, weeping tree with narrow, willow-like leaves. These

Below left:
Eucalyptus nicholii
Below right:
Eucalyptus ficifolia

bluish green leaves have a lovely peppermint scent. Quite a tough tree, it tolerates poor or heavy soils, frost and wind. It makes the ideal instant tree for a new housing suburb or bare garden. Native to Queensland and New South Wales in Australia. Height 40–52 ft (12–16 m) x width 15–40 ft (5–12 m). ZONE 8.

Nicholii = Richard Nichol (1866–1947) of the Sydney Botanical Gardens.

Euodia

KOREAN EVODIA
Rutaceae

A perfect small tree. There, I have said it. *Euodia* are perfect and much neglected by the horticultural world. These fine trees have been one of my most cherished plants since I first encountered *Euodia* while working at the Chelsea Physic Garden, London, on the banks of the Thames in the early 1970s. I have been trying to convince anyone who would listen ever since—without much success, I might add. The plants grew happily in sandy Thames soil with 24 in (600 mm) of rain per annum and now they grow in my clay garden with 100 in (2500 mm) of rain a year. So you get the picture—they are not fussy about soil and are not too particular about the conditions given. They are happy in any climate from zones 5 to 10.

Euodia have a very tidy structure, and beautiful clean branches. The young stems are smooth, light brown and the older branches are furrowed and black. The plants are relatively small, making them ideal shade trees for small suburban gardens. In a warm climate, I think *Melia* is the perfect shade tree, but if you cannot grow a *Melia*, then grow this, as it is more cold-hardy.

Euodia would also be an excellent choice for avenue planting. The trees tolerate city atmosphere and pollution and will cope with wind, cold and hot sun.

The leaves of *Euodia* look good all summer. They do not get tatty as some deciduous trees do. The fall color is usually a pale yellow and reasonably worthy without being world-beating. The ash-like leaves are pinnate, with three or four pairs of opposite leaflets and one terminal leaflet.

The flat heads of tiny, sweetly scented, yellowish flowers are

laden with bees during early summer, and these are followed by tiny, black, gunshot seeds.

Euodia are found across Asia, into Madagascar and even Australia. The hardy, deciduous species are from China and Korea and were all collected by E. H. Wilson (1876–1930).

Euodia = sweet-smelling, from Greek "eu," meaning good and "odia," meaning odor.

Above: *Euodia daniellii*

Euodia daniellii

This fast-growing plant is a gardener's dream, as in its youth it grows speedily to produce a good-size tree in just a few years, and this is just what all impatient gardeners desire. Then, having done that, it endears itself by slowing down and the tree remains of modest proportions. In other words, it stays a small tree, having rapidly grown to, say, 12 ft (4 m). There are fast-growing trees aplenty but most of them carry on, becoming forest giants overwhelming house and garden. So *Euodia* becomes a tidy mop-top tree (the sort children paint), easily fitting into any suburban garden. It does occasionally send up a sucker or two but these are easily dealt with. Named for William Daniell, a British surgeon who first discovered this plant in China. Height 12–18 ft (4–6 m) x width 30 ft (10 m). ZONE 5.

Euodia henryi

Euodia henryi has bold, ash-like leaves with reddish petioles in the sun, dark green above and light beneath. The terminal bud is an unusual furry affair, like a seagull's beak. Smooth, gray-brown stems have a few raised lenticels. It forms a tidy cherry-sized tree in just a few years. Named after Augustine Henry (1857–1930),

Left: *Euodia henryi*, with *Paulownia* (left) and *Idesia* (right).

an Irish doctor whose passion was plant collecting. Based in China for nearly 20 years from 1880, he sent thousands of dried plant specimens as well as seeds to Kew Gardens in London. Height x width 15–20 ft (5–6 m). ZONE 5.

Euonymus

SPINDLE TREE
Celastraceae

*E*uonymus is such a very large group of plants it is hard to have a good grasp of it. They vary from small, evergreen creepers and ground covers to small deciduous trees, and then on to big, wide-spreading, evergreen trees. You can never really be comfortable saying, "That's a *Euonymus* because it looks like so and so." Some evergreen types are grown for their dense ball shape and sometimes for hedges, while the deciduous ones are more commonly grown for their lovely winged fruits, although the fall colors can be good, too.

Many species have a peculiar habit of holding the seeds half in and half out of the fruits, usually in strongly contrasting colors (like pink and orange). Most have tiny, nondescript flowers.

They are quite tough, robust shrubs, not fussy about soil, growing in heavy clays and alkaline soils as well as in hot sun and coastal gardens. Most species are very wind-hardy, the evergreen ones being especially tough in this respect.

Euonymus = good name or good repute, from Greek "eu," meaning good and "onoma," meaning a name.

Euonymus alatus
BURNING BUSH, WINGED SPINDLE TREE
This is a bushy, deciduous shrub with scintillating fall colors in rich reds. Gaudy, purple fruits with bright orange seeds within are on show at the same time. The seeds remain half in the fruit, providing a flamboyant contrast. *Euonymus alatus* is usually seen as a wide-spreading, twiggy shrub. The stems have corky, winged bark. Originates from China. Height 15–20 ft (5–6 m) x width 10 ft (3 m). ZONES 4 TO 9.

The form **'Compactus'** is compact and dense, and usually wider than it is high. Height 10 ft (3 m) x width 10–15 ft (3–5 m).

Alatus = winged.

Euonymus europaeus
SPINDLE TREE
Spindle tree is a small, deciduous tree earning its keep in the fall with a twin display of yellow fall color and the unusual, pinkish red fruits holding shiny, orange seeds. As you would gather from the name, it is native to Europe, including Britain. Height 10 ft (3 m) x width 8 ft (2.5 m). ZONES 4 TO 8.

The form **'Aldenhamensis'** is a more prolific fruiting variety.

Europaeus = from Europe.

Euonymus fortunei
WINTERCREEPER
Euonymus fortunei is an evergreen creeper usually grown for ground cover, though it can be trained as a climber. It is more often seen in the various variegated forms rather than the straight green-leaf species. I can vouch for its hardiness, having seen it growing on freezing cold mountain tops in Korea. The creamy flowers are tiny and easily missed. It is happy growing in sun or shade, thus making a great ground cover. It is named after Robert Fortune (1812–1880). Wintercreeper is a native of China, Japan and Korea. Height 24 in (60 cm) or 15 ft (5 m) as climbers x width indefinite. ZONES 5 TO 9.

There is a multiplicity of forms available, including the new 'Emerald' series from the U.S.A. **'Emerald Charm'**, **'Emerald Cushion'** and **'Emerald Leader'** are rich green forms. 'Emerald Cushion' is to 12 in (30 cm) high x 18 in (45 cm) wide. **'Emerald Gaiety'** is green with a white margin. Height 3 ft (1 m) x width 5 ft (1.5 m). **'Emerald n' Gold'** has a bright gold margin. Height 24 in (60 cm) x width 36 in (90 cm).

Euonymus japonicus
JAPANESE SPINDLE TREE
Euonymus japonicus is a tough customer just made for those hard-to-fill places: poor soil, too much wind or hot baking sun. This dense evergreen will grow anywhere—in shade, on chalk, by the

Right: *Euonymus fortunei* growing on a rock.

Far right: *Euonymus japonicus* 'Ovatus Aureas'

Above: *Euonymus japonicus* 'Ovatus Aureus'

leaves. These leaves quickly become lush, dark and glossy, turning yellow or red in the fall.

The plant is usually a multi-stemmed, upright bush but it will become a small tree in time. Plant it in a sheltered site with moist soil. It is not too fussy about the soil as long as it is well drained, and is capable of growing on very acidic and alkaline soils. *Euptelea* are very prone to root diseases when first planted and can be tricky in the first year or so, but if you get them past that stage everything will be fine. It is one of the few plants I would recommend staking to prevent wind rock and any damage to the roots in those vital early stages of development. There are no pests or problems other than the root diseases. Being deciduous, it is cold-hardy. It originates from western China where it was discovered by Père Armand David (1826–1900) in 1869. Height 25 ft (8 m) x width 20 ft (6 m). ZONES 6 TO 9.

The other species, *Euptelea polyandra*, is from Japan and very similar.

Euptelea = good shrub; Greek "eu," meaning good and "ptelea," meaning a shrub with similar elm-like fruits; *pleiosperma* = having thick seeds.

sea. It has the added advantage that it can be clipped and therefore used as a hedge. Heavy pruning is also tolerated. It makes a neat, compact plant that can also be grown in tubs and containers. It is an ideal plant for tough city sites, or those drafty corners where no other plant wants to grow. From Japan, and also native to Korea. Height 12 ft (4 m) x width 6 ft (2 m). ZONES 6 TO 9.

We usually see the variegated forms grown only for their leaves and robust nature. **'Albomarginatus'** has white or silver edges, while **'Aureovariegatus'** has gold-edged leaves. **'Ovatus Aureus'** has a pale green center and broad, gold edges to the leaves.

Japonicus = native of Japan.

Euonymus myrianthus, syn E. sargentianus

A big, slow-growing, evergreen shrub with lustrous green leaves, *Euonymus myrianthus* has horizontal branches holding its canopy of pendulous leaves. Orange fruits hold the red seeds in the typical "half in, half out" pattern for weeks. A native of western China. Height 10 ft (3 m) x width 12 ft (4 m). ZONES 7 TO 9.

Myrianthus = numerous flowers (*myrio* = myriad; *anthus* = flowers).

Euptelea

Euptelea pleiosperma
Eupteleaceae

*E**uptelea* is a genus of just two deciduous species in a family of their own and so they are often overlooked. But if you look at the bright, shiny, luscious leaves, you will agree they are worthy of more attention. These attractive leaves look as good near the end of summer as they did in the spring. It is really a three-season plant because the tiny red, bristly flowers (there are no petals) appear on the stems before the new spring bronzy

Above and left:
Euptelea pleiosperma

Fagus

BEECH
Fagaceae

Beeches have a slow, ponderous look to them and such is their nature. They grow in a very leisurely way and can be planted as a large shrub. It will be many years before you have a problem tree. My own beech is over 30 years old and has only recently gone from large shrub size to what could be called a tree.

Beeches are worth growing for their simple, shiny, waxy leaves and their clean, smooth trunks. The generally oval leaves

Right: *Fagus sylvatica* in spring.

are hard and leathery and take years to rot down and so they form a dense mulch under the trees.

They are happy in any kind of soil as long as it is well drained. The beech will grow in extremely alkaline or acidic soils and along with the ash and the elm make up the trio which tolerates extremes of alkalinity.

Beeches are quite hardy to cold but do not relish coastal or windy places. In very exposed sites they tend to look ragged or one-sided. Being very shallow-rooted, they are frequently toppled by storms. The next time you see a beech blown over, take note of how all the roots have traveled along the soil surface rather than searching downwards. It is these ground-robbing surface roots that prevent any plant competition around the base of a beech tree. A combination of these thirsty roots, the dense shade and the carpet of fallen leaves prevents any plants other than bluebells from growing in a beech forest. This is what makes beech forests so amazing, the pillars of smooth, gray trunks emerging from the ground, with no other plant life to distract the eye.

Fagus sylvatica
EUROPEAN BEECH

This forms a stately, spreading, deciduous tree. It has fall colors of copper and rich golds, unsurpassed in the good years, and dreary at other times. The newly emerging leaves are one of the highlights of a Northern Hemisphere spring when, just for a day or two, the tree is pink and glistening. A beech tree in spring is a treasure. The leaves then become a glossy dark green. The flowers are tiny, nondescript affairs. Edible nuts, or "mast" as they are called, are produced, though its takes 40–50 years before the tree begins

Right: The fall color of *Fagus sylvatica*.

Left and below:
Fagus sylvatica
'Purpurea'

producing mast and then they only yield a crop every four or five years. Height 80 ft (25 m) x width 50 ft (15 m). ZONES 5 TO 9.

Various forms are available to the discerning gardener, including many purple-leafed forms, often called 'Purpurea' or copper beech. However, it is worth selecting and paying a little more for a really good purple such as 'Riversii' or 'Swat Magret'. All of the forms grow happily from zones 5 to 9.

'Dawyck' forms a narrow column and keeps a neat, erect shape without pruning. Height 60 ft (18 m) x width 22 ft (7 m). **'Dawyck Gold'** is an erect, golden hybrid prone to burning in strong sun. It is golden yellow in the spring and fall with a period of light green in the summer. Height 60 ft (18 m) x width 22 ft (7 m). **'Dawyck Purple'** is another pencil-shaped hybrid with purple foliage. Height 70 ft (20 m) x width 15 ft (5 m).

Fagus = from Greek "phago," meaning I eat; *sylvatica* = of the woods (a reference to the nuts).

Fagus sylvatica **'Pendula'**
WEEPING BEECH
'Pendula' forms a spectacular tree in time but is not a plant for impatient gardeners. The main or structural branches are almost horizontal, while the smaller twigs and outer branches tend to hang almost vertically, like a waterfall or curtain. There is a black-ish purple-leafed version called **'Purpurea Pendula'**. Height x width 50 ft (15 m).

Fagus sylvatica **'Riversii'**
'Riversii' has very shiny, blackish leaves in spring, tending to keep a good strong color throughout the summer. It drops its leaves cleanly; they do not hang on in drab fashion as some do. It forms

a wide-crowned tree, creating a dramatic and imposing sight wherever suitably placed, but it is so bold it can easily dominate a garden scene. Plant it among numerous large trees in a suburban setting. Little fall color. Height 80 ft (25 m) x width 50 ft (15m).

Fagus sylvatica **'Swat Magret'**

This tends to come into leaf eight to ten years earlier than other purple beech, but has other serious claims to fame, including gorgeous pink growth in the spring and the ability to retain its blackish red color all summer long without fading. Height 80 ft (25 m) x width 50 ft (15 m).

Fagus sylvatica **'Zlatia'**

The spring growth is soft yellow, moderating to pale green through summer and reverting to yellow in the fall. 'Zlatia' is one of the few beech cultivars to have a distinct fall color. It is slow-growing with very glossy leaves. Height 60 ft (18 m) x width 50 ft (15 m).

Above: *Fagus sylvatica* 'Rohanii'

Below: *Fagus sylvatica* 'Swat Magret'

Fagus sylvatica **'Rohanii'**

'Rohanii' is a beech that looks more like an oak, with undulating, wavy leaves. In spring, the purple leaves are covered in white hairs. It is easily accommodated in any small garden and can be treated as a shrub for many years. Ten years ago I planted a 3 ft (1 m) bush and now it is 6 ft (2 m) high, so it is best treated as an upright shrub. Should it get too big, it is no bother to prune it a bit or to move it, as beech are fairly easy to transplant. There is a gold version, too: **'Rohan Gold'**.

x *Fatshedera*

x *Fatshedera lizei*
ARALIA IVY, BOTANICAL WONDER, TREE-IVY
Araliaceae

This tropical-looking shrub is usually seen as a houseplant and yet it is perfectly hardy to 15°F (-10°C). It is a hybrid between *Fatsia japonica* (see next entry) and *Hedera helix* var *hibernica* (ivy) and thus the leaf size is intermediate between the two parents. So while the evergreen leaves are not as bold as *Fatsia*, they are still quite conspicuous and make a terrific leafy statement. Its semi-rambling nature is understandable given that one parent is short and stocky and the other a climber capable of reaching the tops of the trees. The mixture of genes is equally shared. Like both parents it is capable of putting up with dense shade and poor soil. It also handles pollution, and maritime climates.

Light greenish to white flowers arise in long panicles, usually in fall. It was bred by Lizé Frères in Nantes, France, in 1910. Height 4–6 ft (1.2–2 m) x width 10 ft (3 m). ZONE 8.

Of a couple of variegated forms, **'Annemieke'** has a bright yellow blotch in the middle of the leaf, while **'Variegata'** has gray-green leaves with a white margin.

Fatshedera = a combination of the two parents' names;
lizei = after the breeders.

Above: x *Fatshedera lizei*

Fatsia

**Fatsia japonica, syn *Aralia japonica*,
*A. sieboldii***
JAPANESE ARALIA, JAPANESE FATSIA
Araliaceae

Fatsia japonica holds a special place in my heart as it was the first plant I ever learned to distinguish as a child—after the roses, of course, which pricked my hands when I attempted to retrieve a lost or wayward ball. In retrospect it is easy to see why it is child's play to recognize a *Fatsia*. With their big, fat leaves it would be hard to confuse it with any other shrub.

I love plants that fill a variety of roles and *Fatsia japonica* is a splendid example. It will grow in full sun but can sometimes look bleached, with a yellowish appearance, but it is in the shade that this shrub sparkles. It is the perfect shrub for gloomy places including dry shade, the most difficult of sites in a garden. These parched gardens in the lee of a building or perhaps under trees where the roots compete for moisture are nigh on impossible to fill. So use *Fatsia*, *Aucuba* or *Sarcococca* for these inhospitable places. As a nurseryman, gardeners are always asking me for plants to grow in dry shade and yet the shrubs that tolerate and thrive in these conditions are considered second rate. Gardeners are scathing of *Fatsia*, *Mackaya*, *Aucuba* and *Sarcococca*, all rock-solid stalwarts for shade. You may need to water these plants to help them get established, but thereafter they are invincible.

Easy to transplant when young, it is probably not a good idea to shift *Fatsia japonica* later. The plant is equally happy in alkaline or acidic conditions, which is unusual for shrubs. No pruning is required as it keeps a good natural shape with its thick, club-like stems and whorls of stiff leaves. The base of the petiole (or leaf stalk) hangs on to the thick stems like a hand catching on to a branch.

The flowers are quite impressive, with starry showers like exploding fireworks. These creamy white flowers are followed by black berries. *Fatsia* is frequently used to add a tropical look to a fernery or shade house. Big, bold, glossy leaves are like a giant hand. It certainly has one of the biggest leaves of any hardy plant,

to 12 in (30 cm) or more across. Being evergreen and free from pests and diseases, it is always a picture of health. It hails from Japan, which probably accounts for its hardiness. Height x width 5–12 ft (1.5–4 m). Frosts to 15°F (-10°C) are fine, so it is quite hardy. ZONE 8.

The clone **'Variegata'** has creamy white margins to the leaf and is prone to sunburn.

Fatsia = a Latinised version of the Japanese name; *japonica* = from Japan.

Above: *Fatsia japonica*

Firmiana

**Firmiana simplex, syn *F. platanifolia*,
*Sterculia platanifolia***
CHINESE PARASOL TREE, VARNISH TREE
Sterculiaceae

Firmiana simplex is a tropical-looking tree from China. The bright green trunk is smooth and tactile, and simply demands to be touched. It is impossible to pass this tree without stroking the bark. The green trunk is a sure sign of the tropics. Hardy trees from cold climates need their tough old bark to protect them from the elements.

Amazingly, the parasol tree is reasonably hardy and, even more surprisingly, it is deciduous. This decidedly exotic-looking plant adds a touch of the tropics to any garden scene and does not take up too much room, forming an upright, tidy tree. Look up into the canopy and the rich, glossy green leaves have all the hallmarks of the tropics. Held out in perfect symmetry, the five-lobed, *Fatsia*-like leaves can be up to 18 in (45 cm) long.

Long spikes of tiny, yellow-green flowers in summer come and go without any fanfare. The resulting seed cases, like mini-

Left: *Firmiana simplex* with *Anigozanthos*.

parasols, are far more exciting. They are initially a pinkish green before drying to a papery cinnamon color, ideal for floral art work and winter decorations. As these pods split open, a brown fluid looking like varnish is released, making a mess on cars and tarmac below, thus the common name varnish tree. These pods also give rise to the other common name of parasol tree.

It is not at all fussy about soil, coping with heavy clay and other poor ground. In fact, it almost seems happier in hard, heavy ground.

Finding a climate that suits it is a bit trickier. It definitely needs full sun to thrive and needs all the summer heat it can get. In a mild winter and cool summer climate, it dithers and does not really want to grow, while places with colder winters can grow this well, providing there is enough summer heat to ripen the wood and get it motivated. It is capable of putting up with dry summers and drought, and is generally described as a zone 7 plant.

It needs shelter, as do most plants with big leaves. Apart from an occasional caterpillar hole I have never seen a pest or disease bother it in any way.

It forms a neat, round-crowned tree, fitting easily into a small garden. It is used as a street tree in China, Japan and France.

The genus is named after Karl Josef von Firmian (1716–1782), Governor of Lombardy Province in what is now Italy, then a part of the Austrian Empire. It is a native of Asia, from Vietnam to southern Japan. Height 50 ft (15 m) x width 30 ft (10 m). ZONE 7.

Simplex = entire leaf, or single flower or stem (in this case it is likely to be the single stem, as it is one of those clean, single-trunk trees and is never multi-trunked); *platanifolia* = leaf like a *Platanus* or plane tree.

Fraxinus

ASH
Oleaceae

"Ash before the Oak—In for a soak
Oak before the Ash—in for a splash"
This was a rhyme I learned as a small child. "In for a soak" means a wet summer is likely should the ash come into leaf before the oak tree, while "in for a splash" means a good summer with only a splash of rain if the oak tree comes into leaf first.

Ash trees are a common sight in the cooler regions of the Northern Hemisphere, with *Fraxinus excelsior* being one of the dominant trees of the European landscape. They are mostly big, round-headed trees with clean, smooth gray stems when young and tactile, furrowed bark as they mature. The distinctive black or very dark brown buds are a feature in winter.

Ash are familiar to us all. We often describe plants as having ash-like leaves, those pinnate leaves with the opposite leaflets along a central leaf stalk. Unblemished all summer, these leaves delight with their fall colors of yellows and purples.

Ash trees are tolerant of a wide range of soils, including very acidic as well as extremely alkaline soil. Not many woody plants will thrive as well as ash on limestone hills. Hard, packed clays and occasional waterlogging also pose no threat to these trees. In fact, the harder or heavier the soil, the happier they are. The taller-growing species have deep, searching roots. Windswept

Above: *Fraxinus excelsior*

Above: *Fraxinus excelsior* in the fall.

sites pose no problem and they are among the toughest deciduous trees for coastal sites. All ash are easy to transplant at any size.

Most have panicles of small, greenish-yellow or white flowers in the spring. The flower heads are usually at the tips of the stems, and some are deliciously scented.

There are a few bush-sized ash and a few evergreen species found in botanical collections. Some of the smaller-growing species will cope with drought and very hot climates. Generally they are grown from seed, which may take two years to germinate. Choice species and named clones are grafted onto seedling rootstocks.

Fraxinus = the old Roman or Latin name for the tree (ash is a Saxon word).

Fraxinus americana
WHITE ASH

If ever you are fortunate enough to go to Thomas Jefferson's Academic Village at the University of Virginia you will see some magnificent white ash trees. Laid out in the 1820s, the campus buildings were designed by the great man himself and the ash trees were especially chosen by him to give unity and shade to the campus. After seeing these trees in such an elegant setting, you will be hooked ever after, and such an idyllic campus makes you want to be a student again.

Fraxinus americana is fast-growing and broadly columnar, bearing long, dark green leaves, turning yellow or purple in fall. Height 80 ft (25 m) x width 50 ft (15 m). The tree originates in eastern U.S.A. and Canada. ZONES 6 TO 9.

Several good cultivars are available. **'Fall Purple'** has lovely purple fall color, making it even more intense, and is an outstanding male clone. Deep purple fall foliage puts on a great show for several weeks. Height 60 ft (18 m) x width 40 ft (12 m). **'Rose Hill'** has dark green, lush leaves on a fast-growing male clone (therefore no messy seeds to gather up). The fall color is bronzy-red fall. Height 50 ft (15 m) x width 30 ft (10 m).

Americana = from America.

Fraxinus angustifolia 'Raywood', syn *F. oxycarpa*
NARROW-LEAVED ASH, CLARET ASH

This is by far the best form of this southern European ash. A good choice for warmer climates as it colors reliably every fall, even in warm coastal climates where fall color is often a non-event. Its dark green leaves turn a reddish purple in a phenomenal display. The tree is fast-growing with an open, clean appearance, showing off the lovely smooth branches. Height 70 ft (20 m) x width 50 ft (15 m). ZONE 5.

Angustifolia = narrow leaves.

Fraxinus chinensis rhyncophylla
CHINESE ASH

This forms a small tree, fitting comfortably into small gardens. In fact it is more like an open, airy shrub for years and years. The clean green foliage is fine during summer but the highlight is the beautiful butter-yellow and bronze fall color. Height x width 12–15 ft (4–5 m). ZONE 6.

Chinensis = from China; *rhyncophylla* = leaf like a bird's beak.

Fraxinus dipetala

An ideal ash for small gardens. The glossy leaves, with five leaflets, are more capable of surviving hot sun and drier climates than most ash. Creamy white panicles of flowers appear in spring and have a pleasant musty hay scent. From California and Mexico. Height x width 12–15 ft (4–5 m) x width 10 ft (3 m). ZONE 9.

Dipetala = two petals.

Fraxinus excelsior
EUROPEAN ASH

European ash is a very familiar plant, and one that you will recognize from a distance with its clean, open habit and smooth gray stems. The furrowed trunks on older trees have a neat bark pattern and even bole, up to the first branches. Then there are the leaves—so healthy all through summer, not moth-eaten like so many trees. The dark green leaves turn yellow in fall.

A big, bold tree, happy in extremes of lime and acidity, it will grow willingly in wet or heavily compacted soil. In fact, it seems to prefer it that way. It is wind-hardy, too, though it has a habit of

Above: *Fraxinus angustifolia* 'Raywood' in fall color with *Pinus wallichiana*.

dropping dead branches and twigs during a storm. *Fraxinus excelsior* is native to Europe. Height 100 ft (30 m) x width 70 ft (20 m). ZONES 5 TO 9.

Excelsior = lofty or tall.

Above: *Fraxinus ornus*

Fraxinus excelsior 'Jaspidea', syn. *F. e.* 'Aurea'
Vivid yellow foliage throughout summer turns rich gold before leaf fall. 'Jaspidea' needs full sun to bring out the best colors for

Right: *Fraxinus excelsior* 'Jaspidea'

Above: *Fraxinus spaethiana*

Fraxinus ornus
FLOWERING ASH, MANNA ASH

Manna ash is from the sunny, drier parts of the Mediterranean. The shrub-like habit of *Fraxinus ornus* makes it ideal for small gardens or as a street tree in warm to hot climates. Scented, fluffy white flowers are an added bonus. Height x width 50 ft (15 m). ZONES 6 TO 9.

Ornus = from Latin word "orno," to furnish.

Fraxinus pennsylvanica 'Summit'
GREEN ASH, RED ASH

This is a fast-growing, tall shade tree suited to campus planting or perhaps a large yard. The 'Summit' clone has reliable golden-yellow fall color. Height 45 ft (14 m) x width 25 ft (8 m). ZONE 4.

Pennsylvanica = from Pennsylvania.

Fraxinus spaethiana

A small Japanese tree with exceptionally beautiful leaves, *Fraxinus spaethiana* has beautiful butter-yellow fall color. The large, swollen petiole base or leaf stalk wraps itself around the bud and stems. Large panicles of flowers occur in spring. The name refers to the Spaeth Nursery in Berlin, Germany. Height x width 12–15 ft (4–5 m). ZONE 6.

Fraxinus velutina
ARIZONA ASH, VELVET ASH

This is a shrub to small tree suited to hot, dry climates. The leaves and stems are covered in soft, velvety hairs, turning yellow in fall. Originates from western Texas to southern California. Height x width 30 ft (10 m). ZONE 6.

The variety **'Fan-Tex'** is fast-growing, with a tidy shape and larger, dark green leaves. ZONE 6.

Velutina = velvet.

summer and fall. It is generally a tidy mophead tree. Bright yellow stems and prominent black buds feature in winter. As it has to be grafted, nurseries can choose a rootstock to suit the local conditions, such as *F. excelsior* for moist, cool regions. Look for a plant that is grafted low to the ground, so there is no obvious graft union, and remove any suckers. It tends to drop dead twigs and branches, which can be a nuisance if planted in a lawn or parking area. Height x width 20 ft (6 m). ZONE 5.

Ginkgo

Ginkgo biloba
MAIDENHAIR TREE, GINKGO
Ginkgoaceae

Ginkgo is a genus of one species. If you look closely, the parallel veins in the leaf of *Ginkgo biloba* are different from any other hardy tree. Ginkgos have been on this planet since the days of the dinosaurs and are one of the oldest and most primitive plants. Fossil remains show they used to grow across Europe and North America. Their closest relatives are conifers and cycads, but it is hard for most of us to see any similarity with these groups of plants. Cycads are ancient, palm-like plants and most of the familiar conifers are evergreen, while ginkgos are deciduous.

The name maidenhair tree refers to the similar shape of the leaves to the *Adiantum* (maidenhair fern). Some gingkos have fan-shaped leaves without any split at all, while others have two lobes so split they are almost separate (thus *biloba*). Other forms have *Adiantum* fern-like multi-split leaves.

While the tree is very cold-hardy, it also loves summer heat. It is tolerant of any kind of soil, and grows well in dry or sandy regions and is equally happy in clay soil with a high rainfall. It not only grows but thrives in a range of locations. The ginkgo is probably more tolerant of city and atmospheric pollution than any other tree and, with human help, is now reconquering lands it formerly dominated.

Ginkgos are easily propagated from seed or layering, or by grafting. Cultivated trees are usually grafted males cloned to avoid the smelly, disagreeable, apricot-like fruits produced by the females. These fruits are unpleasant in the garden and a real nuisance on paved streets.

Above and below:
Ginkgo biloba

Ginkgos are reasonably wind-tolerant, having thick, waxy leaves, though they need to be away from the seashore. The trunks are quite attractive, with furrowed bark in a soft gray-brown. No pests or diseases attack the tree and when you include the superb fall color in rich butter-yellow, it all adds up to the perfect garden tree.

Plant a ginkgo for its very unusual leaves, the rich butter-yellow fall color, because it is such an easy plant to please, growing in hot summers and cold winters, and because of its ability to cope with pollution. Last but not least you will be planting a piece of our planet's history. The tree originates from southern China. Height 100 ft (30 m) x width 25 ft (8 m). ZONES 5 TO 9.

Some varieties to try are: **'Fall Gold'**, initially upright, eventually forming a wide-spreading tree, selected for its rich fall color. Male. Height 50 ft (15 m) x width 30 ft (10 m). **'Fairmount'**, a fast-growing pyramidal form with good structure. Male. Height 50 ft (15 m) x width 20 ft (6 m). **'Fastigiata'** has an upright columnar habit, ideal for confined city streets. Height 50 ft (15 m) x width 15 ft (5 m). **'Pendula'** is a spreading semi-weeper. Height x width 30 ft (10 m). **'Princeton Sentry'** is a male clone, similar to 'Fastigiata'. Height 50 ft (15 m) x width 15 ft (5 m). The leaves of **'Variegata'** are streaked with creamy white. This variegation is not very stable and the plant may easily revert to green. Height 30 ft (10 m) x width 20 ft (6 m).

Ginkgo = Chinese word; *biloba* = two-lobed (referring to the leaves).

Gleditsia

Gleditsia triacanthos inermis
HONEY LOCUST
Fabaceae

Honey locust is a tree of many colors, both literally and figuratively. You have a choice of yellow, green and bronze, and it is willing to grow in a variety of places and niches. For example, it is grown as tall, upright street trees in cities, coping with the industrial pollution and poor root conditions. You often see it as park trees providing shade for rhododendrons and azaleas. Or you can take one home as a small, weeping, mop-top tree for your back garden.

Gleditsia have the delightful habit of producing new growth throughout summer, creating an attractive effect with the old and new foliage together. The compound leaves are made up of many tiny leaflets, casting a delicate and gentle shade. The network of crooked, twisty, black branches and stems seen through the leaves in summer becomes a major feature after leaf fall.

The small, green, pea-like flowers usually go unnoticed, but it is hard to miss the huge sickle-shaped pea pods up to 18 in (45 cm) long. These pods have a sweetish, edible pulp within. Hanging down like twisted Christmas tinsel and finally falling in late winter, they play havoc with the mower in grassy areas. The pods are also a problem in city streets. The vicious long thorns on the trunks and the stems are also very off-putting, which explains why most people grow the form *G. triacanthos inermis*, as it is thornless. The trees are prone to suckering from the roots, especially if the roots are damaged, say, by digging up underground services. The roots can cause further problems by

Above: *Gleditsia triacanthos* 'Sunburst'

Above: *Gleditsia triacanthos* 'Sunburst' and *Lavendula stoechas*.

lifting and damaging paving. Virtually any soil with reasonable drainage is suitable and it is very drought-tolerant. Large specimens can be safely transplanted with bare roots in the winter.

Honey locust may need staking and training until a good shape is achieved. It is brittle and prone to wind damage and therefore best grown in a sunny, sheltered site. It needs full sun to thrive and so looks jaded when shaded. It will grow in extremes of heat and cold, performing best in climates with hot summers and cold winters. A good city tree in some respects as it does not mind pollution and because the leaves are so small, they soon disintegrate after they have fallen, reducing the need to brush them up. All have rich, golden yellow fall color.

A host of pests and diseases have made them difficult to grow in parts of the U.S.A. Webworm, mites, galls, cankers and borers all take a fancy to them. Not many people realize that this

Above: *Gleditsia triacanthos* 'Ruby Lace'

ferny foliage deciduous tree is a native of the eastern States. It was named after Herr Gleditsch, a former director of Berlin Botanischer Garten. Height 30–80 ft (10–25 m) x width 25–35 ft (8–11 m). ZONE 3.

There are some wonderful cultivars available, such as **'Bujotii'**, a small tree with pendulous branches and bright green foliage. **'Elegantissima'** is a slow-growing, shrubby form, ideal for small gardens where you can enjoy the foliage at eye level. It has a narrow, upright shape, in no danger from strong winds. For both height 15–25 ft (5–8 m) x width 15 ft (5 m). **'Majestic'** has a good upright habit, bright green,

attractive foliage and is thornless. **'Moraine'** forms a tall tree with a broad crown, and the dark green leaves turn golden yellow in the fall. It is thornless and fruitless, i.e., male, resistant to webworm and very popular. **'Ruby Lace'** is a marvelous purple-red leaf form. **'Shademaster'** is a vigorous form with upright branches and dark green leaves. It has the great advantage of being thornless, and nearly podless. Height 45 ft (14 m). **'Skyline'** is also thornless, with a pleasing symmetrical shape. Dark green leaves in summer turn golden-yellow in fall. Height 50 ft (15 m). **'Sunburst'** features bright yellow young leaves that gradually turn green. It is not as hardy as most other cultivars and it is brittle, but makes an ideal small-garden tree as it is fast-growing, thornless and has a pleasing horizontal habit. Deservedly popular. Unless specified, height 40 ft (12 m) x width 30 ft (10 m). There are several other species of *Gleditsia* from Texas, Japan, Korea and China.

Triacanthos = three spines; *inermis* = unarmed or without thorns.

Hedera

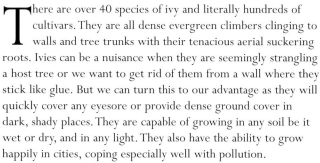

IVY
Araliaceae

There are over 40 species of ivy and literally hundreds of cultivars. They are all dense evergreen climbers clinging to walls and tree trunks with their tenacious aerial suckering roots. Ivies can be a nuisance when they are seemingly strangling a host tree or we want to get rid of them from a wall where they stick like glue. But we can turn this to our advantage as they will quickly cover any eyesore or provide dense ground cover in dark, shady places. They are capable of growing in any soil be it wet or dry, and in any light. They also have the ability to grow happily in cities, coping especially well with pollution.

Hedera = an ancient name for the plant.

Hedera canariensis
CANARY ISLAND IVY, NORTH AFRICAN IVY
This is a very pretty ivy with bright grass-green new leaves becoming slightly darker as they harden up. The leaves are 4–8 in (10–20 cm) long and can be heart-shaped, rounded or just slightly lobed. Unfortunately being from the Canary Islands off the coast of Spain it is slightly sensitive to frost, but makes a superb ground cover in warmer regions. Height 30 ft (10 m). ZONE 8.

Canariensis = from the Canary Islands.

Hedera helix
COMMON IVY, ENGLISH IVY
When climbing as a young plant the juvenile leaves have three or five distinct lobes and very pointy leaf tips. As the plant reaches the light and becomes mature the leaves change to adult mode with entire oval or rhomboid leaves, 1.5–2.5 in (4–6 cm) long. If you take a cutting from this mature growth you can grow it as a shrub rather than a vine. These older portions are the only parts to have clusters of greenish white flowers followed by little black berries. Ivy is used to cover unsightly tree stumps and walls and is often used as an indoor plant growing over a wire frame to any shape you want to create. It grows naturally all through Europe through to Turkey and Iran. Height 30 ft (10 m). ZONE 5.

Left: *Hedera helix* 'Variegata'

There are all sorts of varieties ranging from variegated forms with white, cream or yellow markings and some with purple or near black leaves and others with distorted or wavy leaves.

Helix = spiral or twisted.

Hydrangea

Hydrangeaceae

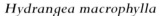

ydrangeas make popular, hardy and resilient shrubs, well known to us all. They can so easily be taken for granted as they fill so many roles, and can grow in wet, windy or coastal sites. As well as growing in difficult garden sites, they are also commonly used as a pot plant or for window boxes.

We all know that hydrangeas are famous for their fabulous summer flowers, but they are wonderful foliage plants, too. Somehow we never seem to regard them as such, probably because the leaves are hidden behind a blanket of flowers. No other plant keeps its flowers for so long and it is only in the spring, before the riot of colorful blooms, that we may see the foliage in all its glory.

Hydrangea = water (*hydra*) vessel (*angeion*), describing the shape of the flower.

Hydrangea macrophylla
BIGLEAF HYDRANGEA, FLORIST'S HYDRANGEA
As the common name and species name *macrophylla* imply, this has large leaves, splendid in their own right. Besides having grand glossy, wind-tolerant leaves, the plant is also remarkably tough. Many of the glossy-leaf cultivars such as **'Ayesha'** and **'Seafoam'** will grow on clifftops, surviving the worst salt-laden gales. Needless to say, they thrive and look their best given better conditions

Above: *Hydrangea quercifolia*

than this and grow to perfection in a sheltered, moist site. They will grow under conditions of shade as well as some waterlogging. Acidic soil gives blue and alkaline soil pink and red flowers. Virtually free of pests and diseases, they are really easy-care plants. A native of Japan. Height 6 ft (2 m) x width 8 ft (2.5 m). ZONES 6 TO 9.

Macrophylla = big leaves.

Hydrangea quercifolia
OAKLEAF HYDRANGEA
This unusual hydrangea is perhaps not as robust as *H. macrophylla*, but quite beautiful in its own way. It forms an arching shrub with cones or panicles of white flowers in late summer, and the flowers

Right: *Hydrangea macrophylla*

sssssssss

(body)

take on a reddish tinge as fall approaches. The real surprise is the fall color of the leaves in stunning reds, purple and burgundy. This is the only hydrangea with spectacular fall color, and the contrast with the reddish tinged flowers is wonderful. This plant grows in full sun or semi-shade and enjoys good drainage. It is not very happy in climates with cool summers, though it will take cold winters if the summers are hot. It hails from the southeastern U.S.A. Height 6 ft (2 m) x width 8 ft (2.5 m). ZONES 5 TO 9.

There is an exciting double-flowered form called **'Snowflake'**, which prefers partial shade, and a superb single clone called **'Snow Queen'**.

Quercifolia = oak-foliaged (reputedly in reference to American red oaks).

Idesia

Idesia polycarpa
CHINESE WONDER TREE
Flacourtiaceae

Now this tree is an enigma to me: it is deciduous and therefore you would think it was hardy, and yet it is not happy in the cooler parts of Europe or the U.S.A. The truth is, it is hardy to cold winters but needs warm summers to succeed. Continental hot summers and cold winters suit it well, as does a lush, mild climate.

Gardeners often want instant trees—preferably ones that stop growing when they have reached the desired height. This is the nearest I have found to that "perfect" tree, growing to 12 ft (4 m) or so in very quick time and then slowing down to a more sedate growth rate to remain a small tree. Occasionally *Idesia polycarpa* decides it wants to form a larger tree but mostly it is wide-spreading and small. The airy, open habit shows off the animal-like trunks, looking like elephant hide. In a way it is a "designer tree" or, to put it another way, the sort of tree children

Above: *Idesia polycarpa*

Left: *Idesia polycarpa* with new berries.

Above: *Idesia polycarpa* with berries.

love to climb. This flawless structure with a tier of branches, then a gap and another tier and so on shows perfect design, making other twiggy trees look cluttered. Hand-sized, heart-shaped leaves are rich green above and pale below. The striking red petiole or leaf stalk adds to their appeal. It seems as though every leaf has been carefully spaced.

It makes a wonderful shade tree near the house. If you need to step out into some cool shade or somewhere to sling your hammock, then *Idesia polycarpa* should be near the top of your list. The compact, tiered structure and resilient nature also make it an ideal candidate as a street tree.

The flowers are nothing special—the panicles of small, yellowish flowers are easily missed—but you cannot bypass the mass of bright red berries. If you are lucky, these berries will hang on long after the unspectacular leaf fall. Berries are dependent on several factors. There are separate male and female trees and obviously only the females have berries. Many trees are seedlings and so you will not know what you have until the tree matures and flowers. Then, even if you have a female tree, it is not going to have many berries unless there is a male tree nearby. That is why they make such good street trees as an avenue of females can be pollinated by one or two males.

There are one or two named female clones available, such as **'Kentucky Fry'**, so it is worth a dollar or so more for a selected or grafted form. Luck also plays a part in how long the birds leave the berries alone in the fall. In some regions they are untouched for months and elsewhere the birds relish them. Regardless of the berries, the stately *Idesia* is worth growing for its foliage alone and the berries are just a bonus.

It is easily transplanted from open ground with bare roots; even large specimens can be moved with ease. Place it in full sun. It is not fussy about soil, including lime soils. Thankfully it is never bothered by pests and diseases. The tree is reasonably tough when it comes to wind, even growing in coastal cities. This may come as surprise when you see the size of the leaves.

Idesia polycarpa was named after a Dutch plant collector, Eberhard Ides, who traveled in China in the 17th century. The tree comes from China, Korea and Japan. ZONE 6 TO 9, remembering the need for hot summers. Height x width 40 ft (12 m).

There is a subspecies called **I. p. var vestita**, said to be hardier to cold and, appropriately, it has a furry coat in the form of a downy undersurface to the leaf. This subspecies was discovered by Ernest Wilson (1876–1930).

Polycarpa = many fruits.

Ilex

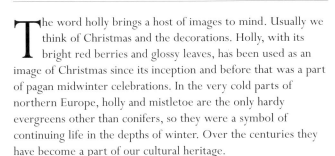

HOLLY
Aquifoliaceae

The word holly brings a host of images to mind. Usually we think of Christmas and the decorations. Holly, with its bright red berries and glossy leaves, has been used as an image of Christmas since its inception and before that was a part of pagan midwinter celebrations. In the very cold parts of northern Europe, holly and mistletoe are the only hardy evergreens other than conifers, so they were a symbol of continuing life in the depths of winter. Over the centuries they have become a part of our cultural heritage.

"Polished" is the word best describing most hollies. It is as if each leaf has been specially waxed and polished until it shines. For gardeners in cold climates hollies are essential, being the most hardy evergreen plants. The tough, evergreen types form the backbone of many a garden in very cold places. They are useful for hedges, especially where we want to direct foot traffic; not many pedestrians are willing to take a shortcut through a holly hedge.

Hollies will cope with city pollution and some species handle windy sites. Nearly all are indifferent to soil types, living in alkaline soil or heavy, compacted clay. They cope with heat and drought, and most are shade-tolerant, too. They are a very tough shrub, practically indestructible. No pests or diseases trouble them, and they are long-lived and will not die out, which is essential for a hedge plant to prevent any gaps occurring.

It may come as a surprise to learn some hollies lose their leaves, having paler, thin leaves more like deciduous *Euonymus*.

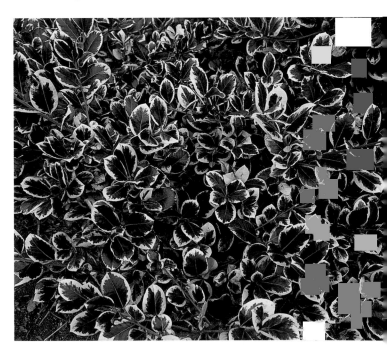

Above: *Ilex* x *altaclerensis* 'Golden King'

The link to the more familiar evergreen types is provided by the flowers and berries.

With hollies, male and female plants are separate and if you want a crop of luscious berries you will need two or more clones. The berries are brilliant for color in midwinter. "Brilliant" is also the word that best describes the shiny leaves of so many of the cultivars.

Ilex = a classical name for evergreen oak or *Quercus ilex* (and so the genus name comes from the similarity to holm oak).

Ilex x *altaclerensis* (*I. aquifolium* x *I. perado*), syn *I. altaclarensis*
HIGHCLERE HOLLY

This is a mixed group of hybrids between *Ilex aquifolium*, the English holly, and the Canary Island *I. perado*. They are quite hardy to cold and wind, even growing in coastal regions. They also cope with city pollution. Numerous clones exist, including some excellent variegated types. Some of them have confusing names, with 'King' being female and 'Queen' being male. Height 70 ft (20 m) x width 40–50 ft (12–15 m). ZONES 7 TO 9.

'**Golden King**' has a deep green leaf edged in golden-yellow. The leaf edges are smooth (no spikes). Female. Height x width 15 ft (5 m). '**Lawsoniana**' is the reverse of 'Golden King', so the yellow is in the center. It is really tri-colored because it has a dark green outer part, then patches of light green and then the pale gold center. Female. Height 20 ft (6 m) x width 15 ft (5 m). '**Wilsonii**' is the best straight, green form with glossy, spiny leaves and a good crop of bright red berries. Female. Height 25 ft (8 m) x width 15 ft (5 m).

Altaclerensis = the latin name for the garden Highclere in England, from which this species is named.

Ilex aquifolium
ENGLISH HOLLY

English holly grows in Britain and all across Europe into north Africa and Asia. It is a very hardy plant, and has had a place in people's lives since early pagan times until the present day. Like *Ilex* x *altaclerensis*, it will grow in polluted cities and coastal windy regions. It is excellent for a hedge or as a solo specimen. Height 80 ft (25 m) x width 25 ft (8 m). ZONES 7 TO 9.

A huge number of clones have been selected over the centuries. '**Ferox**' (hedgehog holly) is an ancient cultivar that has provided a silver-edged and a gold blotched clone as well. The word *ferox* means "fierce," and is appropriate, as this not only has spines along the sides of the leaf but on top of the leaf as well. Male. Height 9 ft (3 m) x width 6 ft (2 m). '**Golden Milkboy**' has a typical spiky holly leaf with a big splash of gold in the center. Male. Height 20 ft (6 m) x width 12 ft (4 m). There are numerous attractive variegated hollies, including '**Silver Queen**' and '**Argentea Marginata**'. Both height x width 12 ft (4 m).

Aquifolium = old name meaning pointed leaves, sometimes thought to refer to the shiny foliage.

Ilex cornuta
CHINESE HOLLY

Ilex cornuta forms a low-growing, dense bush with glossy leaves and bright red berries. It is a tough plant, ideal for heavy soils and poor sites. It takes hot summers and cold winters in its stride. It is native to China and Korea. Height x width 15 ft (5 m). ZONES 7 TO 9.

'**Burfordii**' is an improved form with darker leaves and just a few spines. Free-fruiting. Width 12–15 ft (4–5 m). '**D'Or**' has a

Left: *Ilex aquifolium*

Above: *Ilex* x *meserveae* 'Blue Angel'

crinkly, curled leaf, very different from most hollies. Bright yellow fruits make a change from the familiar reds. Height x width 3–4 ft (1 m). '**O' Spring**' features spiny, rectangular leaves with an obvious trident of three spines at the end. The tri-color leaf with gray and green, and a cream and golden edge in various widths creates a very eye-catching bush. Height x width 3–4 ft (1 m).

Cornuta = horned.

Ilex crenata
JAPANESE HOLLY

Tiny, almost black leaves compensate numerically for what they lack in size. This dense shrub or small tree is ideal for hedges and topiary. It is especially good for creating Japanese-style gardens as it takes regular trimming with no complaint. Although usually seen as a low, dense plant, it can be upright and open (if pruned). It is best in full sun and well-drained soil, but other than that it is not fussy and is a tough little shrub. A native of Japan and Korea. Height 15 ft (5 m) x width 12 ft (4 m). ZONES 5 TO 9.

'**Convexa**' (syn '**Bullata**') is an oldie but a goodie. It is popular as a low hedge for its rich, dark green foliage and crops of berries. Height 8 ft (2.5 m) x width 6 ft (2 m). '**Golden Gem**' has golden-yellow, smooth leaves that add a touch of strong color

Right: *Ilex perado*
with berries.

to any winter garden. It is likely to go green in shade, so plant in full sun. Height 3.5 ft (1.1 m) x width 4–5 ft (1.2–1.5 m). **'Mariesii'** (syn *I.c.* **var** *nummularioides* or *I. mariesii*) is a neat little shrub, ideal for Japanese-style gardens as it can be trimmed to any desired shape. It is naturally an upright, narrow shape and covered in tiny black leaves. Height 24–36 in (60–90 cm) x width 18–24 in (45–60 cm).

Crenata = notched or toothed.

Ilex x *meserveae* (*I. rugosa* x *I. aquifolium*)
BLUE HOLLY

A group of hybrids developed in the U.S. to cope with a continental climate. They all have glossy blue foliage, the blue being more intense in colder places.

Their names give the clue to whether they are male or female clones: **'Blue Angel'** is slow-growing and compact, and the least hardy. Height 12 ft (4 m) x width 6 ft (2 m). **'Blue Boy'** has a spreading habit. **'Blue Girl'** abundant red berries. **'Blue Prince'** is similar to 'Blue Boy'. **'Blue Princess'** is similar to 'Blue Girl'. For all, height 10 ft (3 m) x width 12 ft (4 m). ZONES 5 TO 9.

Meserveae = named for Mrs Kathleen Meserve, the breeder *c.* 1900.

Ilex 'Nellie R. Stevens' (*I. cornuta* x *I. aquifolium*)

This beautiful hybrid has obvious elements of *Ilex cornuta* with its raised, puckered leaves which are shiny as well as spiny-edged. It is a female form, and is laden with soft, orange-red berries. It forms a large shrub and ultimately a small tree. Height 22 ft (7 m) x width 12 ft (4 m). ZONES 7 TO 9.

Ilex perado

Ilex perado forms a bold, evergreen shrub with glossy, dark green, almost smooth-edged leaves up to 4 in (10 cm) long. The plant is surprisingly hardy given its country of origin, the Canary Islands

Above: *Ilex pernyi*

Above: *Ilex verticillata* with berries.

off the coast of Spain. It eventually makes a small tree, but can be kept at shrub size for years by judicious pruning. Height 20–30 ft (6–10 m) x width 22 ft (7 m). ZONES 7 TO 9.

Ilex pernyi

It must be an *Ilex*, but it is not quite like any holly you have ever seen before. It is a large shrub with very distinctive, shiny, black leaves, edged with sharp spines. So it looks like a typical holly except that the leaves are very small, although the plant itself becomes a large shrub or even a tree. You can prune it to open it up Asian-style, making a real feature of the smooth branches. It was named after a French missionary, Paul Perny, who collected the plant in its native China.

Ilex pernyi is happy in extremely wet or cold climates but not so good in dry areas. Height 28 ft (9 m) x width 10 ft (3 m). ZONES 6 TO 9.

Ilex verticillata
BLACK ALDER, WINTERBERRY
This deciduous shrub is grown primarily for the red berries in winter. The mass of berries can last for months and it is definitely worthy of a space. You need at least one male plant to ensure a

crop of berries. There are some named fruiting forms. It fruits best in full sun, though it will grow in shade. The fall leaves sometimes take on a yellow tinge. The plant needs acidic soil and grows naturally in wettish places but seems to handle dry places, too. Originates from eastern U.S.A. and Canada. Height x width 15 ft (5 m). ZONES 5 TO 8.

Verticillata = whorled (referring to the placement of the fruits).

Juniperus, syn Sabina

JUNIPER
Cupressaceae

Junipers have to be one of the most diverse and versatile groups of plants on the planet, growing in climates as varied as Mexico, China, Africa and the Arctic Circle. They are far more tolerant of extremes than most conifers. As if to prove the point, they can even be grown in tubs, coping with the extremes of drought and hot sun. In fact any soil seems to suit as they will grow in clay or alkaline soils. Even hot, dry banks, which are anathema to most conifers, pose no problems for the resilient juniper, making them the king of the ground covers for windy, exposed gardens.

Garden cultivars tend to be extreme shapes, such as upright pillars, prostrate ground covers or the shooting stars of *Juniperus chinensis* 'Kaizuka'. Many junipers are fierce to touch with spiky, pointed leaves, so take care where you place them, keeping them well away from paths.

Juniper = a Celtic word meaning rough,
that was taken up by the Latin scholar Virgil.

Juniperus chinensis
CHINESE JUNIPER
Juniperus chinensis is a tough, drought-tolerant plant from China and Japan. It is usually seen in gardens as one of the blue or yellow forms listed below. Height 70 ft (20 m) x width 20 ft (6 m). ZONES 3 TO 9.

'**Blue Vase**' is a very small blue-foliaged form, ideal for rockeries. Height x width 2–3 ft (60–90 cm).

Others include:

Juniperus chinensis '**Aurea**'
'Aurea' is an upright, slender bush with bright golden-yellow foliage in sun or shade. It can burn if given too much sun, but that is where it gets the best color, so you have to find a happy medium. It is okay in dry places, too.

It grows slowly, and forms a dense, compact plant. Height 35 ft (11 m) x width 15 ft (5 m).

Juniperus chinensis '**Kaizuka**'
HOLLYWOOD JUNIPER
The common name was given presumably because this spreading shrub was overused in that Los Angeles suburb when first on the market.

It is a real impact plant with shooting stars of twisted, bright green foliage. It has the appearance of being pruned by an eccentric gardener. This is the natural shape, although they can be trimmed for greater effect. A true architectural plant. Height 20 ft (6 m) x width 10–12 ft (3–4 m).

Chinensis = from China.

Right: *Juniperus chinensis* 'Kaizuka'

Above: *Juniperus* x *pfitzeriana* 'Dandelight' and the trunk of *Pinus pinea*.

Right: *Juniperus chinensis* 'Blue Vase' (back left), *Chamaecyparis obtusa* 'Rigid Dwarf' (front left) and *Picea glauca* 'Echiniformis' (front right).

Juniperus x *pfitzeriana*, syn *J.* x *media*

Popularized as the ideal ground-hugging, weed-smothering ground cover, this juniper is tough as old boots and considerably more attractive. Gray-green leaves lie flat along the shoots. Height 4 ft (1.2 m) x width 10 ft (3 m). ZONES 4 TO 9.

There are several named cultivars, including **'Dandelight'**, a beautiful, lemon-yellow form recently introduced into cultivation. It turns rich gold in winter and is splendid ground cover. Height 2 ft (60 cm) x width 6 ft (2 m).

Pfitzericana = named for German nurseryman, W. Pfitzer, *c.* 1900.

Juniperus scopulorum

ROCKY MOUNTAIN JUNIPER

Juniperus scopulorum is a small, conical tree with peeling brown bark and bluish foliage. It is native to the Rocky Mountains. Height 50 ft (15 m) x width 20 ft (6 m). ZONES 4 TO 7. *Juniperus scopulorum* **'Moonglow'** has a neat, narrow, upright habit. The silver-blue foliage color is maintained all through the year. *J. s.* **'Blue Heaven'** is very similar.

Scopulorum = brush-like.

Juniperus scopulorum 'Skyrocket'

Juniperus scopulorum **'Skyrocket'**, syn *J. virginiana* **'Skyrocket'**

One of the first plant names I learned, probably because the plant is unique. Even a rookie student could recognize this from 20 paces. A superb, pencil-thin, gray-blue conifer that is able to contend with heat and drought. It is ideal near steps and paths where you want a statement or strong vertical line. Height 20 ft (6 m) x width 20–24 in (50–60 cm).

Above: *Juniperus squamata*

Juniperus squamata
SINGLESEED JUNIPER

Singleseed juniper forms a prostrate shrub, spreading bush or small upright tree, with gray-green to silvery blue foliage and flaky brownish bark. It grows native in Afghanistan, the Himalayas and western China. Height 30 ft (10 m) x width 3–25 ft (1–8 m). ZONES 5 TO 8.

'Blue Star' is a common variety, ideal for rockeries. It is compact and rounded with bluish gray-green leaves. Height 16 in (40 cm) x width 3 ft (1 m). **'Meyeri'** is an unusually shaped bush that always wants to grow at an angle. While most garden-worthy junipers are ground-hugging or narrow, pillar shapes, this one has a mind of its own and shoots off like a missile. The effect is enhanced by the sparkling blue foliage. Best in full sun, it can cope with heavy, wet soil and hot climates. 'Meyeri' is named for Frank Meyer (1875–1918), the American plant collector most famous for the Meyer lemon. Height 12–30 ft (4–10 m) x width 20–25 ft (6–8 m). ZONE 4.

Squamata = scaly.

Juniperus taxifolia var *lutchuensis*

This forms a very spreading and prostrate ground cover with a blue tinge. It is an ideal plant for covering banks and will even cascade down vertical rock walls. Height 1–2 ft (30–60 cm) x width 10 ft (3 m). ZONE 9.

Taxifolia = foliage like a *Taxus* or yew.

Juniperus virginiana
PENCIL CEDAR, RED CEDAR

Pencil cedar is a variable species from eastern and central U.S.A., thus the name *virginiana* from the state of the same name. It can be columnar or wide-spreading, and has gray-green foliage and brown bark. It is extremely hardy. Height 50–100 ft (15–30 m) x width 15–25 ft (5–8 m). ZONES 3 TO 9.

'Silver Spreader' is a spreading, ground-hugging plant ideal for warm climates and yet equally happy in cold regions.

Right: *Kalopanax pictus*

Kalopanax

Kalopanax pictus, syn *K. septemlobus*
CASTOR ARALIA
Araliaceae

*K*alopanax is a genus of one species, and *K. pictus* is one of the most ornate plants in my garden. It is also sometimes known as *K. septemlobus*, meaning "seven-lobed leaves." This is an obscure species deserving far wider recognition as a fine, garden-worthy plant. In the wild it is a tall, upright forest tree with a leaf like a maple and overall shape and trunk like an ash. In a garden it forms a sparsely branched shrub or small tree with chunky stems. As a young plant the leaves are the main feature but in time the fierce, thick prickles all along the stems and branches become a major talking point. Beware, and do not plant it anywhere where people are likely to brush against it, as the prickles are very sharp.

The leaves add a tropical touch by their size and appearance, although the plant is perfectly hardy and easy to please, being equally content in hot and dry, or wet climates. For good overall shape give it good light or full sun. Any soil from acidic to alkaline is acceptable.

Typically the large leaves are five- to seven-lobed, looking just like a five-pronged maple with prominent red petioles. It is

only the showers of creamy white flowers like exploding pompoms that make you think otherwise. They are reminiscent of *Fatsia* flowers, which is hardly surprising as the plants are closely related.

The fall color is occasionally a rich butter-yellow but not consistently enough to be grown for fall color alone. Consider it more of a bonus when it comes. Perhaps if the plant were to be grown from selected forms and given cultivar names, we could have both the tropical look and fall color.

Reasons the plant is not more popular include the variability and inconsistency when grown from seed, and the difficulty of propagating it vegetatively. It resists attempts to grow from cuttings and is usually grown from root cuttings, a time-consuming and difficult task. Most plants in cultivation have been grown from seed thus the variation in leaf shape and fall color. A native of China, Korea, eastern Russia and Japan. Height x width 30 ft (10 m). ZONES 5 TO 9.

The smaller-growing subspecies, **Kalopanax pictus var maximowiczii**, is probably the better garden plant as the leaves are larger, more obviously lobed and tropical-looking and the plant does not grow so fast or so tall. It forms a bushy shrub around 6 ft (2 m) high and wide after 10 years' growth.

Kalo = beautiful; *panax* = ginseng (a related medicinal plant);

pictus = ornamental.

Larix

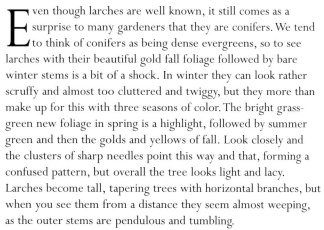

LARCH
Pinaceae

Even though larches are well known, it still comes as a surprise to many gardeners that they are conifers. We tend to think of conifers as being dense evergreens, so to see larches with their beautiful gold fall foliage followed by bare winter stems is a bit of a shock. In winter they can look rather scruffy and almost too cluttered and twiggy, but they more than make up for this with three seasons of color. The bright grass-green new foliage in spring is a highlight, followed by summer green and then the golds and yellows of fall. Look closely and the clusters of sharp needles point this way and that, forming a confused pattern, but overall the tree looks light and lacy. Larches become tall, tapering trees with horizontal branches, but when you see them from a distance they seem almost weeping, as the outer stems are pendulous and tumbling.

All larches hail from the cooler regions of the Northern Hemisphere, often growing on mountain slopes. They like a cool, moist climate and are very cold-hardy but are not too happy in warm or dry regions. They like a good deep soil, be it acidic or alkaline, and preferably in a high rainfall area, though it should be well drained.

They suffer from a few pests such as aphids and larch blight, which is actually a white woolly chermid insect, and also some devastating diseases like canker and larch blister.

Larix = an old Roman name for larch.

Larix decidua, syn L. europaea
EUROPEAN LARCH
European larch forms an upright tree, with the crown spreading as it ages. The upturned branches have pendulous pale green foliage, giving a weeping effect from afar. The tree originates in

Above: *Larix decidua* in fall colors.

northern and central Europe. Height 100 ft (30 m) x width 12–20 ft (4–6 m). ZONES 3 TO 8.

'Pendula' has a more pronounced weeping habit.

Decidua = deciduous.

Larix kaempferi
JAPANESE LARCH
This is a large vigorous tree similar to *Larix decidua* but with bigger leaves. The reddish twigs look great in the wintertime. It will tolerate cold, harsh, open sites. *L. kaempferi* was introduced from Japan in 1861 by John Gould Veitch (1839–1870) for the English Veitch Nursery, and is named after German doctor and botanist Engelbert Kaempfer (1651–1715), who was stationed in Japan. Height 100 ft (30 m) x width 12–20 ft (4–6 m). ZONES 5 TO 8.

'Blue Haze' has brighter bluish foliage.

Larix occidentalis
WESTERN AMERICAN LARCH
Potentially the most magnificent of all the larches, this is a narrow tree when young, and spreading with age. The trunk has reddish brown bark. The blue-green to gray-green leaves are like the European larch but the cones have little tongues protuding. Larch cones are small, the size of a walnut, and can be very decorative. They are often painted and used for Christmas ornaments.

A species from western North America, found by David Douglas (1798–1834), who introduced the Douglas fir into cultivation. Height 80 ft (25 m) x width 15 ft (5 m). ZONES 4 TO 8.

Occidentalis = western.

Leucothoe

Ericaceae

*L*eucothoe is a genus of about 50 species of shrubs, cultivated mainly for their variably shaped leaves, often glossy and dark green, and for their panicles of usually white flowers.

The genus was named after Leucothoe, daughter of Orchamus and loved by Apollo. This is the same Apollo who killed Daphne's bridegroom and drove her to seek refuge as a plant.

Leucothoe fontanesiana, syn *L. catesbaei*, *L. walteri*

DROOPING LEUCOTHOE, FETTERBUSH

Leucothoe fontanesiana is the most well known of the genus and was formerly called *L. catesbaei*. I can remember as a student being enthused by the variegated version of this plant. It is one of the best evergreen shrubs for shade, and forms a dense ground cover, ideal for covering banks with its arching stems.

Once established it is a weedproof cover that will give pendulous racemes of white, *Pieris*-like flowers in the spring. The foliage is a rich, dark green through summer, taking on purplish bronze tinges in winter, depending on the setting and how cold it is. Grow it on a bank if you can and allow it to drape down gracefully, showing off its foliage and flowers.

If it gets tatty, cut it back to ground level and start again, as it regenerates easily if pruned in early spring. It is easy to transplant at any age, as the fibrous root system is similar to the related rhododendrons. It tolerates wind, but performs so well in shade that, with so few shade-loving shrubs available, this is the ideal place for it. It is not happy in hot, sunny sites and tends to get a leaf spot disease when stressed, so keep it in moist, acidic, shady glades where it luxuriates. Dry soils are fine once it is established and cool or cold places are fine, too.

The species was named for René Louiche Desfontaines, an 18th century botanical author. *Leucothoe fontanesiana* is found native in southeastern U.S.A. Height 3–6 ft (1–2 m) x width 10 ft (3 m). ZONES 5 TO 9.

There are few named types worth seeking out. A smaller version of the species is **'Nana'**. Height 2–3 ft (60–90 cm) x width 4–5 ft (1.2–1.5 m). The variegated **'Rainbow'**, which enthused me as a student, has dark green leaves mottled with pale green, cream, yellow and pink. It needs shade to prevent sunburn. Height 5 ft (1.5 m) x width 6 ft (2 m). **'Scarletta'** has shiny reddish bronze new growth and often colors up in the fall even though it does not lose its leaves. Height 5 ft (1.5 m) x width 6 ft (2 m).

Leucothoe grayana

This is a Japanese shrub with a rough surface and oval leaves taking on bronze or scarlet color in fall. It is semi-evergreen, depending on clone and climate. The leaves have a rough, puckered surface. The pale green-white midsummer flowers sometimes take on a red tinge. Height 3 ft (1 m) x width 5 ft (1.5 m). ZONE 6.

Grayana = named for Asa Gray (1810–1888).

Leucothoe keiskei

Another Japanese species with curled leaves, rolled back around the edges, giving it a manicured appearance. The evergreen leaves turn bronzy in winter. Creamy white cup flowers appear in

summer. It is a tidy little plant worthy of a place in a shady spot. Height x width 24 in (60 cm). ZONES 6 TO 8.

Keiskei = named for Japanese botanist Keisuke-Ito (1803–1901).

Above: *Leucothoe fontanesiana*

Lindera

Lauraceae

*T*his little-known group of shrubs deserves greater popularity. The great majority are Asian, while two or three originate in eastern U.S.A. and Canada. Some are evergreen while most are deciduous. They are really quite diverse—just because you like one *Lindera* does not mean you will like them all as they vary so much. Most have clusters of tiny, yellow flowers early in the spring and some have superb fall color. Generally they are easy to grow, given neutral or acidic soil. They are happy in wet climates and quite drought-tolerant, too. Grow them in sun or part-shade, though the deciduous ones need full sun to have stunning fall tones. Their natural setting is the forest edge, but plants seem to cope with windy sites. Occasionally they suffer dieback and rust.

Lindera = named for Swedish botanist Joseph Linder (1676–1723).

Lindera benzoin

SPICE BUSH

If you live in the Appalachians, you know spring is on its way when the spice bush comes into flower. In early April the bare black stems are laden with tiny, yellow flowers, followed by bright red berries. It is not the sort of flower to set the gardeners talking, but it does raise your spirits to know winter is waning. Then all through summer it fades into the background until fall when it displays its bright yellow fall color. The small, simple, bright green leaves color up more when the bush is in full sun. Spice bush makes an attractive addition to a woodland garden.

Early land surveyors in the Carolinas used this as an indicator plant. The presence of spice bush meant it was good land. Early settlers used the aromatic twigs, leaves and berries for drinks and for spicing up meals. Height x width 10 ft (3 m). ZONES 5 TO 9.

Benzoin = spice.

Above: The fall color of *Lindera obtusiloba*.

Right: *Lindera benzoin*

Lindera erythrocarpa

A rather plain shrub for most of the year, with a brief splash of color when the yellow flowers emerge in spring, but it is fall when this shrub claims center stage. The fall colors are a combination of reds, burnished orange and yellows. It forms a sparse, rather spindly shrub in shade, but grow it in full sun and the dense foliage sits pleasingly on horizontal branches. The oval, thumb-sized leaves are simple and smooth.

Like its Appalachian sister, this Korean plant is only likely to be granted a place in larger, woodland gardens, but should you decide to grow one, you will not regret it. Height x width 15–20 ft (5–6 m). ZONE 6.

Erythro = red; *carpa* = fruit.

Lindera obtusiloba

You are unlikely to confuse this with any other plant. It is almost ginkgo-like or perhaps a ginkgo crossed with a maple. It is an exciting plant but, unfortunately, is not readily available. It is certainly one of my most cherished shrubs.

As a young plant it is an upright bush with waxy, almost rounded, leaves with three distinct lobes. It has prominent, round, red buds in the leaf axils and some forms have reddish stems.

The fall color is scintillating—the clear butter-yellow simply sings in bright sunlight. The plant appears to color well in mild climates as well as in colder, more traditional, fall-color regions.

Some forms have purple, *Cercis*-like new spring growth, the best of which should be selected and named.

I have seen this as a tree in Korea, but in most garden situations it is best regarded as an upright shrub. Native to Korea, China and Japan. Height x width 20 ft (6 m). ZONES 6 TO 9.

Obtusiloba = blunt lobes (referring to the strangely shaped leaves).

Liquidambar

SWEETGUM
Hamamelidaceae

You know you are making progress with plant identification when you can tell a *Liquidambar* from a maple. Here are two or three little tricks to help you distinguish liquidambars. One, they have alternate leaves compared to the opposite leaves of maple. Two, the young stems of liquidambars are often corky and ridged, though this is not always so and therefore it is not foolproof. Three, if the tree has seeds, then identification is easy as the maple has the typical winged seeds while liquidambars have a round, spiky ball enclosing the seeds. Fallen fruits can be a problem for pedestrians in streets and parking lots, causing people to twist an ankle.

Liquidambars, of which there are six species, all have delightfully aromatic, maple-like leaves. The Mediterranean version, *Liquidambar orientalis* (Oriental sweetgum), used to be tapped for storax, a fragrant gum used in cosmetics and medicines. *L. styraciflua* (sweetgum), from the U.S.A., yields sweet gum used as a medicine for common colds and as an additive for chewing gum.

Liquidambars detest strong winds; their branches are ripped and torn by even modest storms. To compensate for this they have no serious pests or diseases. Ideally, plant them in reasonably well-drained soil, but they will grow in moist sites. Conversely they handle drought pretty well, too.

Liquidambar = liquid gum.

Left: *Liquidambar styraciflua* 'Variegata'

Above: *Liquidambar styraciflua*

Left: *Liquidambar formosana* fall leaves.

Above left and right: *Liquidambar styraciflua* 'Lane Roberts' in the fall.

Liquidambar formosana, syn *L. formosana* var *monticola*

This good-looking tree varies according to the seed source. Some are rather plain while others have fabulous spring and fall color. The new growth is a strong purple, changing to bronzy-red and eventually dark green. It has lovely, strong, red petioles or leaf stalks. The smooth leaves somehow invite you to caress them, rewarding you with the essence of freshly picked apples. The maple-shaped leaves usually have three lobes and intense purple fall color. The smooth trunks are distinctly gray when young and take on a typical furrowed bark as they age. The tree originates in mainland China and Taiwan. Height 40 ft (12 m) x width 30 ft (10 m). ZONES 7 TO 9.

Formosana = native of Taiwan (Formosa being the old name for the island).

Liquidambar orientalis
ORIENTAL SWEETGUM

A small tree, slow-growing and similar to *Liquidambar styraciflua*, but not as ornamental. Its mid-green leaves turn yellow and orange in fall. Oriental sweetgum comes from Greece and Turkey. Height 20 ft (6 m) x width 12 ft (4 m). ZONES 7 TO 9.

Orientalis = oriental.

Liquidambar styraciflua
SWEETGUM

A fabulous garden or park tree where space permits, *Liquidambar styraciflua* is equally stunning in the wilds of the Appalachians where it occurs in moist valley sites, even growing in areas inundated after heavy rain. The tree is, however, quite tolerant of dry summers and more drought-hardy than commonly supposed. Strong winds bruise the leaves, eventually tearing and splitting branches. It is easily transplanted at any stage, so large trees can be moved for "instant" city beautification. The plant is often grown from seed but the seedlings are very variable. It's worth spending a few dollars more for a named cultivar, guaranteed to please. Without a doubt, this is one of the best trees for fall color. In mild, warm climates where fall color is a scarce commodity, choose a *Liquidambar* for your garden, as it will not let you down. Native to the eastern U.S.A. and Mexico. Height 80 ft (25 m) x width 40 ft (12 m). ZONE 6.

'**Burgundy**' has burgundy new spring leaves and long-lasting, deep purple fall color. '**Festeri**' has purple-red fall color, which lasts long into winter in warm climates. '**Festival**', a clone from the U.S., offers great orange-red fall color. '**Golden Treasure**' is an appropriately named Australian form. The leaves have a bright yellow margin in summer, turning to cream and then white in fall. The central green leaf goes orange-red or maroon, creating a vivid contrast. Height 30 ft (10 m) x width 20 ft (6 m). '**Lane Roberts**' is one of the best clones for fall color with sustained, rich, blackish crimson shades. It has smooth bark, which is unusual for a *Liquidambar*. '**Palo Alto**' has a wonderful combination of orange and fiery red fall color, lasting several weeks. For all the above cultivers, unless otherwise stated, height x width 60 ft (18 m).

'**Rotundiloba**' has smooth, rounded leaves and is instantly recognizable compared to the usual pointed lobes of a *Liquidambar*. It is sterile, and is therefore ideal as a street tree, as there is no fruit to trip over. Height 40 ft (12 m) x width 20 ft (6 m). '**Variegata**' has gray-green leaves edged in creamy yellow. Height 50 ft (15 m) x width 25 ft (8 m). '**Worplesdon**' is a very distinctive clone, having neater, narrow leaves turning orange and apricot. The tree is more graceful than some, with drooping branches. Height 50 ft (15 m) x width 25 ft (8 m).

Styraciflua = sweet gum flowing.

Liriodendron

TULIP TREE, TULIP POPLAR
Magnoliaceae

This is a genus of deciduous trees of stately habit and curiously shaped leaves, which turn yellow in fall. The flowers are quite large, about the size of a tulip, in fact. They are brightly colored when in your hand and yet the tree manages to disguise them among the yellow-green summer foliage. A big specimen can be laden with hundreds of apricot-colored flowers and hardly a soul sees them.

There are only two species of *Liriodendron*, one from China and the other more familiar one from eastern U.S.A. Their unique leaf shape has the appearance of someone having diligently cut out the end of each leaf with a pair of scissors.

Liriodendrons are willing to grow in clay and extremes of acidity and alkalinity. Both the species relish good, deep, moist soil and are best shifted into a permanent position when young, as older plants do not transplant easily or well.

They resent root disturbance and are best in a woodland setting where they will remain undisturbed. This environment also helps protect them from wind, as they are quite brittle and easily damaged.

Lirion = lily; *dendron* = tree.

Liriodendron chinense
CHINESE TULIP TREE

Liriodendron chinense has a shinier, smoother leaf with a narrower waist between the lobes than *L. tulipifera*, and a flatter, straighter outer edge. The green and yellow flowers are also smaller than those of *L. tulipifera*. Having said that, it is still instantly recognizable as a tulip tree. It is also a smaller tree in cultivation, which may be an asset. Generally, it is only grown as a novelty because of

its relationship with its American cousin. It is a native of China and Vietnam, and provides a link between plants from this region and those of North America. Height 80 ft (25 m) x width 40 ft (12 m). ZONES 7 TO 9.

Chinense = from China.

Liriodendron tulipifera
TULIP TREE, TULIP POPLAR, YELLOW POPLAR

Liriodendron tulipifera grows native all along the American east coast. With such a climatic range it is remarkable there are not more variations and forms. It is very hardy, tall-growing and fast-growing, forming one of the dominant trees of the natural forests. In the U.S. it is known as tulip poplar and yellow poplar, although it is not related to poplars.

The fragrant lime-green and apricot flowers are followed by large, pointed seed cones. Seedling trees take longer to flower than grafted clones. The bright green leaves turn brilliant butter-yellow and golds in fall. A tree is simply magnificent on a sunny day when dressed in gold. Height 100 ft (30 m) x width 50 ft (15 m). ZONES 5 TO 9.

'**Aureomarginatum**' has a bright yellow leaf with a splash of green in the center. It looks stunning in the spring and then gradually becomes almost one shade of green by midsummer. Also colors well in the fall. Height 70 ft (20 m) x width 30 ft (10 m).

'**Compactum**' is a smaller tree, ideal where space is limited. Height 40 ft (12 m) x width 25 ft (8 m). '**Fastigiatum**' is an erect form, ideal for confined spaces or where you need height. Height 70 ft (20 m) x width 25 ft (8 m). The clone '**Arnold**' has a similar upright habit. Height 70 ft (20 m) x width 25 ft (8 m).

Tulipifera = tulip flower.

Above: *Liriodendron tulipifera* 'Aureomarginatum'

Left: *Liriodendron tulipifera* in fall color.

Lonicera

HONEYSUCKLE
Caprifoliaceae

*L*onicera is a rather unusual genus, as half of the plants are shrubs and the others are climbers. Two of the bushy loniceras are discussed below. One is hardly ever seen as a single shrub, instead being almost exclusively used for hedges, and the other has been in cultivation for over a century but is only now becoming popular.

The genus was named by Carl Linnaeus (1707–1778) after Adam Lonitzer (1528–1586), a German botanist and physician.

Lonicera korolkowii

This plant was a huge hit at the Chelsea Flower Show a few years ago, and the only surprise is that it has taken so long to become popular. It is easy to grow and has the most marvelous leaves in a

Right: *Lonicera korolkowii*

Right: *Lonicera nitida* 'Baggessens Gold' trimmed into a column with olearias either side and *Ilex crenata* 'Golden Gem' front left.

glorious shade of blue. In late spring and early summer the pink flowers are a delightful contrast to the leaves.

It forms a very hardy, deciduous shrub, with a tidy habit for a *Lonicera*. It can easily be pruned should it become unkempt. Happy in any soil and quite drought-tolerant, it needs to be in full sun as it enjoys heat, and for the leaves to keep their blue luster.

The species is named for General Nikolai Iwanowitsch Korolkow (born 1837), who was Governor of Sirdarja in Turkestan, the home of this plant, along with Afghanistan, Pakistan and other central Asian areas. Height 10 ft (3 m) x width 15 ft (5 m). ZONES 5 TO 9.

Lonicera pyrenaica is very similar.

Lonicera nitida

BOXLEAF HONEYSUCKLE

Now here is a strange plant, so different to the climbing honeysuckles. The house we lived in when I was a child had a hedge of this *Lonicera*. It was my job to clip the hedge if I wanted to earn some pocket money. *Lonicera nitida* has a neat, tight habit, ideal for hedges, and I remember just how easy it was to clip, no effort at all for a youngster. The flowers are small and insignificant.

Boxleaf honeysuckle is similar to boxwood, except it is faster growing, creating a more instant hedge. It always has a rich, dark green look and could be described as a "constant" evergreen hedge.

Trim it every two or three months to keep it tidy, not that it ever becomes rank and unkempt. It can be used for mini-hedges in the same way as boxwood, remembering a tiny 4 in (10 cm) hedge needs more frequent clipping. The natural shape is rangy and more open.

Full sun is best for *L. nitida*, but it will take a little shade. It is not at all fussy about soil, growing in very acidic or alkaline ground as well as sand or clay. Likewise, high or low rainfall makes no difference, and it is reasonably robust in wind and cold winters. Heavy snow can distort and ruin the shape of the hedge, so shake off any snow with a broom or rake as soon as possible. This species is native to southwestern China. Height 11 ft (3.5 m) x width 10 ft (3 m). ZONES 6 TO 9.

'Baggessens Gold' is a yellow-leaf form that does best in partial shade. Height x width 5 ft (1.5 m).

Nitida = brilliant or shining (referring to the shiny leaves).

Lyonia

Ericaceae

*L*yonia is a genus of American and Asian shrubs grown primarily for their glossy, leathery foliage. Most of them are deciduous but some are handsome evergreens. They have clean-looking oval leaves, but these can vary from cold-hardy humble leaves to lush and almost tropical-looking examples. The flowers show the family connection with *Pieris* as they have chains or racemes of white bells. Sometimes the flowers are pretty but often they are overlooked.

Lyonia must have acidic or neutral soil that is free-draining. Some species grow in swamps in the wild but, like so many similar plants, they do not like wet feet in the garden. Most are cold-hardy and grow in sun or part shade. They can be useful low shrubs for shady woodland gardens or some of them could

Above: *Lyonia mariana*

Above: *Lyonia ovalifolia*

even be used for ground cover. The taller species are worthy of a space for their elegant habit and lush leaves. Like most of the Erica family they are easy to transplant and can be shifted to another location. You can prune them at any time to improve the shape, although it is not essential.

Lyonia is named after John Lyon (died 1814) who industriously collected plants in the eastern U.S.A. to take to England for sale. *Lyonia* are found native in the Himalayas, east Asia, the U.S.A. and Mexico.

Lyonia ligustrina

The clusters of small white flowers on this shrub in late summer are often hidden by the hard, finely toothed leaves. In the wild this bush often grows in wet places but it also seems to tolerate drought. It is deciduous and some leaves turn red in the fall. It originates in the eastern U.S.A. Height 3–4 ft (1 m) x width 6 ft (2 m). ZONE 5.

Ligustrina = Ligustrum or privet leaf.

Lyonia lucida
FETTERBUSH

The shiny pointed leaves of fetterbush have an almost citrus look about them. The prominent central vein splits the handsome leaf in two. Being evergreen and dense, this bush fits in well in rhododendron gardens. Clusters of soft pink or white bell-shaped flowers hang beneath the leaves near the tips of the stems in summer. It is native to the warmer coastal regions of eastern U.S.A. Height 3–4 ft (1 m) x width 6 ft (2 m). ZONE 7.

Lucida = shiny.

Lyonia mariana
STAGGERBUSH

Lyonia mariana forms a small, dense bush with erect stems and clean, attractive oval leaves. It is a great plant where you want a tidy low-growing shrub that is easy to trim. The leathery leaves look good all summer and change to orange and reds in the fall. Quite large hanging white- or pink-tinged bells appear in late spring. Originates from eastern U.S.A. Height 6 ft (2 m) x width 4 ft (1.2 m). ZONES 5 TO 9.

Mariana = Maryland.

Lyonia ovalifolia

The gem of the genus, this splendid shrub has tall, arching branches with big, glossy grass-green leaves. It is worth growing simply for the leaves alone, but the racemes of white bell-shaped flowers are also very pretty. Although not an easy plant to blend into a suburban garden, it will look just fine in a woodland setting. This plant grows naturally across a vast area including western China, Japan and Taiwan, and there does seem to be considerable variation. In western China whole hillsides of a fine flowering form exist while the Japanese version is best grown as a foliage plant. We will need to wait for selected cultivars for consistency. Height x width 15 ft (5 m). ZONE 6.

Ovalifolia = oval leaf.

Lyonothamnus   UNIQUE

Lyonothamnus floribundus var *aspleniifolius*
CATALINA IRONWOOD
Rosaceae

This unusual shrub is found growing naturally only on the islands just off the Californian coast: Santa Catalina, Santa Clemente, Santa Rosa and Santa Cruz. The straight species has simple, toothed leaves and is not very pretty. However, the variety with ferny leaves, *Lyonothamnus floribundus* var *aspleniifolius*, is one of the finest foliage plants to be found. The slender, notched leaves are spread out in a pinnate, finger form, like a bird's footprint. They look like they have been cut out of paper. The opposite leaves are a rich, dark green color and are doubly pinnate. It is monotypic, meaning there are no close relatives. A most unlikely member of the rose family, it is related to peaches and strawberries.

Maackia

Maackia amurensis
Fabaceae

*M*aackia amurensis is a very hardy, small, deciduous tree with subtle charm. The overall shape is a wide canopy, making it a suitable shade tree. The interesting peeling trunks are light brown in color and smooth and shiny in parts. The young stems have a hammered look, while the thicker branches have paper-thin bark peeling away as the trunk expands. It is like a stocking being stretched by a very large leg.

The opposite leaves are divided into seven leaflets in a fairly typical legume fashion and they have yellow fall color. All through spring and summer the leaves maintain a clean, healthy appearance with a hint of blue. *Maackia* is related to *Cladrastis* but is easily distinguished by the the fact that the leaf buds are visible on the stems in *Maackia*. On *Cladrastis* these buds are hidden beneath the leaf stalk or petiole. The *Maackia* buds are dark, shiny black and very pointed. From these buds, *Maackia* puts out new growth in the spring and the flowers appear on the tips. Short, chunky racemes packed with white pea-like flowers appear in midsummer. The flowers are not pure white but have a hint of cream or lemon.

Being a legume, *Maackia amurensis* is easy to grow in any soil including alkaline, and it seems content in wet or dry climates. They form fairly robust, easy-care plants and the only problem I have encountered is an occasional borer attack. Choose a site in full sun and plant the tree when quite young, as most legume plants do not like being shifted.

Maackia amurensis was discovered by Richard Karlovic Maack (1825–1886), a Russian naturalist in the Amur region of Siberia and Manchuria. The genus is named after him and the species after the region. Height 50 ft (15 m) x width 30 ft (10 m). ZONES 5 TO 8.

Above:
*Lyonothamnus
floribundus* var
aspleniifolius

Clusters of small, white flowers almost like *Spiraea* add a foamy, frothy appearance to the plant in early summer. It has fabulous trunks of reddish chestnut bark, peeling like that of redwoods. It tolerates drought and is definitely happier in hot climates. It will grow in a moist climate if the drainage is particularly good. It copes quite well with poor, rocky ground but does need shelter as it is prone to root rock and may blow over. If it gets past this wind-susceptible juvenile stage it seems to be quite resilient to wind and gales. Plant securely and stake it until it is established.

It is difficult to propagate from cuttings, and seed is not always easy to acquire or to germinate. Height 40 ft (12 m) x width 20 ft (6 m). ZONE 9 OR 10.

Lyono = for American plant collector W. S. Lyon (1851–1916); *thamnus* = shrub; *aspleniifolius* = leaves like *Asplenium* fern; *floribundus* = lots of flowers.

Right: *Maackia
amurensis*

Far right: *Maackia
amurensis* and
*Liquidambar
acalycina.*

Magnolia

Magnoliaceae

We tend to think of magnolias as flowering plants and perhaps neglect the wonderful array of leaves. Several magnolias are evergreen and bless us with their magnificent foliage all year, while one of the deciduous species, *Magnolia macrophylla*, has the biggest leaves of any hardy tree. Magnolias not only put up with hard, poor, clay soil, they seem to positively thrive on it. Most have thick, fleshy roots like fingers and perhaps this is the reason they prefer heavy soils to light, loamy ground. Some will even cope with occasional flooding, and in general perform better in wet climates or wet ground. Most need acidic to neutral soil, as highly alkaline conditions turn the leaves yellow and chlorotic.

Magnolias are one of the many link plants between Asia and the eastern U.S., and are thought to be the oldest flowering plants, not counting conifers.

Named after Professor Pierre Magnol (1638–1715), an Italian botanist, author and teacher.

Magnolia delavayi

The magnificent, paddle-like leaves on *Magnolia delavayi* are probably the largest of any supposedly hardy evergreen shrub. It is fairly easy to grow, being happy in sun or shade. It is ideally suited to big, woodland gardens where the huge leaves are sheltered from winds. It needs a large garden to be in proportion to its surroundings, looking too cumbersome in smaller suburban plots.

Rather than stand-alone specimens in a lawn, plant them in a shrubbery among other large leaf plants like rhododendrons, and they will repay you handsomely.

Magnolia delavayi can be knocked back by severe frosts but regenerates if the bush is established. A hard frost in the first year or three of its life may be the end of it. Well-drained, acidic soil is best but, unlike most magnolias, it will tolerate lime soil. Those of you with alkaline soil will be pleased to hear this is a magnolia willing to grow in your patch. It is happy in wet or dry climes.

The leaves have a wavy or undulating edge and are typically 12 in (30 cm) long. They are gray-green, in what one might describe as camouflage colors, and slightly gray underneath.

The flowers appear on the tips of new growth in late spring over a period of several weeks. In warm climates the bush then sprouts two or three new stems below the spent flower, and each of these new growths has a terminal flower as well, generously having two bursts of flower each year. The flowers are very short-lived, usually only lasting for one day. They are slightly scented and creamy white. In recent times, pink and brown forms with smaller, bronzy leaves have been seen. It is easy to propagate from seed or cuttings. This plant originated in China. Height x width 30 ft (10 m). ZONES 7 TO 9.

Delavayi = from French missionary and botanist based in China, Abbé Delavay (1838–1895).

Magnolia grandiflora

BULL BAY, SOUTHERN MAGNOLIA

The southern states of the United States are the homeland of this magnificent tree, conjuring up images of Scarlet O'Hara, *Gone With the Wind*, and big, white-painted southern mansions. It was widely planted in the gardens of these plantation homes. You really need a home of grand proportions to show off this huge, wide-spreading tree, as it will dominate any garden scene.

One of the more unusual magnolias, on account of it being wind-hardy, even coping with coastal gales. The big, glossy leaves are protected by the shiny top surface and the felty underside. The new leaves have a coating of fawn-brown indumentum or "fur," protecting the emerging leaf from dehydration. Some cultivars, such as **'Russet'**, retain this indumentum on the underside of the leaf.

The huge, white, terminal flowers are endowed with an intoxicating perfume. *Magnolia grandiflora* says it all, a very appropriate

Left: *Magnolia delavayi*

Above: *Magnolia* x *soulangeana*

Right: *Magnolia grandiflora*

Magnolia macrophylla
LARGE-LEAVED CUCUMBER TREE, UMBRELLA TREE
This majestic tree has gigantic leaves up to 3 ft (1 m) long, like enormous paddles. Somehow the leaves manage to look in proportion on such a big tree, though they can look a trifle silly on a young plant. The leaves are shiny, pale green above and silvery beneath. They are quite brittle and easily damaged by wind and storms, so shelter is the first priority. The size of these leaves can make the tree look out of place in a small garden. It is happy growing in sun or part-shade and not too fussy about soil. My own plant is growing in a swamp, where it can be flooded at times, and yet I have seen some fabulous specimens in dry climates, too.

The flowers appear above the new spring growth and are easily missed, especially as they tend to be way up above you, facing the sky. They are white and scented. It makes an interesting tree viewed from above if you have sloping terrain, and then the leaves and the flowers can be seen and enjoyed. Native to the southeastern U.S.A. Height x width 30 ft (10 m). ZONES 6 TO 9.

The form ***M. m. ashei*** is sometimes listed as a separate species (*M. ashei*). It has equally large leaves on a smaller, manageably sized shrub and could perhaps find a place in smaller gardens. Height x width 10–15 ft (3–5 m). ZONES 6 TO 9.

Macrophylla = big leaf (an understatement in this case).

Magnolia x soulangeana (*M. denudata* x *M. liliiflora*)
SAUCER MAGNOLIA
Usually an upright bush at first, it spreads with age. The thick stems are shiny brownish purple and the leaves are bold, rich green. Most of us would happily grow this plant for foliage alone, but the flowers are amazing too. Large, chalice-like blooms appear in spring before the new leaves, and invariably have purple or red at the base of the tepals, thinning out toward the tops to be paler or white. The inside of the tepals is white and if you cut them for a vase the flowers open right out to reveal a beautiful porcelain-white inner. Named in honor of the Chevalier Etienne Soulange-Bodin, who first raised them in 1820 in a garden at Fromont near Paris, France. Height x width 20 ft (6 m). ZONES 5 TO 9.

There are lots of lovely clones including **'Alexandrina'**, with a very upright habit ideal for small gardens; **'Lennei'** with

name. If you are lucky enough to have a plant with accessible flowers you will be drawn again and again to enjoy the perfume. Unfortunately, the flowers are short-lived, but the tree will produce many of them over a period of several weeks in midsummer.

In the cooler parts of Europe and North America it is grown as a wall shrub, giving the effect of an evergreen climber. It helps that it is wind-hardy or it would get battered. Grow it on the sunny or shady side of house, though it flowers best on the sunny side. Height 20–60 ft (6–18 m) x width 50 ft (15 m). ZONE 6.

Grandi = big or grand; *flora* = flower.

Magnolia hypoleuca, syn *M. obovata*
JAPANESE BIG-LEAF MAGNOLIA, WHITEBARK MAGNOLIA
Magnolia hypoleuca forms a bulky, upright tree, often multi-stemmed and grown primarily for its gigantic leaves. These mid-green leaves can be up to 16 in (40 cm) long, so they are very impressive. It is a pity the flowers appear after the leaves, as they tend to be forgotten when hidden among such sumptuous foliage. These creamy white flowers are scented and the size of the flower depends on the seedling source. The smooth young stems are purple brown and the older trunks the typical gray of a magnolia. The tree is native to Japan. Height 50 ft (15 m) x width 30 ft (10 m). ZONES 5 TO 9.

Hypoleuca = white undersides
(referring to the silvery white underside of the leaf).

Above: *Magnolia macrophylla* with a form of *Hydrangea heteromalla* at the front.

dark purple flowers, and **'Rustica Rubra'** with rosy red-colored outer tepals. The flowers are scented like ice. For all, height x width 20 ft (6 m).

Magnolia virginiana, syn *M. glauca*
SWEET BAY OR SWAMP BAY

An unusual, open, gaunt little tree, *Magnolia virginiana* is evergreen, or almost so, with glossy, dark green leaves up to 6 in (15 cm) long. It is more popular as a foliage bush than for its flowers, which emerge from the terminal round buds from midsummer into fall. These fragrant, creamy white flowers are not very obvious among the lustrous green leaves.

It seems to tolerate wet places and heavy clays. Native to eastern U.S.A. and named after the state of Virginia. Height x width 15 ft (5 m). ZONES 5 TO 9.

Mahonia

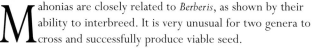

Berberidaceae

Mahonias are closely related to *Berberis*, as shown by their ability to interbreed. It is very unusual for two genera to cross and successfully produce viable seed.

Typically, mahonias are upright shrubs with flashy, pinnate, evergreen leaves and long, thin panicles of yellow or orange flowers. They are some of the most beautiful foliage plants and all the more valuable to gardeners as they will grow in shade, though they will just as easily grow in sun. They are not fussy about soil type or quality and will grow in wet or dry climates. Most are quite drought-tolerant. A few species from Mexico are almost desert plants and these tend to have smaller, glaucous, blue-gray leaves. Even these dry land plants will grow in a wet region.

Although the leaves look and feel quite tough they are sensitive to wind. Mahonias in a windy site always looks ragged and unloved, though they do survive. The bold evergreen leaves make this the ideal architectural shrub. Most have sharp spines on the tips of the leaflets so have a care where you plant them. They transplant easily; even large plants can be moved in winter if cut back a little. Like *Berberis*, some species are host to a rust disease, otherwise they are easy-care plants.

Mahonia was named after Bernard McMahon (1775–1816). Of Irish birth, McMahon became a famous horticulturist in the United States as an author and nurseryman. A friend of Thomas Jefferson, he helped sponsor the Lewis and Clark expeditions yielding *Mahonia aquifolium*, among other exciting discoveries.

Mahonia aquifolium
OREGON GRAPEHOLLY

This low-growing and spreading bush is a terrific ground cover for sun or shade. It is excellent in areas with deciduous shrubs to provide a visual backdrop, keep down the weeds and provide winter interest. The leaves take on a reddish purple tinge in the colder months and then in spring the stems are topped with fragrant canary-yellow flower spikes. The tree comes from western North

Right: *Mahonia japonica*

America, as the common name suggests. Height 3 ft (1 m) x width 5 ft (1.5 m). ZONES 6 TO 9.

Aquifolium = old name meaning pointed leaves.

Mahonia fortunei
CHINESE MAHONIA

Mahonia fortunei is quite different from most, with very small, toothed leaves nowhere near as vicious as typical mahonia. The finger-length leaflets are dark green above and have a texture like plastic. The plant forms a multi-stemmed bush and being small, is easy to accommodate. Terminal yellow flowers in summer are small and insignificant. Like all mahonias, it is evergreen and tolerant of a wide range of conditions. Named after plant collector Robert Fortune (1812–1880), who introduced it to the west from China in the 1840s. Height 4 ft (1.2 m) x width 3 ft (1 m). ZONES 8 TO 9.

Mahonia japonica

A wonderful foliage and flowering plant. The pinnate leaves with their spiky edges are a shiny dark green all summer and take on hints of red and yellow in winter. The racemes of late winter or spring flowers arch out and droop away from the center of the crown and are nicely scented. A terrific architectural plant near

Right *Mahonia lomariifolia* with berries.

Above: *Mahonia lomariifolia*

lower leaves fall, the furrowed trunk becomes prominent. Bright yellow flowers on terminal spikes are followed by brilliant blue berries. A native of western China. Height 10 ft (3 m) x width 6 ft (2 m). ZONE 8 OR 9.

Lomariifolia = after *Lomaria*, a genus of ferns.

Mahonia mairei

If you are lucky enough to see this in flower you will be taken aback by the splendid heads of orange bells. They are really quite stunning, and the bees think so too as they busy themselves looking for nectar. Just as this floral display is fading, the bush keeps our attention with a stunning exhibition of reddish bronze new growth. The fully extended leaves are shiny gray-green and possibly the largest of any mahonia. Named after Edouard Maire, a missionary based in Yunnan, a province in China. Height 10–12 ft (3–4 m) x width 6 ft (2 m). ZONE 8.

Above: *Mahonia mairei*

Mahonia x media (M. japonica x M. lomariifolia)

This group of hybrids has magnificent foliage and brilliant flowers. They form multi-trunked, upright bushes with beautiful pinnate leaves. The contrast between the older darker leaves and the lovely bright green new foliage is a highlight of any spring garden. The bright yellow spikes of flowers are scented and very impressive, popular with bees and gardeners alike. Some, like **'Lionel Fortescue'**, have upright flower spikes and others, like those of **'Charity'**, swoop. Height 12–15 ft (4–5 m) x width 12 ft (4 m). ZONE 8 OR 9.

Media = intermediate between two plants.

buildings, it eventually grows in a nicely rounded fashion. It is a Chinese native long grown in Japan and was thus assumed to be a native of that country, hence its name. Height 6 ft (2 m) x width 10 ft (3 m). ZONE 7 OR 8.

The leaflets of **'Bealei'** are often so broad they overlap each other. The flower racemes are shorter and more erect. It is usually thought to be hardier to cold than the straight species. Height 6 ft (2 m) x width 10 ft (3 m).

Japonica = from Japan.

Mahonia lomariifolia

Every genus has its gem and this is it. We often think of deciduous plants as being tops for new foliage, but wait until you see the glossy new leaves of this evergreen shrub. Even the old leaves are glorious, and a great contrast with the new ones.

It is the archetypal architectural plant with rigid structure, a rounded shape and scalloped leaves. The opposite leaves are pinnate and each leaflet has five spikes. Take care where you plant it, the spines are quite vicious. Pick the plant up by the base of the stem, otherwise it is like trying to pick up a hedgehog.

As a young plant it is vertical with a single trunk, then as it ages it becomes multi-trunked with a rounded outline. As the

Melia

Melia azedarach

BEAD TREE, CHINABERRY, PERSIAN LILAC, PRIDE OF INDIA
Meliaceae

*M*elia azedarach is one of the best foliage trees in the world if you are lucky enough to have a sufficiently warm climate for this prize to thrive. It appears to need warm summers or else a permanently warm climate to perform at its best. However, it will tolerate winter cold as long as the summers are hot enough to compensate or there are high sunshine hours. For instance, British summers do not seem to be

Above left and right:
Melia azedarach

consistently hot enough and so the cool wet winters probably finish it off. But the southern States provide a suitable climate.

In a cold climate it does not tolerate much frost, but if you have hot summers to ripen the wood it will endure severe cold. Even dry, semi-desert situations suit this tree. It copes with poor soil, including sand, rock or clay as long as the drainage is good, and is free of pests and diseases.

It is a tree that must be grown in full sun and is obviously light-sensitive. Some avenue trees under streetlights will hold their leaves for longer in the fall than neighboring trees. In some regions the tree has become a pest, seeding naturally on waste ground.

The large, glossy leaves are doubly pinnate, meaning side branches of leaflets come off the main leaf petiole. The overall effect is a full and rather lacy look. These leaves can be up to 30 in (80 cm) long, although 10–15 in (25–35 cm) is more typical, and they are lush enough to attract comment.

Furrowed black trunks and purple-black stems are features in winter. The structure is quite sparse and the tree has a gaunt, antler-like appearance in winter. This distinguishes it from other, more twiggy deciduous trees.

Melia makes a great avenue or campus tree as it does not get too big, making it useful for old city lots with overhead power lines. Likewise, its roots do not protrude above ground. It is surprisingly wind-hardy for a deciduous tree, enduring coastal gales. The plant is easy to transplant at any size and makes an excellent instant tree if a large specimen is moved into your garden. It grows speedily, too, if you should plant a small specimen. It is easy to propagate from seed or cuttings. In some hot regions this plant has naturalized from seed so inquire at your local garden center before planting one.

Large panicles of sweetly scented, lilac-colored flowers come with the new leaves. The small, light-purple flowers are hermaphrodite, meaning both sexes are present and so seed is freely set. Clusters of light yellow to apricot fruit hang from the branches in summer through into fall. The berries persist long after the leaves have fallen and give rise to its common name, bead tree. The berries are mildly poisonous. The "beads" were used by monks for rosaries. In fall, the tree colors in stages. Bright yellow leaves contrasting against the green parts of the

tree are a dazzling sight. The ensuing carpet of yellow leaves is attractive.

The tree seems to be a native of vast areas of the globe and possibly was spread by early traders. It seems to grow naturally in much of Asia, including the Middle East. Height 30–50 ft (10–15 m) x width 15–25 ft (5–8 m). ZONE 7.

There is a named form from Texas, **'Umbraculiformis'** (the Texas umbrella tree), which forms a flat, wide-spreading crown and is popular as a street tree. It is said to have appeared originally on the battlefield of San Jacinto, Texas. Height x width 30 ft (10 m).

Melia = Greek for ash tree (which has similar leaves);
azedarach = an old Persian name for this tree.

Melianthus

Melianthus major
HONEY BUSH
Melianthaceae

Although considered a weed in warmer regions because of its suckering habit, honey bush is one plant most of us would be happy to accommodate. The strong-jointed stems have a fan of ferny blue-hued leaves, like folded fabric, at every node. The steely blue effect is more pronounced in hot or dry climates. The deeply toothed, pinnate leaves are huge and can be 20 in (50 cm) long. As if the stunning dramatic foliage is not enough, *Melianthus* bombards your senses with huge spikes of rusty red flowers in early summer. These big trumpets of burnt-toffee red are laden with such delicious nectar that honey-eating birds lose all fear and bees become drunk at these "horns of plenty." In English gardens it is treated as a tender perennial and it was at Chelsea Physic Garden on the banks of the Thames in London where I first fell in love with this nectariferous beauty. It tends to have a heady effect on gardeners as well as bees.

It is hardy, drought-tolerant and copes with everything from stones to sand to clay as long as it is not too wet. Best in full sun and happy in windy sites, and it can be grown near the sea. It

Right: *Melianthus major*

tends to fall over if given lush conditions or too windy a site. It can be cut back to ground level if it gets too tall or ragged. If the suckering habit is likely to be a problem in your climate then it is possible to grow it in raised beds where the plant can be restrained. This tends to keep the plant smaller, neater and more compact, adding to the leafy beauty. No obvious pests or diseases attack this species. Height 6–10 ft (2–3 m) x width 3–10 ft (1–3 m). ZONE 8.

Melianthus minor is a smaller, poor imitation, never rivaling the majesty of its relative. Both are from South Africa.

Melianthus = Greek "meli," meaning honey and "anthus" flowers; *major* = big.

Nandina

Nandina domestica
HEAVENLY BAMBOO
Berberidaceae

This has one of the largest leaves of any plant I know, and yet to look at it, you would think I had just made that up. Huge triangular leaves up to 36 in (90 cm) long are made up of dozens of leaflets, giving the impression of a small-leafed bush. Each leaflet is shiny, narrow, pointed and surprisingly tough, although the overall effect is rather ferny and lacy. I have never seen a plant with more leaflets per leaf.

The "bamboo" of its common name comes from the cane-like stems and the plant's suckering habit. Like other plants

Above: *Nandina domestica* 'Richmond' with berries.

traditionally grown in Asian temple grounds, you know it will grow in any soil. When thousands of feet and hundreds of years have compacted the soil to such a degree, there is no structure left. The bare grounds never have a weed and any woody plant growing there has to be tough as nails, as is true of *Pistacio*, *Tilia* and *Ginkgo*.

The multiple, upright stems rarely branch. Eventually an old plant suckers and makes the bush wider, although this takes years. They do not sucker vigorously enough to concern the tidy gardener. The furrowed bark on the older canes is just like *Mahonia* and both are in the Berberis family. They all have furrowed bark, yellow wood and even yellow roots.

Nandina domestica is best in acidic or neutral soils. It thrives in poor soil, even heavy clays or in light, dry soils. In fact, tougher conditions give rise to more intense leaf color. No pests or diseases seem to bother it.

Spring leaves are tinged with red, go to green for summer and take on red hues again in winter. The plant is happy in sun or shade, though flowering and winter leaf color are better when the plant gets sufficient sunlight. It is evergreen, but can tend to be deciduous in cooler climates.

Erect panicles of sweetly scented, white flowers occur in spring and summer. The flowers will not set your heart aflutter, but the resulting berries might. They are bright red in winter and persist for months as the birds ignore them.

Both male and female plants are required for fruit, although there are some hermaphrodite clones such as **'Richmond'**. Oddly, they fruit prolifically if there is more than one plant, even if both plants are the same clone and therefore genetically the same. Height 6 ft (2 m) x width 5 ft (1.5 m). Native to India, China and Japan. ZONES 6 TO 9.

Nandina = a variation of a Japanese name; *domestica* = used in or around the home (although it could refer to it being grown near temples).

of gold, rich reds and bronze. The leaves are tri-pinnate with nine leaflets, green in the shade and colored in sun. The tops are smooth, and because of the puckered, rigid quality they "sing" when rattled. Height x width 2–4 ft (60–120 cm).

Nandina domestica 'Gulf Stream'
Attractive bronzy leaves in spring, green in summer, then glowing red in fall and winter. Height 3 ft (1 m) x width 4 ft (1.2 m).

Nandina domestica 'Harbor Dwarf'
Perhaps the most graceful of the Pygmaea types. Semi-deciduous. Height 3 ft (1 m) x width 4 ft (1.2 m).

Nandina domestica 'San Gabriel'
This has unusual foliage, which looks like a caterpillar has chewed it, leaving just the thin leaf blades. Rich, red wine color in fall. Height 3 ft (1 m) x width 4 ft (1.2 m).

Above: *Nandina domestica* 'Nana'

Nandina domestica 'Firepower'
Appropriately named, as its striking red leaves certainly gives it "firepower." It forms a very tidy, compact plant. Height 18 in (45 cm) x width 24 in (60 cm).

Nandina domestica 'Nana', syn 'Pygmaea'
This is guaranteed to grow whatever the site, and is small enough to fit in any garden. It is evergreen, has multi-colored leaves and in fact has everything except pretty flowers. Great for tubs and pots and tough sites, such as shade underneath pines. Strangely, it takes on fall colors. Evergreen plants by definition do not change color in the fall, but *Nandina* defies the rules and changes to shades

Neolitsea

Neolitsea sericea, syn Litsea glauca, N. glauca
Lauraceae

When giving out prizes for top foliage plant, *Neolitsea sericea* is one of my nominations, along with *Mahonia lomariifolia* and *Magnolia grandiflora*. It is an evergreen shrub, which in its native habitat becomes a small tree. It is so slow-growing that this is unlikely to happen in your lifetime. The leaves are a dull gray-green above and white beneath.

The most appealing aspect, however, is the phenomenal new spring growth, which decorates the plant with a dusting of gold. Each new leaf is covered in silky hairs that demand to be stroked. They are as silky as my labrador's ears, and the plant is sometimes known as spaniel's ears. While it is nice to think this spring show is for our benefit, the covering of fine hairs is protecting the new leaves from hot sun and salt-laden winds. As soon as the leaf has hardened, the soft hairs fall off. The three-veined adult leaf is

Left and far left:
Neolitsea sericea

similar to the related cinnamon. Fully grown leaves are silver-backed and satiny, and aromatic when crushed.

Clusters of small, greenish yellow flowers in the fall are easily missed. They appear below the top whorl of leaves and have a slight bottlebrush look about them.

It is perfectly hardy to frosts and is extremely wind-hardy as it grows naturally on the windswept Island of Cheju to the south of Korea.

In Cheju it is a tidy, rounded, evergreen tree growing among the stone walls in a setting reminiscent of the windswept west coast of Ireland. In gardens, it is more of a flat-topped, small shrub. Should it ever get too big for a garden situation, it can easily be pruned.

It looks best in full sun but will grow in shade. Any soil appears to be acceptable, no matter how poor, and it is not too fussy about wet or dry climates. A native of China, Taiwan, Korea and Japan. Height 20 ft (6 m) x width 10 ft (3 m). ZONE 9.

Neo = almost or new; *litsea* = a genus of tropical plants; *sericea* = silky.

Nothofagus

SOUTHERN BEECH
Fagaceae

These Southern Hemisphere beeches were once included with the northern *Fagus*, but are now in their own genus. They are one of the plants that link the countries that once made up the supercontinent Gondwanaland. *Nothofagus* is a genus common to Australia, New Zealand, Antarctica and South America. (Those in Antarctica died, as you might expect, and are only found there as fossils.) In New Zealand and Chile especially, they form huge forests of almost pure *Nothofagus*.

A mixture of deciduous and evergreen trees, some are of slow enough growth to consider planting in suburban gardens. As young plants they have an open, airy nature and could be used instead of silver birch. They do not like drought and although they grow in windy places in the wild, a single specimen in a windy site will look ragged. Moist, acidic soil and a sheltered site are the ingredients for success.

Notho = false; *fagus* = beech.

Above: *Nothofagus menziesii*

Nothofagus menziesii
SILVER BEECH
Silver beech features dainty leaves on an elegant, upright tree. Each leaf is small, round and doubly toothed around the edge. A unique and fascinating leaf pattern that will delight your garden visitors. Although mature trees have silvery trunks, it takes too long for garden trees to acquire this attribute. This evergreen is native to New Zealand. Height 50 ft (15 m) x width 25 ft (8 m). ZONES 8 TO 9.

Menziesii = named for Archibald Menzies (1754–1842).

Nothofagus obliqua
ROBLÉ BEECH
One of the hardier deciduous species from the wet forests of Chile, this is a quick-growing, elegant tree with a slightly weeping habit. The leaves take on orange colors in fall. Originates from Argentina and Chile. Height 70 ft (20 m) x width 50 ft (15 m). ZONES 8 TO 9.

Obliqua = oblique or unequal sides (at the base of the leaf).

Above: *Nothofagus menziesii* with *Pittosporum eugenoides* back right.

Nothofagus procera, syn N. alpina
RAULI
Faster growing and with larger leaves than most species, this deciduous tree is used for timber plantations. The deep green leaves have fall colors of yellow, orange or red. From Argentina and Chile. Height 80 ft (25 m) x width 50 ft (15 m). ZONES 8 TO 9.

Procera = tall or slender.

Nothofagus solandri
BLACK BEECH

As a young plant, this forms a slender, upright tree with layers of branches, and almost lends itself to Asian-style pruning. The tiny, smooth-edged, evergreen leaves are held in fans of foliage on thin, black stems. It was named after Daniel Solander, the Swedish botanist who accompanied Joseph Banks and Captain James Cook on the first voyage of discovery to New Zealand and Australia in 1769. Native to New Zealand. Height 50 ft (15 m) x width 30 ft (10 m). ZONES 8 TO 9.

Nyssa

Nyssaceae

*N*yssa is one of the few trees, along with *Liquidambar*, that is guaranteed to color up, even in warm, mild climates. They are unremarkable trees for the most part, but they do have some surprises in store, such as their ability to grow in wet soils or places prone to flooding. *Nyssa* can also grow in very dry soils, and in the wild are found on dry ridges as well as valley bottoms.

Being slow-growing makes it an ideal garden tree, succeeding in any acidic garden soil. If you have some difficult-to-fill boggy ground, then consider *Nyssa* along with *Taxodium* and *Metasequoia*. Nyssas resent root disturbance, so choose your site carefully and do not be tempted to shift the plant later.

Flowers of all *Nyssa* species are insignificant and easily missed. *Nyssa* are one of the many plants linking the Appalachians with China. Three species are worthy of mention, of which only *Nyssa sylvatica* is at all common.

They are reasonably wind-hardy and definitely cold-hardy. Plant in full sun to get the best fall colors.

Nyssa = a water nymph in Greek mythology
(reflecting the plant's predilection for moist places).

Nyssa aquatica

This is not renowned for its fall color but is a great conversation piece for parks and large gardens. Huge leaves and the ability to grow in water are its attributes. *Nyssa aquatica* is especially tolerant of wet conditions and therefore well named. I was staggered to see them with their trunks emerging from 3 ft (1 m) of water in a *Taxodium* swamp. Originates from the southeastern United States. Height 30–50 ft (10–15 m) x width 20–30 ft (6–10 m). ZONE 5.

Nyssa sinensis
CHINESE TUPELO

The Chinese *Nyssa* is possibly even better for fall color than its American cousin. Long, lush leaves tapering to a point can be 8 in (20 cm) long. These larger, upturned leaves are more attractive than the downturned *N. sylvatica*. It is a shame it is so rare. A native of central China. Height x width 30 ft (10 m). ZONES 7 TO 9.

Sinensis = from China.

Nyssa sylvatica
TUPELO, BLACK GUM, SOUR GUM

It is a funny thing about *Nyssa*; all summer you wonder if it

Above and right:
Nyssa sinensis

Left: *Nyssa sylvatica*
'Pendula' with
Taxodium distichum.

deserves a place in your garden. The glossy leaves are nothing special and the overall habit of the tree is rather scruffy. Then suddenly, for two weeks in fall, it is the best thing on the planet, let alone your garden. Although the display is brief compared to other fall trees, I prefer quality rather than quantity and so does *Nyssa sylvatica*. The fiery reds, scarlet and orange do justice to any fall display.

Young plants have smooth, gray stems, but despite these clean-looking stems, the bush always looks cluttered, as if it has too many branches. Older trunks become furrowed, almost like the trunk of an ash tree.

Although they are moderately drought resistant, they do not like city pollution. There are no serious pests or diseases. The plant originates from eastern North America. Height 70 ft (20 m) x width 30 ft (10 m). ZONES 5 TO 9.

Individual trees vary in color, and named forms are worth a few dollars more. **'Dirr's Selection'**, **'Jermyns Flame'** and **'Sheffield Park'** are all dependable cultivars. For all, height 70 ft (20 m) x width 30 ft (10 m). **'Pendula'** forms a dome 15 ft (5 m) high and wide, and is therefore better suited to small gardens.

Sylvatica = growing in woods and forests.

Osteomeles

Osteomeles schweriniae
Rosaceae

*O*steomeles schweriniae forms a charming shrub bearing the daintiest little pinnate leaves with minute gray-blue leaflets. It looks so feathery and delicate and yet it is surprisingly tough, growing in any soil, even hard clays and rocky places. It handles drought, hot sun, wet climates, warm climates as well as frosts. Even the bush itself is tough with wiry stems that you can almost tie in knots, but beware the primitive spikes defending the bush. Plant one in a sunny border near a path. It is not going to get too big, and you can always thin it or shape it. The summer clusters of small, white flowers look a little like the related *Pyracantha* or *Crataegus*. But it is almost exclusively grown for those pretty fern-like leaves. It is deciduous in cool regions and evergreen if there are no winter

Above: *Osteomeles schweriniae,* with flowers.

Left and below: *Oxydendrum arboreum* in fall colors.

frosts. The plant was first found in western China by Abbé Delavay and introduced by Ernest Wilson (1876–1930). The fruits are dry-looking, little red berries, which turn black. Height x width 10 ft (3 m). ZONE 7.

The subspecies **O. s. microphylla** has dainty, smooth leaves on a smaller bush.

Osteo = bone; *meles* = fruit; *schweriniae* = for F. K. Schwerin (1856–1934).

Oxydendrum

Oxydendrum arboreum
SORREL TREE, SOURWOOD
Ericaceae

Here is a neat little tree just made for small gardens. It has some truly great qualities. It is small, compact, tidy and rounded, making it the perfect small-garden tree in terms of size. As well, this deciduous tree with scrumptious colors in reds and scarlets will be one of the highlights in any fall garden. The fall colors sometimes include shades of yellow and maroon depending on the season, and perhaps the seedling variation. If ever there was a plant needing some named selected clones, this is it. Most of them are good anyway, but they do vary in leaf color and even more so in flower size and profusion.

Exquisite flowers arise in long racemes of creamy white bells, a little like *Pieris*, and they last a very long time. Even after the flowers have fallen, the flower stalks and developing seed cases still look like flowers from a distance. The flowers have two other virtues. They are deliciously fragrant and therefore popular with bees as well as gardeners. And they appear in mid to late summer when few other woody plants are in flower. Most woody plants flower in spring to give them a whole summer's growth to put energy into the seeds.

As the flowers might tell you, it is related to *Pieris* and is in the Erica family along with rhododendrons and azaleas. Like them, it needs rich, moisture-retentive soil with a degree of acidity. Plant in full sun to give the best fall colors, and provide a plentiful supply of rain or hose water. Being related to rhododendrons, it is easy to transplant, but unfortunately suffers from the same root rot.

If you have a sheltered garden, with a need for a small tree that has several seasonal displays, then this could be just the plant for you.

Right: Parrotia persica in fall colors.

It is cold-hardy and yet it is equally at home in warm zones. It originates from eastern North America. Height 30–50 ft (10–15 m) x width 25 ft (8 m). ZONES 5 TO 9.

Oxy = sharp; *dendron* = tree; *arboreum* = tree.

Parrotia

Parrotia persica
PERSIAN IRONWOOD

*P*arrotia persica is a tough plant, growing in virtually any soil, and is surprisingly wind-hardy for a deciduous bush. Less surprising is its drought resistance, as it hails from northern Iran. It is capable of withstanding baking hot summers and freezing cold winters, and it is best grown in full sun to bring

Right:
Parrotia persica

out the fall colors. In regions noted for fall color this plant never fails, although some seedlings are better than others. Surprisingly, no one has selected a top coloring form and named it.

Parrotia persica is most commonly seen as a park tree and sometimes appears in suburban gardens or as a street tree. No pruning is necessary except to shape it as a young plant and maybe to select one stem as the main leader. Seedlings often have wayward, almost horizontal, leaders and may need some help to show them which way is up.

The plant tends to be a rangy, wide-spreading bush and is usually multi-stemmed with a flat-topped, horizontal shape. The branches often self-graft where they intertwine, meaning the touching branches join together to form one. There are smooth, gray trunks on young plants, while older trunks have lovely hammered bark in grays, green and almost black.

The rich red, fluffy flowers are easily missed, they are so tiny. They appear in late winter and early spring before the new season's leaves emerge. They are appreciated as a cut flower, and worth venturing out into the winter cold to collect.

On first glance the alternate leaves could be mistaken for witch hazel or *Hamamelis*. They are related, so there is a connection. The new spring growth is often bronzy or pink, but it is the fall color that is truly outstanding. A stunning mixture of golds, reds and yellows often make this plant the highlight in an arboretum, even with all the competition.

Parrotia persica grows in any soil, acidic or alkaline, heavy or light, wet or dry. Hot summers and cold winters bring about the best fall colors. It is extremely wind-hardy and generally an easy plant to grow.

It was named for German naturalist and traveler F. W. Parrot. It grows native in the Caucasus and northern Iran. Height 25 ft (8 m) x width 30 ft (10 m). ZONES 4 TO 9.

The only named clone is a rare weeping form, **'Pendula'**. Height 5 ft (1.5 m) x width 10 ft (3 m).

Although it is monotypic (only one species in the genus) there is a related plant some include in the genus. **Parrotiopsis jacquemontiana** is a large deciduous bush from the Himalayas. Its leaves look like *Parrotia* and turn yellow and gold in the fall. The flowers are clusters of yellow anthers surrounded by white bracts appearing in late spring and early summer. *Parrotiopsis* means like a *Parrotia* and *jacquemontiana* is after Victor Jacquemont, a French botanist who died at just 31 while botanizing in India. Height 20 ft (6 m) x width 12 ft (4 m). ZONES 6 TO 9.

Persica = Persia, the old name for Iran.

Parthenocissus

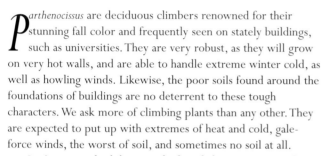

Vitaceae

*P*arthenocissus are deciduous climbers renowned for their stunning fall color and frequently seen on stately buildings, such as universities. They are very robust, as they will grow on very hot walls, and are able to handle extreme winter cold, as well as howling winds. Likewise, the poor soils found around the foundations of buildings are no deterrent to these tough characters. We ask more of climbing plants than any other. They are expected to put up with extremes of heat and cold, gale-force winds, the worst of soil, and sometimes no soil at all.

Parthenocissus climb by using leaf tendrils twining around any support available, or failing that, they attach themselves with adhesive pads directly to the wall. These versatile plants can be grown as a ground cover, a self-clinging climber on walls and fences, or up a tree trunk. Bear in mind that any climber will grow as high as the host or support it is given.

Parthenon = virgin; *cissus* = ivy or vine.

Parthenocissus henryana, syn *Vitis henryana*
The leaves are a rather unusual color. The base color is olive to bronzy maroon with the unique silver veins taking prominence. So you will not mistake this vine for any other. The silver veining is most conspicuous when the vine is grown in partial shade, but the fall color is better on sun-ripened growth. Not content with giving us interesting leaf color all summer, this benevolent vine serves up scintillating fall colors as well. Rich scarlet reds are resplendent, even in warm mild regions. The plant was named for Augustine Henry (1857–1930) who spent many years in China as a customs agent and enthusiastic plant hunter. Discovered by him in 1885 and introduced by E. H. Wilson (1876–1930) in 1900. Height 30 ft (10 m). ZONE 7 OR 8.

Parthenocissus quinquefolia, syn *Vitis quinquefolia*
VIRGINIA CREEPER
What to do when faced with a large expanse of boring concrete wall? Cover it in Virginia creeper and let nature take its course. Not only will it cover your bare wall with its tenacious clinging stems and a lattice of foliage, but in fall you will get the full dividend when the leaves turn fiery orange, crimsons and clarets. You will take one look and give yourself a pat on the back for planting one of the most spectacular climbers on Earth. It is happy in sun

Left: *Parthenocissus henryana*

Below: *Parthenocissus tricuspidata*

or shade and virtually any kind of soil. It can also be grown up tree trunks but will quickly smother other plants, so take care. Originates from eastern North America. Height 50 ft (15 m). ZONES 3 TO 9.

Parthenocissus himalayana is similar, but with larger leaves.

Quinquefolia = five-pointed leaf.

Parthenocissus tricuspidata
BOSTON IVY

Called Boston ivy because it was popular in that city, and ivy for the three-pronged, pointed leaf to easily distinguish it from Virginia creeper, which has five. The leaves are bronzy green in summer, changing to stunning burnished reds. The plant climbs by means of suckers on the ends of tendrils and it speedily covers any wall. Do not put one on a wall that you want to be able to access easily. Once you have planted a *Parthenocissus* you should leave it alone, apart from pruning away from windows or you will never get to see out. This fast-growing creeper hails from East China, Korea, Taiwan and Japan. Height 70 ft (20 m). ZONES 4 TO 8.

The selected form, **'Veitchii'**, has smaller leaves and purple new foliage.

Tricuspidata = three-pronged (leaves).

Paulownia

Scrophulariaceae

Paulownias are very similar to *Catalpa* with their huge leaves and upright panicles of foxglove flowers. The surprise is they are from different families, *Catalpa* being in the Bignoniaceae, a semi-tropical family with lots of climbers, while *Paulownia* is the big daddy of the foxglove family. Paulownias are tidier, less straggly trees than the somewhat wayward catalpas. Incredibly fast-growing, they quickly form a tremendous tree, and in just three years can have a trunk 8 in (20 cm) thick.

While paulownias tolerate cold winters, they need heat or warm summers to thrive. Plant in full sun in a sheltered site, as strong winds mash the huge leaves. They are not fussy about soil as long as it is well-drained, and both dry and wet climates seem to suit most of them. *Paulownia tomentosa* is probably better for cooler, wetter climates while *P. fortunei* is ideally suited to hotter, drier climes.

They sometimes send up suckers and can therefore be grown from root cuttings. Transplanting is easy. They have fantastic flowers for a deciduous plant, with the appearance of giant purple-blue foxgloves. Because the flowers are way up in the tree, they are hard to see. If you can find a gully to plant one in and then view the tree from above you will get a spectacular view of the flowers and the leaves.

Even in winter they look stately with their open, clean trunk. Given that the timber is so hard, it is surprising it is also palatable to borer grubs. The timber is very valuable, being used for dowry boxes in Asia.

This outstanding deciduous tree was named after Anna Paulowna (1795–1865), daughter of Tsar Paul I of Russia, and is sometimes known as the Princess or Empress Tree. Anna Paulowna became Princess of the Netherlands. All species are from China.

Paulownia fargesii
This has smaller, smoother, tidier leaves than other species. They tend to be triangular and slightly pointed. The mauve-violet flowers are spotty in the throat. It is probably the best species for cooler climates. A mature tree has a neater, tidier look than *P. tomentosa*. Paul Farges (1844–1912) was a French missionary based in China. Height 25 ft (8 m) x width 20 ft (6 m). ZONE 6.

Above: *Paulownia fargesii*

Paulownia fortunei
Paulownia fortunei has creamy white, very big florets with purple or brown markings within the trumpet. The fragrant flowers vary considerably in size and color. The plant needs hot summers to thrive. Named for Robert Fortune (1812–1880). A native of China and Taiwan. Height x width 25 ft (8 m). ZONES 6 TO 9.

Paulownia tomentosa, syn *P. imperialis*
EMPRESS TREE, FOXGLOVE TREE, PRINCESS TREE, ROYAL PAULOWNIA

The rich purple-blue flowers are much darker than *Paulownia fargesii*. The enormous, light green leaves are up to 12 in (30 cm) long and very impressive, unless it is a breezy site, in which case they look a bit ragged. Very tolerant of atmospheric pollution and poor soil. A native of China, it has become naturalized in eastern U.S.A. Height 40 ft (12 m) x width 30 ft (10 m). ZONES 5 TO 8.

Tomentose = woolly (referring to the woolly underside to the leaf).

Above: *Paulownia tomentosa* with seed pods.

Phellodendron

Phellodendron amurense
AMUR CORK TREE
Rutaceae

Here is a tree that has not yet lived up to expectations. *Phellodendron amurense* has great potential as a street or campus tree but seems to be overlooked every time that choice is made. It forms a small, flat-topped tree, not unlike a *Melia* or the closely related *Evodia*.

The plant needs a continental climate or at least warm summers. It does not thrive in Britain where false springs and late frosts do it damage. This is typical of plants from Korea and North China where every spring day is slightly warmer than the previous one. These plants like a definite winter followed by a consistent, steady spring. Other than that, it is a tough plant, tolerating clay, alkaline, poor, dry or rocky ground, anything, in fact, as long as the drainage is good. It is easy to transplant, even as large specimens.

The ash-like leaves emit a smell of turpentine when crushed. They have a rich butter-yellow fall color and old trees have attractive furrowed, corky bark which gives rise to its common name. The tiny male and female flowers appear on separate trees and the females have shiny black berries.

Grow in full sun for good health and for the best fall colors. Originates from northeast Asia. Height 46 ft (14 m) x width 50 ft (15 m). ZONES 3 TO 9.

The clone called **'Macho'** is male and non-fruiting, with a spreading crown and very corky bark.

> *Phellos* = cork; *dendron* = tree; *amurense* = from Amur, a region of north China and Siberia, where the Amur River flows.

Above: *Phellodendron amurense*

Photinia x *fraseri* (*P. glabra* x *P. serratifolia*)
RED TIP
This forms an upright evergreen shrub or small tree with dark green leaves. Height x width 15 ft (5 m). ZONE 8 OR 9.

The hybrid forms are popular. **'Birmingham'** is an American hybrid with bronzy new growth more similar to the *P. glabra* parent. It is spreading and bushy-headed. Height x width 15 ft (5 m).

Photinia, syn Heteromeles, Stranvaesia

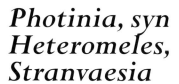

Rosaceae

Need a tough, dense, evergreen shrub or hedge for your front yard? Look no further than the stylish *Photinia*. The leaves are radiant all year but are at their most spectacular in the spring with dazzling red new growth. The big, waxy leaves are tough but handsome, too, with their shiny, smooth surface. Most species are from China and Japan, and there are over 40 in all, including deciduous as well as the more familiar evergreen types. Evergreen *Photinia* endure regular pruning and thus make excellent hedges and topiary plants. They will even regenerate when pruned drastically. Being so robust, there is no danger of them dying, an essential attribute for hedge plants. Like most plants in the rose family, it is prone to fire-blight but it is not common. In some regions it can suffer various diseases, but elsewhere seems untouched. *Photinia* can be transplanted from open ground up to 3 ft (90 cm) high or from pots. Their good root system means they are wind resistant.

> *Photinia* = from Latin "photeinos," meaning shiny, glossy leaves.

Right: *Photinia* x *fraseri* 'Red Robin'

Photinia x fraseri 'Red Robin'

'Red Robin' is a phenomenal shrub for its spring display of brilliant red new growth, the equal of any *Pieris*. This hardy shrub is used for hedges and as a street bush. When the startling red color fades to green, get out there and trim it all over, making the plant put on a second burst of growth. It colors best when in full sun.

It is a tough plant, coping with poor soil and strong winds, and quite heavy frosts. As well, it tolerates hard pruning if ever needed to drastically reduce it to a manageable size, not that it forms a particularly big bush, and it always keeps a tidy habit, growing evenly without any rank or untidy growth. Just as much at home near the sea as it is at higher altitudes. Developed in New Zealand. Height x width 10–15 ft (3–5 m). ZONE 7.

Photinia x fraseri 'Robusta'

'Robusta' is bigger, tending toward the *P. serratifolia* parent and therefore a larger plant. This Australian hybrid seems to be the most cold-hardy of the group. Height 30 ft (10 m) x width 20 ft (6 m). ZONE 7.

Photinia glabra

JAPANESE PHOTINIA

Photinia glabra has big, bold, leathery, dark green leaves, red when young. It is tough, though not as hardy as some other species. Height x width 10 ft (3 m). ZONE 7.

The form called **'Rubens'** is worth seeking out for its brilliant red new leaves. Height x width 10 ft (3 m).

Glabra = smooth.

Photinia serratifolia, syn P. serrulata

Photinia serratifolia makes a large shrub, eventually forming a tough backdrop tree or ideal shelter tree. The big, oblong leaves are dark, glossy green with a hint of red. The new foliage is bright red in spring. Flat corymbs of *Pyracantha*-type, creamy white flowers arise in late spring. Has winning ways in that it is more lime- and frost-tolerant than other evergreen species. From China and Taiwan. Height 30–40 ft (10–12 m) x width 25 ft (8 m). ZONE 7.

Serratifolia = serrated edges (of the leaves).

Photinia villosa

ORIENTAL PHOTINIA

The only deciduous species worthy of a space, this makes a very small, flat-topped tree, easily accommodated in gardens. Bright bronzy new leaves in the spring could almost be mistaken for a small-growing *Malus* or *Prunus*. The fall color is brilliant, a combination of orange and red, scarlet and gold, with a bonus of bright red, shiny berries.

The plant is not happy on limestone, but otherwise any rough, tough soil will do. Originates from China, Korea and Japan. Height x width 15 ft (5 m). ZONES 4 TO 9.

'**Village Shade**' is a new cultivar with more oval leaves and excellent fall color. Height x width 15 ft (5 m).

Villosa = shaggy or hairy.

Physocarpus

Physocarpus opulifolius, syn *Spiraea opulifolius*

Rosaceae

*P*hysocarpus is a rugged, deciduous shrub which, I have to confess, is rather drab. It would not attract a second glance except that there are two rather lovely yellow leaf clones: '**Luteus**' and '**Dart's Gold**'. *Physocarpus opulifolius* is a gardener's friend, growing in those seemingly impossible sites.

Below right: *Photinia villosa* var *sinica*

Above: *Physocarpus opulifolius* 'Luteus' with seed capsules.

While cold-hardy, its real toughness comes in its ability to handle dry, shady positions, such as under big, old conifers. Although you may have to water the plant for the first summer to establish it, once away it will cope with extreme drought and shade. It is also capable of growing well in very warm regions as well as extremely cold. Acidic to moderately alkaline soil as well as clays are acceptable. So virtually any kind of site and soil will suit this rugged plant. The bright yellow versions are brilliant for lighting up a dark corner of the garden or as a contrast to the dark green of camellias. They will of course also grow in full sun.

The spring growth is a delicious shade of greenish yellow, taking on more gold tones as the leaves mature. The leaves are pointed, serrated and vaguely like a *Crataegus* or hawthorn. The clusters of white *Spiraea*-like flowers tend to be lost among the yellow leaves, but when the seed cases change to red and the bush has a startling new lease on life.

The peeling, striated bark can be made into a feature by cutting off the lower branches, but generally it remains unseen. Just to prove it is the ultimate in tough plants, you can prune it any way you fancy and there are no pests or diseases. Plants of any size can be shifted in winter when the plant is dormant. A native of eastern North America. Height 10 ft (3 m) x width 15 ft (5 m). ZONE 3.

Physa = a bladder; *carpus* = pod or fruit; *opulifolius* = guelder rose leaf, the guelder rose being *Viburnum opulus*.

Picea

SPRUCE
Pinaceae

Spruces are, for the most part, cool-climate conifers with a typical Christmas tree shape. Mostly they come in rich, dark greens with a few blue-gray species. Some of our most stunning blue garden plants are cultivars of *Picea*, such as *Picea pungens* 'Koster' (Koster's blue spruce). Provide them with a rich, deep, cool, acidic soil, a cool climate and a home in the sun and you will have a happy *Picea*. The shape is ruined and the shrub will be sparse and ragged-looking when grown in the

Left: *Picea glauca* var *albertiana* 'Conica' and three *Pseudopanax* trunks.

Right: *Picea abies* 'Aurea'

covered in evergreen needles, which are rough or sharp to touch. The older needles fall off, leaving a raised little peg on the stem.

Picea = from the Latin "pix," meaning pitch (*Picea* exude a sticky resin).

Picea abies
NORWAY SPRUCE

This is the "true" or traditional Christmas tree, with blunt, dark green leaves. A huge tree is sent to Britain every Christmas and erected in London's Trafalgar Square as a special thank you from the people of Norway for the help they received during the Second World War.

On a smaller scale, it is an ideal tub plant, which may be kept from one Yuletide until the next. It grows native in southern Scandinavia, and central and southern Europe. Height 70–130 ft (20–40 m) x width 20 ft (6 m). ZONES 3 TO 8.

'Pyramidalis' is an upright, narrow, tidy form, with very short needles. The yellow-needle form is *Picea abies* **'Aurea'**. For both, height 50 ft (15 m) x width 15–20 ft (5–6 m).

Abies = looks like the similar *Abies* genus.

Picea breweriana
BREWER SPRUCE

Picea breweriana is one of the most spectacular trees in the world. It is worth a visit to an arboretum just to see one. You will think your eyes deceive you when you see a waterfall of blue-green foliage, possibly making it the most pendulous of all natural trees. Unfortunately, it is not an easy plant to please. It grows naturally on dry, gravelly soil in deep ravines at high altitude. So it does not like wind, or being too moist or in too mild a climate. Even if it does like your climate, it is very slow-growing. Many a gardener has, like me, given up and planted the easier but similar *Picea smithiana*.

Picea breweriana is named after William Henry Brewer (1828–1910), who botanized in California and later became a professor at Yale. The tree originates from northern California and southern Oregon. Height 30–50 ft (10–15 m) x width 10–12 ft (3–4 m). ZONES 6 TO 8.

Picea engelmannii
ENGELMANN SPRUCE

This forms a narrow, conical tree with bluish green foliage. The four sided sharp needles are very fragrant, if you are brave enough to investigate. It is very cold-hardy and likes a cool, moist climate. A native of North America's Rocky Mountains. Height 70–130 ft (20–40 m) x width 15 ft (5 m). ZONES 3 TO 8.

'Glauca' is the best garden form, often grown for its superb blue foliage.

shade. Growing in the wild, they endure various hardships and thus are wind- and cold-hardy. They are easy to transplant in winter if root pruned properly.

They are not a good choice for coastal areas as they abhor salt-laden winds. Piceas also suffer devastating attacks of aphids and mites in warmer regions, leading to total defoliation. They are really cold, mountain-loving plants.

Piceas form neat, upright trees with branches in whorls,

Picea glauca var *albertiana* 'Conica', syn 'Albertiana Conica'
DWARF ALBERTA SPRUCE

This form was found in the Canadian Rockies in Alberta, thus the name. It is very slow-growing and forms a neat, pyramidal shape, ideal for rockeries and as a statement plant. Height 3–6 ft (1–2 m) x width 2–4 ft (60–120 cm). ZONES 3 TO 8.

Picea glauca **'Echiniformis'** is an especially dwarf blue-gray shrub. Height x width 3 ft (1 m).

Glauca = blue.

Left: *Picea glauca* var *albertiana* 'Conica'

Above: *Picea likiangensis purpurea* with *Buddleia globosa*.

Picea likiangensis purpurea
LIJIANG SPRUCE

This is known for its vibrant purple candles of new flowers. The bluish green foliage is pretty good, too. A native of southern and western China and southeast Tibet. Height 100 ft (30 m) x width 20–28 ft (6–9 m). ZONES 6 TO 8.

Likiangensis = from Likiang, a region of western China; *purpurea* = purple.

Picea omorika
SERBIAN SPRUCE

Picea omorika forms a narrow, spire-like tree with dark green needles. It seems more tolerant of pollution and poor soils than other spruces, and is rarely attacked by mites or aphids. Perhaps this is the spruce to try in warmer regions. A native of Bosnia and Serbia. Height 70 ft (20 m) x width 6–10 ft (2–3 m). ZONES 5 TO 8.

Omorika = the Serbian word for spruce.

Picea orientalis
CAUCASIAN SPRUCE, ORIENTAL SPRUCE

Picea orientalis has a neat conical habit with horizontal branches. It features very ornamental, rich, dark green foliage and a dense habit. It tolerates cold, drought and seems to resist mites. Originates from Turkey and the Caucasus. Height 100 ft (30 m) x width 20–25 ft (6–8 m). ZONES 5 TO 8.

Orientalis = oriental, as in Turkey.

Picea pungens 'Koster'
KOSTER'S BLUE SPRUCE

Grown in the right climate this bluest of blue spruces is an unforgettable sight. The right conditions are cold winters or a continental climate. The trees are not easy to blend with other plants and are difficult to place in a garden scene because of the strong color. Good clones are grafted and very slow-growing, therefore plants are expensive (but worth it). It does not enjoy warm, mild

climates or hot places. The cultivar name is taken from the Koster Nursery in Boskoop, Holland. Boskoop is an area totally given over to nurseries intersected by canals used for transporting the plants. Height 50 ft (15 m) x width 3 ft (1 m). ZONES 3 TO 8.

Pungens = pungent (because of the sap).

Picea sitchensis
SITKA SPRUCE

Sitka spruce is a very large, upright tree often grown for timber. The sharp, dark green leaves cover all of the twigs in every plane and are white underneath. It is happy in moist, cool climates and grows naturally from northern California up to Alaska. The plant

Above: *Picea orientalis*

Left: *Picea pungens*

was first discovered in 1792 by Archibald Menzies, a surgeon and naturalist on Captain Vancouver's voyage. Height 80–160 ft (25–50 m) x width 20–40 ft (6–12 m). ZONES 7 TO 8.

Sitchensis = of Sitka, the place.

Picea smithiana
HIMALAYAN SPRUCE

Himalayan spruce is the next best drooping weeper after *Picea breweriana*, and this one is happier in warmer climates where the latter will not survive. It grows easily in wet climates and makes faster, speedier growth. The leaves are dark green. *Picea smithiana* is named after Sir James Smith of Norwich (1759–1828). He is famous for buying the collections of Carl Linnaeus on his death in 1778 and founding the Linnaean Society. Height 70–100 ft (20–30 m) x width 20–28 ft (6–9 m). ZONE 8.

Picrasma

Picrasma quassioides, syn *P. ailanthoides*
QUASSIA
Simaroubaceae

This is a really tidy tree, ideally suited to small gardens. Its small size, tidy habit and fall color should make this one of the most well known of all deciduous trees and yet it is not. But it is so easy to grow and so beautiful it should be known by every keen gardener. It is one of the best small shade trees you could imagine and a firm favorite of mine.

The tree has a truly pyramidal habit, sloping up to the topmost point. The leaves turn brilliant orange and scarlets in the fall, starting with the tips and gradually working on down into the center of the tree, so at any one time the inner part of the tree may be green, the midsection yellow or orange and the tips bright, sunny reds. Even in a warm climate it produces startling colors. Possibly the best thing about it is the length of time the fall show lasts. It is often one of the first trees to color up and yet still glows when many other plants are stark and bare.

The dark green leaves are vaguely ash-like, or perhaps more like a *Koelreuteria*. The stems are interesting, being a blackish, reddish brown with prominent creamy yellow lenticels and a distinct terminal bud. The bark is very attractive, especially to the touch.

The structure of the tree is appealing too, as it has a central leader with whorls of branches at regular intervals, all sloping up at the same angle, and so the tree has a very tidy habit, winter or summer. It provides light shade for shrubs such as *Rhododendron* and *Pieris* without taking up too much room. The flowers are cute rather than showy. Yellowish green clusters in spring are followed by red fruits.

It is cold-hardy, growing all through the cooler parts of China, Japan and Korea. As well as moist areas, it is equally happy in drought-prone regions. It prefers an acidic to neutral soil, though will grow on lime.

Picrasma is one of the many plants in our gardens first collected by that tireless plant hunter Ernest Wilson

Left: *Picrasma quassioides*

(1876–1930), who went on to become curator of the Arnold Arboretum in Boston. The tree is native to northern India, Nepal, Bhutan, China, Korea and Japan. Height x width 25 ft (8 m). ZONES 6 TO 9.

Picrasma = refers to the bitterness of the bark; *quassioides* = like a *Quassia*, a medicinal plant from India.

Pieris

Ericaceae

From a gardener's perspective, *Pieris* are one of the best-value shrubs available, giving great joy for little effort. If you can grow rhododendrons and camellias then you can easily grow a few *Pieris* as they have the same requirement for acidic, free-draining, soil rich in organic matter. Like rhododendrons, they will appreciate a mulch of bark or woodchips to keep their roots cool, moist and shaded.

While some plants have a brief fling of flowers in spring, the *Pieris* is laden with lily-of-the-valley-type blooms for weeks and then, having favored us with its flowers, it tops it off with a stunning display of brilliant new growth.

Pieris have several other fine qualities that make them ideal for small gardens. They are evergreen and so add substance to any garden scene and, being compact, they will fit into even the tiniest gardens. They vary from tiny dwarf cultivars to over 10 ft (3 m), and some will grow in pots and tubs.

These dome-shaped evergreens with narrow leaves are happy in sun or shade depending on your climate. Generally they are much happier and healthier in full sun as long as you keep the roots mulched and cool. In a very hot climate, some shade is advisable. A plentiful supply of water keeps them in tiptop condition. Easy as rhododendrons to transplant and even ancient specimens 20 years old can be shifted in winter without any major setback, as they have a mat of fine, fibrous roots. You do not even have to root prune or prepare them in any way, just dig them up and move them.

In hot climates they can be prone to thrips and some regions have lacewing attack. They may also die from root rot, especially after heavy rain in a hot summer climate. In alkaline soils they tend to look anemic. There are numerous clones including some with cream or salmon-pink new growth. This is yet another plant genus linking the Appalachians to China.

Pieris = from Pieria, a place in northern Thessaly, reputedly home of the Muses who in Greek myth were any of the nine nymphs—young, beautiful, modest virgins who presided over the fine and liberal arts.

Pieris floribunda
FETTERBUSH, MOUNTAIN PIERIS
This forms a compact, rounded shrub with glossy, dark green leaves. Found in open mountain situations in the Appalachians. Height 6 ft (2 m) x width 10 ft (3 m). ZONES 5 TO 9.

Floribunda = flowers in abundance.

Pieris formosa
Pieris formosa is a large, upright shrub with glossy, dark green leaves and red new growth. Native to China and the Himalayas. Height 15 ft (5 m) x width 12 ft (4 m). ZONES 7 TO 9.

Left: *Pieris formosa* var *forrestii*

Above: *Pileostegia viburnoides* climbing up a trunk. *Itoa orientalis* is at left.

Pileostegia

Pileostegia viburnoides, syn *Schizophragma viburnoides*
Hydrangeaceae

This exciting plant has two main claims to fame. It is a hardy evergreen climber, and that is a rare commodity, and it is a *Hydrangea*, though you would never guess to look at the leaves or the flowers. The rich, dark green, waxy leaves are thick, lush and tropical. Clinging tenaciously, like ivy, it will soon cover any structure. Plant it only on a surface you are happy to leave alone, because if you ever want to remove it to paint the wall or fence, you are out of luck. It grows and climbs easily on brick, concrete or timber, in fact, anything solid. Like so many climbers it has to make do with poor, dry soil at the base of trees and walls, though it prefers moist, well-drained soil. It will grow with its roots in shade, though the plant would enjoy some sun, as do most climbers. The more light it receives, the better it will flower. The creamy white flowers on this Himalayan creeper are in large panicles in summer. Each flower is tiny, but the overall effect of hundreds of them is quite charming. Native to India, China and Taiwan. Height 20 ft (6 m). ZONE 7.

Pileostegia = from *pileus*, a Roman felt cap; *stegia* = stigma; *viburnoides* = like the leaf of *Viburnum odoratissimum*.

Pieris formosa **var** *forrestii*
This shrub has bright carmine-red new leaves. It was collected by George Forrest in Yunnan, China. ZONE 8.

Cultivars include **'Charles Michael'**, with red young growth. **'Jermyns'** has spreading and arching branches and dark red new growth. **'Henry Price'** has very dark green leaves, bronze-red when young. **'Wakehurst'** has brilliant red new foliage. For all, height x width 8 ft (2.5 m).

Formosa = beautiful.

Pieris japonica
LILY-OF-THE-VALLEY BUSH
This *Pieris* has given rise to numerous cultivars. It forms a compact, rounded shrub with glossy, mid-green leaves. It is native to eastern China, Taiwan and Japan. Height 12 ft (4 m) x width 10 ft (3 m). ZONES 6 TO 9.

Japonica = from Japan.

Pieris taiwanensis
From Taiwan, this small shrub flowers early, so they can be frost damaged. Height 3–5 ft (1–1.5 m) x width 5 ft (1.5 m). ZONE 7.

Taiwanesis = from Taiwan.

Pinus

PINE
Pinaceae

Pines, love them or hate them, they are hard to ignore. Personally I love them, there is so much variation there is bound to be some you will like. And they are so distinctive, even rookie horticultural novices can recognize a pine, be it a knee-high dwarf or a forest giant. Their unique, billowy habit and characteristic needles are world famous. Most pines are easy to please, growing in any soil as long as it is a sunny site. They hate shade. Generally they are wind-hardy, with only the long-needle

Above: *Pinus elliotii*

Mexican pines being sensitive to wind. Some of the most wind-hardy plants are pines such as *Pinus radiata* from the Californian coast and *P. pinaster* from the Mediterranean. Most pines are easy to grow, being oblivious to soil type or wet or dry climates, providing the drainage is good. Most are cold-hardy, too. Pines are useful park trees, while some of the miniature forms can be grown in city gardens. They have been popular subjects for bonsai for hundreds of years.

Pinus elliotii
SLASH PINE

Slash pine from southeastern U.S.A. has very long needles in twos and threes. It makes a good small "character" tree for gardens in warm areas. Height x width 30 ft (10 m). ZONE 9.

Pinus flexilis var *reflexa*
LIMBER PINE

Limber pine lives on rocky sites and therefore needs good drainage. It is happy in dry sites. A slow-growing tree, it sits easily in suburban gardens. The dark green needles are crowded toward the end of the stem, creating an effect of tufts above bare stem. Originates from the Rocky Mountains, from Alberta to Arizona. Height 50–70 ft (15–20 m) x width 20–28 ft (6–9 m). ZONES 3 TO 8.

Flexilis = flexible; *reflexa* = reflexed (referring to the leaves).

Pinus koraiensis
KOREAN PINE

This grows into a neat, small pyramid in garden situations. It is slow-growing in the early stages and easily accommodated in a suburban garden. It has bluish needles, and grows with a narrow, upright habit when young. Native to the Pacific coast of Russia, Korea and northeast China. Height 70 ft (20 m) x width 25 ft (8 m). ZONES 4 TO 9.

The form **'Compacta Glauca'** is a better garden plant, being bluer, and of a dense, compact nature. Height 10–20 ft (3–6 m) x width 6–10 ft (2–3 m)

Koraiensis = from Korea.

Pinus mugo
MOUNTAIN PINE, MUGO PINE

Pinus mugo is probably the most well-known of the smaller pines, suitable for rockeries and small gardens. It prefers a cool, wet climate, as you would expect, coming from the mountains of Europe. Various named forms are available. Height 11 ft (3.5 m) x width 15 ft (5 m). ZONES 3 TO 8.

Mugo = old Tyrolean name for the plant.

Pinus parviflora
JAPANESE WHITE PINE

This is a conical or columnar, five-needle pine with short, blue-green needles. Most forms for sale have a distinct blue-green appearance. Although a tree in the wild, it is very slow-growing in gardens and is ideal for small plots and even for bonsai. A native of Japan. Height 30–70 ft (10–20 m) x width 20–25 ft (6–8 m). ZONES 6 TO 9.

Parvi = not much; *flora* = flowers.

Pinus wallichiana, syn *P. chilla, P. excelsa, P. griffithii*
BHUTAN PINE, BLUE PINE, HIMALAYAN PINE

Possibly the most attractive pine for small gardens, the slow-growing nature of *Pinus wallichiana* and its beautiful blue, plumed growth make it an attractive garden tree. It will reach 9 ft (3 m) in 10 years, and eventually become a large tree after very many years. The needles hang down, creating a cheerleader's pompom effect. Smooth, gray trunks on young plants are impressive and the tree can be opened up to view the trunk to good effect.

The tree needs moist, acidic, well-drained soil and shelter from strong winds. Nathaniel Wallich, a Dane employed by the British East India Company, traveled widely in the East and collected many new plants in northern India and Nepal, including this pine. He was director of the Calcutta Botanic Gardens for 30

Above: *Pinus wallichiana* (back) with *Pinus bhutanica* (front).

Left: *Pinus mugo* (front) with *P. engelmannii* (right). The yellow hedge is *Chamaecyparis pisifera* 'Filifera Aurea'.

Right: *Pinus yunnanensis*

stems look primitive, with scales like a fish. Older branches have soft orange-brown, flaking bark. Very long needles in billowy swirls add to the prehistoric look. It rarely goes unnoticed, so if you want a conversation piece for your garden, consider this plant. Yunnan province in western China is the origin of, and gives its name to, this plant. Height x width 20–30 ft (6–10 m). ZONE 9.

Pistacia

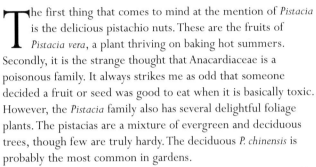

PISTACHIO
Anacardiaceae

The first thing that comes to mind at the mention of *Pistacia* is the delicious pistachio nuts. These are the fruits of *Pistacia vera*, a plant thriving on baking hot summers. Secondly, it is the strange thought that Anacardiaceae is a poisonous family. It always strikes me as odd that someone decided a fruit or seed was good to eat when it is basically toxic. However, the *Pistacia* family also has several delightful foliage plants. The pistacias are a mixture of evergreen and deciduous trees, though few are truly hardy. The deciduous *P. chinensis* is probably the most common in gardens.

Pistachio = from Latin "pist," meaning fodder.

years. He died in 1854 aged 68. Dr. William Griffith also worked for "the Company" and botanized in Assam with Wallich. Native to the Himalayas, from Afghanistan to northeast India. Height 70–120 ft (20–35 m) x width 20–40 ft (6–12 m). ZONES 6 TO 9.

Pistacia chinensis
CHINESE MASTIC
Pistacia chinensis is one of the biggest trees found in China and some ancient specimens can be found in temple grounds. Thankfully it takes a few hundred years to reach this kind of size and you can plant it with safety in your garden knowing it is not going to

Pinus yunnanensis
This is a three-needle pine, forming a small ungainly tree, with a rather primeval appearance. It is not a typical pine at all, even the

Right: *Pistacia chinensis*

outgrow its allotted space in a lifetime. In fact it is a very tidy tree, often seen as a rounded shrub, ideal for small gardens, with glossy, green, pinnate leaves.

A tough plant, it will survive any drought, but is equally at home in wet climates or planted near ponds and streams. Any old soil will do as long as it is free draining. Given a sunny position, it is able to grow just about anywhere, thriving on heat, drought and neglect. Being a poisonous family, no pest is willing to tackle it and there are no diseases of any note. Flowers are a mass of tiny blooms at the ends of the stems, but not very exciting. The flowers are followed by red berries. There are no problems transplanting in the winter.

The fall colors are stunning, and it is one of the best shrubs in terms of fall color and duration. Rich orange, red and crimson shades occur even in mild climates. The color does vary because they are usually grown from seed, though most are good. Sometimes the new spring growth is colored, too, in shades of red.

Frank Meyer (1875–1918) introduced good spring coloring forms from China to California. Perhaps some of the better forms should be given cloned names and distributed. The plant can be pruned drastically should you ever need to and it could be coppiced, as are the related *Cotinus* sometimes. A native of central and western China. Height 50–80 ft (15–25 m) x width 22–30 ft (7–10 m). ZONES 7 TO 9.

Chinensis = from China.

Pittosporum

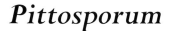

Pittosporaceae

*P*ittosporum is a wonderful group of foliage shrubs. In fact, they are grown only for their leafy evergreen effect and in some parts of the world they are used for the cut foliage trade. The stems are sold in flower markets as a leafy complement to cut flowers. They are a very large genus found naturally in New Zealand, Australia, China and Japan. Gardeners in the Northern Hemisphere are probably more familiar with the Asian varieties.

All the plants are evergreen, most are hardy, and the ornamental ones generally have a narrow, upright, bush shape when young. Some species are extremely wind-hardy, even salt-wind hardy. They like an open, sunny site, and are not hard to

Above: *Pittosporum eugenoides*

please when it comes to soil, pH and moisture. While one or two Australian species have attractive flowers, for the most part you could pass a bush and not know it was flowering other than by the scent from the tiny flowers. The seeds are black and sticky.

Pitto = pitch or tar; *sporum* = seed.

Pittosporum eugenoides
TARATA, LEMONWOOD

An upright, elegant species with shiny, pale green leaves with a distinctive wavy edge. You won't confuse this plant with any other: it is unique. It grows easily and rapidly in any situation where you want a tall, upright, evergreen shrub. Reasonably wind-hardy. It has lemon-scented leaves, thus the common name of lemonwood. A native of New Zealand. Height 15–40 ft (5–12 m) x width 6–15 ft (2–5 m). ZONE 9.

Eugenoides = like a eugenia (an evergreen tree from Australia).

Pittosporum tenuifolium
KOHUHU

Very popular in the cut-flower trade for the pretty foliage, this makes a narrow, upright shrub, easy to please and with unusual, dainty, blackish brown flowers. There are numerous variegated forms with white, yellow and even pink or black foliage. This New Zealand native is an ideal statement plant to replace conifers. Plant it at the end of a border where you need a dense, robust, evergreen bush. It is also an ideal shrub for large hedges. Height 12–30 ft (4–10 m) x width 6–15 ft (2–5 m). ZONE 9.

Tenuifolium = thin- or slender-foliaged.

Pittosporum tobira
JAPANESE MOCK ORANGE

Well known and popular throughout the world, *Pittosporum tobira* is grown for its foliage and because it can be pruned to any shape you desire. The thick, oval, glossy leaves are a rich green color. Creamy flowers have a lovely orange-blossom scent. While most flowers fade, these intensify in color, becoming more yellow as they age. More hardy to cold than most and quite wind-hardy, too. It also tolerates drought. From China, Japan and Taiwan. Height 6–30 ft (2–10 m) x width 5–10 ft (1.5–3 m). ZONE 9.

Tobira = local Japanese name.

Left: *Pittosporum tobira*

Platanus

PLANE TREE
Platanaceae

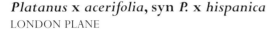

For such a small genus of plants, *Platanus* has certainly had an impact on our lives. The trees are seen in city streets all across the temperate world, surviving pollution, drought, and acres of tarmac and concrete. As if this is not enough, they survive ruthless pruning when cut back to stumps, or pollarding, as it is called. It seems no matter what we do to them, the ancient plane trees just carry on regardless, providing us with shade, greenery and a luxuriance we would surely miss.

Planes have an unusual trait in that the petiole, or leaf stalk, completely encloses next year's bud. Pull a leaf off and you will see what I mean. This protection of the new bud and the shiny top surface of each leaf bolster its defenses against city pollution. Of the six species, we usually only see one hybrid and one species.

Platanus = ancient Greek name for plane tree.

Platanus x *acerifolia*, syn *P.* x *hispanica*
LONDON PLANE

Called the London plane because it is the dominant tree in the streets of London, it even withstood the very polluted period in London's history in the late 1800s and early 1900s when all the buildings went black with the soot and grime. It is widely used in cities around the world because of its ability to thrive in dire conditions. Most people never look up to see this stately tree and probably only notice the peculiar peeling bark. Chunks of bark are constantly being shed, revealing new areas of smooth bark beneath. It has sharply lobed, bright green leaves. The seed clusters are like a knight's mace hanging on a thread. It is a tough plant willing to grow just about anywhere. It is still a botanical mystery where this plant originated. The best guess is as a hybrid seedling in Spain where both *Platanus occidentalis* from North America and

Above and top: *Platanus orientalis*

P. orientalis thrive. Another theory has it originating in Oxford in 1670. Height 100 ft (30 m) x width 70 ft (20 m). ZONE 5.

Acerifolia = leaf like a maple; *hispanica* = Spanish.

Platanus occidentalis
BUTTONWOOD, SYCAMORE

This is a vigorous, wide-spreading tree, with three-lobed leaves and attractive flaking bark. It needs a hot summer climate to thrive and does not grow well in Europe. Grows native from Canada down the eastern seaboard as far as Mexico. Height 80 ft (25 m) x width 70 ft (20 m). ZONE 5.

Occidentalis = Western.

Platanus orientalis
ORIENTAL SYCAMORE

The beautiful glossy green, five-lobed leaves have a lovely toffee scent. This delightful but elusive smell can be overpowering some days and non-existent when you want to enlighten your visitors.

Left: *Platanus* x *acerifolia*

The foliage has rich golds and soft browns in fall. Happy in hot, cold, dry or wet climates. A native of eastern Europe, Greece and Turkey. Height x width 100 ft (30 m). ZONES 7 OR 8.

Orientalis = Eastern.

Platanus racemosa
CALIFORNIA SYCAMORE

This is a vigorous, broadly columnar tree with thick, fleshy leaves, dark green above and slightly hairy beneath. It is capable of growing well in hot, dry, windy climates, but is not as cold-hardy as other species. A native of southern California and Mexico. Height 80 ft (25 m) x width 70 ft (20 m). ZONES 8 OR 9.

Platanus mexicana is very similar to *P. racemosa*. It is evergreen in some regions and hates being transplanted.

Racemosa = flowers in racemes.

Podocarpus

PODOCARPS
Podocarpaceae

Podocarpus is an unusual genus on two counts. The plants are a type of conifer found all across the Southern Hemisphere as well as Mexico, China and Japan. They have managed to inherit a fair bit of the earth, living in places as diverse as New Zealand, Australia, Malaysia, East Africa, New Caledonia, New Guinea and South America. I know it is an ancient genus, but very few woody plants have covered this much territory. Secondly, podocarps are strange bedfellows with other conifers, having fleshy fruits instead of cones.

Conifers are distinguished by having naked seeds: not enclosed in a pod. Many podocarps have seeds enclosed in big red or black fruits, some as big as plums. The botanists get around this dilemma by explaining that the seeds are naked to begin with and the fleshy fruit grows around them.

Nearly every podocarp species is worth growing as a foliage plant and many are becoming popular as potted house and office plants for just that reason. In nature, many are forest giants, but they grow so slowly (especially when contained in a pot) that they show no inclination to lift the roof off.

All podocarps are evergreen, and a few are hardy to cold. Some, like *Podocarpus totara*, are extremely tough, wind-hardy beasts, surviving severe storms. Full sun is ideal for most podocarps, but many will grow in part shade if shade is where you grow your tender plants. They are not too fussy about soil, as evidenced by them growing pot-bound in tubs for years without complaining. Any soil that is not boggy will suffice. They are certainly happy in wet, high-rainfall regions and yet seem equally happy when hardened by drought. Apart from the occasional caterpillar attacking the new growth, they are untouched by pests or diseases. They are excellent textured shrubs, bringing form and stability to any garden. Most have supple, pliable young stems and can be espaliered or topiaried.

Podo = foot; *carpus* = fruit, referring to the fleshy fruit stalk.

Podocarpus alpinus, syn *P. lawrencii*
TASMANIAN PODOCARP

This is a hardy dwarf species growing as a mound or dense ground cover. Dark blackish evergreen leaves create an attractive facade, and there are exciting purple leaf forms available, too. Native to

Tasmania and New South Wales, Australia. Height x width 6 ft (2 m). ZONE 7.

Alpinus = alpine.

Above: *Podocarpus henkelii* with new spring growth.

Podocarpus gracilior

Podocarpus gracilior is grown for its fine, needle-like leaves, which create a plume effect *en masse*. It is the epitome of grace and, as with so many podocarps, the bright green new growth is a delightful contrast with the older, darker, leaves. It forms an upright, dense shrub. A native of east Africa. Height 9 ft (3 m) x width 6 ft (2 m). ZONES 8 OR 9.

Gracilior = slender or graceful.

Podocarpus henkelii

Some gardeners refer to this as the "bamboo bush," as the new pendulous foliage looks very similar to bamboo. It is very slow-growing and makes an ideal plant for pots and entranceways. The leaves are clustered near the stem tip and tend to droop, giving a weeping effect. It is surprisingly wind-hardy for such a tropical-looking plant. This South African species is named after Dr. John Henkell, Conservator of Forests for Natal and Zululand early in the 19th century. Height 6–9 ft (2–3 m) x width 6 ft (2 m). ZONE 9.

Podocarpus macrophyllus
BUDDHIST PINE, KUSAMAKI, SOUTHERN YEW

One of the hardier species, *Podocarpus macrophyllus* has large, dark, blackish green leaves that are firm and leathery. It makes an excel-

Above: *Podocarpus totara* 'Aureus' (center).

lent hedge or topiary plant. A native of eastern China and Japan. Height 50 ft (15 m) x width 20–25 ft (6–8 m). ZONE 7.

'Maki' is a more erect, bushy type and the form most commonly seen in gardens. It has shorter leaves than the species. Popular in Asian cities, where it is often clipped into fantastic shapes. Height 10–15 ft (3–5 m) x width 6 ft (2 m).

Macro = large; *phyllus* = leaf.

Podocarpus salignus
WILLOWLEAF PODOCARP
Podocarpus salignus is most often seen as a large shrub or small tree in gardens. The long, narrow leaves, dark bluish green, and the graceful pendulous habit of the bush make it very appealing. Originates from Chile. Height 70 ft (20 m) x width 20–28 ft (6–9 m). ZONE 8.

Salignus = willow-like (from *Salix*).

Podocarpus totara
TOTARA
A New Zealand forest giant, totara is slow-growing and can be safely planted in gardens without any danger of you being pushed out of house and home. It forms a dense tree when young, similar to yew. It makes an excellent hedge and is an ideal replacement for yew in hot regions. **Podocarpus totara 'Aureus'** is a very handsome yellow-leafed form, that grows best in full sun. For both, height 30 ft (10 m) x width 15 ft (5 m). ZONE 8.

Totara = local New Zealand name for this tree.

Populus

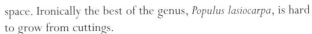

POPLAR
Salicaceae

Poplars provide a tree in no time at all and offer luxuriant foliage and stately nobility. Asian monks must have thought so, too, because they were commonly planted in temple grounds. They are certainly easy to grow. You only have to leave a branch lying on the ground and it puts out roots and "claims" the space. Ironically the best of the genus, *Populus lasiocarpa*, is hard to grow from cuttings.

Do not plant them near pipes, paving or buildings as they can move mountains.

Some gardeners recommend keeping them 100 ft (30 m) from the nearest building or underground services. Most of them prosper in wet, even boggy, ground and they are sometimes used to "dry out" wet areas. All of them are big, upright trees. The drooping male flowers and female catkins are followed by copious amounts of fluffy white seed like kapok, which floats on the wind and can be a nuisance.

Populus balsamifera
BALSAM POPLAR, TACAMAHACA
Balsam poplar is so-called because of the balsam scent of the newly emerging leaves: it is heady and can be overpowering. It is a fast-growing, columnar tree. The shiny leaves are gray-green above and whitish beneath. Height 100 ft (30 m) x width 25 ft (8 m). ZONES 5 TO 9.

Balsamifera = bearing balsam.

Populus deltoides
COTTONWOOD
The lovely upright habit and nice clean trunk make *Populus deltoides* a good outline or horizon tree. The large glossy leaves turn yellow in fall. They make a click-clacking noise in a breeze, but it is a brittle tree in gale-force winds. Otherwise it is very hardy. Native to eastern North America. Height 100 ft (30 m) x width 70 ft (20 m). ZONES 3 TO 9.

Deltoides = river delta.

Populus lasiocarpa
CHINESE NECKLACE POPLAR
This has the biggest leaves of any poplar, with a reddish tinge to the heart-shaped leaf and stalk. It can look fantastic, but is often hard to please and therefore disappointing. Prone to wind damage to leaves and structure. No fall color. A native of central China. Height 70 ft (20 m) x width 40 ft (12 m). ZONES 6 TO 9.

Lasi = hairy or woolly; *carpa* = seeds or fruit.

Above: *Populus deltoides*

Above: *Populus nigra* var *italica*

Above: The fall leaves of *Populus maximowiczii*.

Populus maximowiczii
JAPANESE POPLAR

Japanese poplar forms a narrow, upright column reaching for the sky, and becomes a wide-spreading, billowy tree with age. The attractive leaves are rounded and gray-green with a corrugated surface. Rich, warm, honey colors occur in the fall. Carl Maximowicz was a Russian botanist based at St. Petersburg Botanics, who traveled widely through Manchuria, Korea and Japan in the 1850s and 1860s and was considered an expert on Japanese flora. Height 100 ft (30 m) x width 30 ft (10 m). ZONES 4 TO 8.

Populus nigra var italica
LOMBARDY POPLAR

This black poplar has now conquered the world, being widely planted for its neat columnar habit. If you want a big tree and only have a tiny space, then this is the tree. Brilliant golds in fall. Initially from the district of the same name in Italy. Height 100 ft (30 m) x width 15 ft (5 m). ZONES 3 TO 9.

Nigra = black; *italica* = from Italy.

Populus szechuanica

This is similar to *Populus lasiocarpa*, but is probably a better bet, with even redder leaves and much easier to grow. It is prone to wind damage to leaves and structure. There is no fall color; the leaves somehow just disappear. Named for the province in western China, where it originates. Height 130 ft (40 m) x width 30 ft (10 m). ZONES 4 TO 9.

Szechuanica = from the province in China.

Prunus

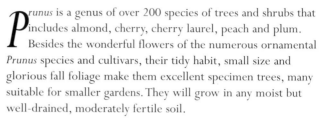

Rosaceae

*P*runus is a genus of over 200 species of trees and shrubs that includes almond, cherry, cherry laurel, peach and plum. Besides the wonderful flowers of the numerous ornamental *Prunus* species and cultivars, their tidy habit, small size and glorious fall foliage make them excellent specimen trees, many suitable for smaller gardens. They will grow in any moist but well-drained, moderately fertile soil.

Prunus = Latin for plum (plums are in the *Prunus* genus).

Prunus cerasifera 'Nigra'
CHERRY PLUM, MYROBALAN

An excellent, fast-growing tree for an instant splash of color in your backyard. The "splash" does not come much brighter than this vibrant blackish purple. *Prunus cerasifera* 'Nigra' makes a wonderful contrast tree against a bright green background, or can add a touch of silver-gray at the front for a sizzling highlight.

Delectable pink blossoms on long sprays just before leafing add to the spring show. The flowers on this small, rounded tree are followed by dark red, cherry-sized fruits.

It is tolerant of virtually any soil, including wet or dry. High rainfall gives luxuriant, brightly colored foliage, while it can look neglected in drier places. It is happy in cold regions, but does not like wind or shade. Leave it unpruned, as you are not trying to get

Below: *Prunus cerasifera* 'Nigra'

Above: Cherry trees showing fall colors.

Right: *Prunus laurocerasus*

a crop of fruit and there is always a risk of introducing disease when you take a saw to *Prunus* species.

Seedlings that spring up in your compost heap are likely to be almost as good for leaf color as the parent plant, and make good gifts for gardening friends. There are numerous cultivars available if you wish to guarantee a good clone. The species originates from southeast Europe and southwest Asia. Height x width 30 ft (10 m). ZONES 5 TO 9.

Cerasifera = bearing cherries, "ceras" is an old Greek word for cherry.

Prunus laurocerasus

CHERRY LAUREL, ENGLISH LAUREL

Prunus laurocerasus comes as a shock to those who think *Prunus* are only plums, cherries and peaches. For a start it is evergreen and that seems all wrong. Then you see the upright sprays of nondescript flowers, very different from cherry blossom. These unappealing muddy white flowers have scent as their saving grace.

A rough, tough kind of shrub, withstanding drought, shade and wind, it is the perfect plant for those seemingly impossible sites. It will grow in any soil from bone-dry sand to wet, swampy ground. The long, waxy leaves are bright green with a shiny surface. The plant transplants easily and is in danger of overuse by landscapers in the Northern Hemisphere, while it is hardly ever seen in the Southern Hemisphere.

There are many dwarf clones, ideal for ground cover in shade. Yes, they will grow in sun, but somehow it seems a waste of their talents when shade-loving plants are so hard to come by. It can take heavy frosts.

If they need pruning, do it with secateurs, removing whole stems rather than making unsightly cuts in the leaves with shears. Originates from eastern Europe and southwest Asia. Height 25 ft (8 m) x width 30 ft (10 m). ZONES 6 TO 9.

Various named forms are available from garden suppliers. The leaves of **'Castlewellan'** are covered in a white speckling-like paint splash. It has a neat, upright habit. Height x width 6 ft (2 m).

'Magnoliifolia' is so called because the leaves are like *Magnolia grandiflora*. Height x width 6 ft (2 m). **'Otto Luyken'** is probably the best clone for flowers. It has a low, spreading habit and therefore makes a good ground cover. Height 3 ft (1 m) x width 5 ft (1.5 m). **'Rotundifolia'** makes an excellent hedge with its tidy nature. Height x width 6 ft (2 m). **'Zabeliana'** is a great ground cover with a low, spreading habit. It has light green, thin leaves. Height 3 ft (1 m) x width 6 ft (2 m).

Lauro = laurus (laurel); *ceras* = cherry.

Prunus lusitanica
PORTUGAL LAUREL, LAUREL

Prunus lusitanica has dark, black-hued evergreen leaves the size of small cherry leaves, although it is hard to imagine this is so closely related to deciduous cherries. It looks more like a bay tree and is in fact used as a topiary substitute for bay in cooler climates. Fragrant white flowers arise in early summer in long, narrow racemes like a *Hebe*. The plant is happy in full sun and is quite wind tolerant, even growing in some coastal regions. It will put up with some shade, though the plant never looks as healthy. Any ground will suffice, even sand and other drought-prone soils. Attacked by thrips in a hot, dry climate. From southwest Europe. Height x width 70 ft (20 m). ZONES 7 TO 9.

Lusitanica = Lusitania, the Roman name for Portugal, its native home.

Prunus sargentii
SARGENT'S CHERRY

This forms a big, flat-topped tree needing sufficient space to show off in all its glory. For me it is worthy of a space for the spring and fall foliage, but the shiny mahogany bark and mass of single pink flowers in spring is impressive, too. So it is a plant of many seasons, having something of interest at every turn. The new spring growth is reddish bronze, opening fully to a dark green. In fall the combination of reds, gold and orange is scintillating. Introduced from Japan to Kew Gardens in 1893 by Charles Sargent (1841–1927) and later to the Arnold Arboretum where Sargent was professor. A native of Japan, Korea and Sakhalin Island, Russia. Height 70 ft (20 m) x width 50 ft (15 m). ZONES 5 TO 9.

Prunus serrulata
JAPANESE CHERRIES

While we refer to the Japanese cherries as *Prunus serrulata* many of them are likely to be of hybrid blood, but they have been cultivated and bred in Japan for over 1,000 years so it has become rather complex. The leaves are bold and beautiful with neat serrated edges. Most are big, wide-spreading trees. Although we think of them as providers of a froth of spring flowers and grow them for their tidy structure and shape, they are often overlooked when we choose trees for fall color. Yet the fall hues of orange and reds can compete with many more famous fall trees. It is a magical display lasting two to three weeks. Height x width 30 ft (10 m). ZONES 6 TO 9.

Serrulata = finely toothed.

Prunus serrulata 'Kanzan' syn P. 'Kwanzan'

Most of the flowering cherries have great fall color but this is worthy of special mention.

'Kanzan' is one of the most familiar spring blossom trees with double flowers in a harsh pink. The flowers open a strong pink and then actually intensify in color. The tree has a very upright habit. The new spring leaves have a bronzy tinge and the fall color is one of the best. Generally considered the hardiest and toughest of the flowering cherries. Height x width 30 ft (10 m). ZONES 6 TO 8.

Prunus subhirtella
HIGAN CHERRY, ROSEBUD CHERRY

This is a small tree renowned for its early pink flowers and excellent fall colors. The beautiful, soft pink, single flowers appear in early spring before the leaves. It is debatable whether this Japanese cherry is a true species and some consider it a hybrid. From Japan. Height x width 25 ft (8 m). ZONES 6 TO 9.

Sub = near or somewhat; *hirti* = hairy.

Prunus subhirtella 'Autumnalis'

This form is worth growing for its habit of flowering at unusual times. As the name suggests, it flowers in fall and often again in

Above: *Prunus lusitanica* pruned to a "mop-top" shape.

Above: *Prunus serrulata* in fall color.

spring. In some years it flowers all through winter. Semi-double white flowers with a hint of pink appear from pink buds. A good cut flower to cheer up the house in winter.

Prunus subhirtella 'Pendula'

There are different forms of this with soft pink or strong pinks and doubles, too. The tree has a genuine weeping habit with branches bending to touch the ground. Because of its tidy dome habit and superb fall color it is more likely to be grown for its shape and leaf than for its flowers.

Above: *Pyrus salicifolia* 'Pendula'

Pyrus

Rosaceae

As well as fruiting pears and ornamental, this genus embraces several other ornamental trees. They generally grow in any fertile, well-drained soil in full sun.

Pyrus = Greek for pear.

Pyrus calleryana

This is one of those plants where the straight species is rather uninteresting, but with a bit of selection work it has turned out fine. It forms a neat, conical, deciduous tree with large, glossy leaves. The wild species is quite thorny but most of the selected

cultivars are free of thorns. Many of the cultivars are used for street and avenue planting as they withstand heat and drought as well as compacted soils. It also endures wind, cold and pollution. The spring flowers are white and quite impressive, but it is grown primarily for its glossy summer leaves and brilliant fall color. Height 50 ft (15 m) x width 30 ft (10 m). ZONE 5.

'Aristocrat' forms a pyramid of glossy, wavy-margined leaves, with bronzy orange fall color. Prone to fireblight disease. Height 40 ft (12 m) x width 20 ft (6 m). **'Bradford'** has leathery, rounded, glossy leaves and lots of flowers. The fall color is splendid. Resists fireblight. However, it tends to have a weak branch structure and literally falls apart as it ages. Height 40 ft (12 m) x width 20 ft (6 m). **'Chanticleer'** has an upright habit. It flowers well, and has a good stable structure. Resists fireblight. The fall color is reddish purple. Height 40 ft (12 m) x width 20 ft (6 m).

Calleryana = fine.

Pyrus salicifolia 'Pendula'

WILLOW LEAF PEAR

This is a very good small-garden plant, clothed to the ground in silver foliage. The new leaves are covered in shiny, silky hairs creating a silver-gray dome. It has a neat, tidy, rounded shape, staying small enough to fit into virtually any garden. A bonus is the fall colors of gold in warm climates and plum red in cooler regions. Simple, white, pear-like flowers appear in spring.

It does suffer attacks of mildew and black spot, though these will be much reduced if the plant is in full sun and in a garden with good air flow. Diseases such as this tend to build up in humid, airless conditions. It is an easy plant in regards to soil and climate, and large plants can be moved in winter for an "instant garden."

The straight species is from southeast Europe, Greece and Turkey, though one hardly ever sees it in gardens, having been superseded by the pendulous form. Height 15 ft (5 m) x width 12 ft (4 m). ZONES 5 TO 9.

Salicifolia = willow or *Salix*-like leaf; *pendula* = weeping or pendulous.

Quercus

OAK
Fagaceae

You would think the mighty oak would have a family of its own, but it is in fact in the beech family, Fagaceae. The similarities between the two are the long, dangling, male catkins and the tiny, greenish, female flowers.

While most oaks are big, deciduous trees, there are many evergreen oaks, some are just shrubs and some have hard, prickly leaves like holly. Somewhat surprisingly, one of the biggest concentrations of oaks is in Mexico, home to dozens of stunning evergreen species.

Some, like the English oak, have bright, grass-green new leaves but are drab through summer and uninteresting in fall. The American deciduous oaks are far more exciting for fall colors. These deciduous oaks are hardy, coping well with very cold winters.

Most ornamental oaks prefer a good deep soil, though they will tolerate less than perfect conditions. They grow best in regions with strong seasonal changes such as hot summers and cold winters. For the most spectacular fall colors a combination of hot, sunny summers and cool, dry fall weather is ideal. While

Left: *Quercus coccinea* 'Splendens'

oaks will put up with some wind, they are not particularly wind-hardy plants. Oaks are attacked by so many different pests and diseases in different regions, but somehow manage to survive them all.

One of the attractive features of oaks is their resilience and stability. You know when you plant an oak that it is for future generations to enjoy.

Quercus = fine tree.

Quercus coccinea
SCARLET OAK

This forms a tall, upright, vigorous tree with deeply lobed, glossy leaves that turn fabulous scarlets in fall. The color lasts for weeks and is especially good when a dry fall follows a hot summer. It makes a good city tree, as it tolerates pollution. Not always easy to transplant. A native of eastern North America. Height 70 ft (20 m) x width 50 ft (15 m). ZONES 5 TO 9.

'Splendens' is a very good colored form for fall.

Coccinea = scarlet.

Left and below left: *Quercus marilandica*

Quercus marilandica
BLACK JACK OAK

A new favorite of mine, this unusual tree has triangular leaves tapered at the base and getting wider at the top, with three lobes. They are thick, glossy and shiny, and a portion of the leaves takes on rich red colors even in summer. It is usually just a large shrub or small tree in cultivation. Native to southeast U.S.A. Height 40 ft (12 m) x width 50 ft (15 m). ZONES 6 TO 9.

Marilandica = Maryland.

Quercus palustris
PIN OAK

Pin oak is a strong, upright tree native to low-lying areas, though it will tolerate dry soils and drought. So you have the option of planting in moist or dry sites. It is a shade tree very popular for its

Above: *Quercus palustris*

Right: *Quercus rubra*

fine habit and slightly weeping nature. The new stems have a reddish tinge and yellowish new growth. The glossy mid-green leaves have a very typical oak shape and superb red fall colors lasting for weeks. Native to eastern U.S.A. Height 70 ft (20 m) x width 40 ft (12 m). ZONE 4.

Palustris = of the marshes.

Quercus robur
ENGLISH OAK

One of the famous oaks, capable of living for hundreds of years and making gnarly old specimens. In England the oak populations have been decimated, with many prime specimens cut down for war efforts, such as for the old wooden naval ships and for trench props in more recent times. Bear in mind that these oaks can live for 700 years, so what happened in Napoleon's time still affects us today.

Nowadays, *Quercus robur* is noted for its rugged appearance, rather than any majesty. The dark green leaves have no fall color of note. Height 120 ft (35 m) x width 80 ft (25 m). ZONES 5 TO 8.

Robur = strength.

Quercus rubra
RED OAK

A fast-growing oak that reaches quite a size, it has reddish new growth in the spring and superb red-brown fall colors. The large, dark green leaves have a matt finish. An established plant will merit attention in any garden. A native of eastern North America. Height 80 ft (25 m) x width 70 ft (20 m). ZONE 3.

Rubra = red.

Rhododendron

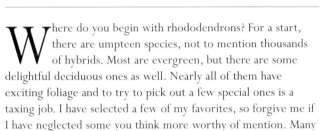

Ericaceae

Where do you begin with rhododendrons? For a start, there are umpteen species, not to mention thousands of hybrids. Most are evergreen, but there are some delightful deciduous ones as well. Nearly all of them have exciting foliage and to try to pick out a few special ones is a taxing job. I have selected a few of my favorites, so forgive me if I have neglected some you think more worthy of mention. Many of the really super leaf *Rhododendron* species are difficult to grow, such as *R. pachysanthum* and *R. pseudochrysanthum*.

Picture rhododendrons and we usually think of the many hybrids with their bold, glossy leaves creating a dense, impenetrable mound. Many of these hybrids have such good leaves it hardly matters if they flower, and yet they are blessed with some of the finest floral displays of any woody plant. Some of the best flowering varieties are also the best foliage plants, too, such as *Rhododendron* 'Crest', *R.* 'Lem's Cameo' and *R.* 'Rubicon'.

Rhodo = red or rose; *dendron* = tree.

Rhododendron arboreum 'Sir Charles Lemon'

Any plant with ferrous or rufus indumentum has almost universal appeal. In this case the underside of the leaves has the rusty appearance and the top surface is dark olive with a rough texture.

Most of the *Rhododendron arboreum* forms have wonderful foliage, but 'Sir Charles Lemon' has the best leaf of any form and is a contender for the best rhododendron leaf of all. The flowers are quite attractive, too, white with purple-brown interior spots in a dense truss.

Above: *Rhododendron arboreum* 'Sir Charles Lemon'

Above: *Rhododendron arboreum* 'Mt Victoria'

The plant forms a large shrub and ultimately becomes a tree. It is reasonably hardy, and tolerates wet or dry climates. Perhaps because they come from dry hillsides in the Himalayas, they are able to put up with hot, dry climates better than most other rhododendrons. They are resistant to many of the usual *Rhododendron* pests and diseases, making them easy-care plants. Wind resistance is another plus, though I would not choose one for a very windy site as it will only cope with rather than grow well in strong winds. Height 40 ft (12 m) x width 12 ft (4 m). ZONES 7 TO 9.

Arboreum = tree-like.

Rhododendron cinnabarinum

The beautiful, glossy, oval leaves have a sheen or luster to the top surface. The edges of the leaves seem to turn down, creating a very clean, neat aspect. This upright bush often has an open, airy look about it. The cinnabar-orange flowers account for the name and hang in clusters at the tips of the stems. These tubular flowers have a rich, strong color at the base, fading to softer orange at the trumpet end. There are numerous forms with apricot, pink, purple or red flowers. Native to the Himalayas. Height 20 ft (6 m) x width 6 ft (2 m). ZONES 8 TO 9.

Rhododendron forrestii

A fascinating *Rhododendron* with a spreading, almost prostrate habit, ideal for ground cover in garden beds. The rounded, rich dark green leaves have a rough, corrugated surface topped off with bright red, bell flowers. It prefers a cool, moist climate. The plant was collected and named after the most successful of all *Rhododendron* hunters, George Forrest (1873–1932). An intrepid Scot, he collected literally hundreds of rhododendrons in China and Tibet in the heyday of *Rhododendron* collecting in the early part of the 20th century. Native to Tibet and China. Height 8 in (20 cm) x width 5 ft (1.5 m). ZONES 7 TO 9.

'Scarlet Wonder' is a superb low-growing *R. forrestii* hybrid, easier to grow than the parent plant.

Rhododendron fortunei series

This series includes the magnificent trio **Rhododendron griffithianum, R. decorum** and **R. fortunei**, all with that typical smooth, oval leaf associated with rhododendrons. *R. decorum* and *R. fortunei* are dense, tidy bushes ideal for gardens and it is easy to keep them around 6 ft (2 m) high, while *R. griffithianum* tends to get leggy and open, though it compensates with beautiful peeling, smooth trunks. They all have flowers with an intoxicating fragrance, making them worthy of a space in our gardens regardless of how pretty the flowers or the fine foliage are. They are typical funnel-shaped flowers in tidy heads, usually in whites and creams.

Hybrids such as the Loderi series and **'Van Nes Sensation'**, **'Lalique'**, and **'Mrs A. T. de la Mare'** have this blood in them and are blessed with a powerful garden-filling scent. Try them as a cut flower and you will be impressed, as they last up to three weeks in a vase and fill the room with their heady fragrance.

This group of rhododendrons was named after Robert Fortune (1812–1880), an early plant collector sent to China in the 1840s. The plants are native to western China and the Himalayas. Height 30 ft (10 m) x width 8 ft (2.5 m). ZONES 6 TO 9.

Rhododendron macabeanum and related big-leaf rhododendrons

Rhododendron grande, R. macabeanum, R. magnificum and **R. sinograde** are all monumental foliage plants. Big-leaf rhododendrons are tricky to grow, but you will think it is worth the effort if you succeed. The giant leaves are simply delectable. "It would not matter if they never flowered," I hear people say, which is just as well as they can take a decade or more to start flowering.

To succeed with these plants you have to have a large garden, and they need a moist situation with regular rainfall throughout the year. They need shade from hot sun, especially when they are young, and are best in full sun when mature. So they are typical forest plants in that they start life in the shade and emerge into sunlight. If you can, arrange to plant them under the shade of a plant you regard as temporary, and years later when the *Rhododendron* is established you can gradually cut back the shade cover

Above: *Rhododendron magnificum*

Right: *Rhododendron pachysanthum*

until the plant has more sun. Good drainage around the roots is also required.

New leaves are covered in white indumentum, protecting the soft growth from sun and wind. This indumentum eventually rubs off the top surface but remains beneath.

The big-leaf species are the first rhododendrons to come into flower in late winter and very early spring, and so there is a danger of frosting of the flowers in many regions of the world.

The sight of these impressive giants in flower is awe-inspiring and you are somehow convinced you are paying homage to them. The flower heads are in keeping with the leaf size. *R. macabeanum* is a native of India. *R. sinograude* is native to Tibet and China; *R. grande*, Nepal and Bhutan; *R. magnificum*, Burma and Tibet. Height x width for all 30 ft (10 m). ZONE 8.

Grande = big; *sinograude* = Chinese and big; *magnificum* = magnificent.

Below: *Rhododendron williamsianum*

Rhododendron pachysanthum

This modest-sized shrub has beautiful new foliage in the spring. The leaves are covered in silver hairs. Gradually the hairs seem to rub off the topside of the leaf as it matures, but the underside remains very furry. This hardy *Rhododendron* is rather tricky to propagate and usually has to be grafted. The flowers are white to soft pink and often have a spotty throat. From Taiwan. Height 5–8 ft (1.5–2.5 m) x width 8 ft (2.5 m). ZONES 7 TO 9.

Pachysanthum = thick or dense flowers, bunched together.

Rhododendron wardii

Rhododendron wardii is a slightly open shrub with smooth-edged, shiny, oval leaves that are as perfect as any leaf can be. Species rhododendrons vary slightly in flower color and size and this one is usually topped off with beautiful lemon-yellow flowers, often with a blotch of red in the center. It is named after the second most successful *Rhododendron* hunter Frank Kingdon-Ward (1885–1958), who collected numerous fine rhododendrons, and this is probably his prize find. He wrote fascinating books about the many trials and tribulations of a plant collector. From Tibet and southwest China. Height 20 ft (6 m) x width 15 ft (5 m). ZONES 7 TO 9.

Rhododendron wardii is the parent of many fine hybrids, notably **'Crest'**.

Rhododendron williamsianum

Rhododendron williamsianum dances to a different tune. It is a miniature bush and often best grown as an epiphyte. The tiny leaves are like small coins and new leaves have a lovely bronze tinge. Tiny, pink bells grace this dainty plant in spring but it deserves a place in any collection worthy of that name just for the leaves alone. The plant is extremely slow-growing, and does best in wet climates with excellent drainage. Give it a sheltered position and a morsel of shade protecting it from hot sun.

J. C. Williams was a keen plantsman, and a sponsor of many plant-hunting expeditions to China during the early 1900s undertaken by George Forrest. It was, in fact, Ernest Wilson who discovered and introduced this fine plant from western China in 1908. J. C. Williams created the famous Caerhays Castle garden in Cornwall, England. Height 5 ft (1.5 m) x width 4 ft (1.2 m). ZONES 7 TO 9.

Rhododendron yakushimanum

A fabulous plant at any season of the year, *Rhododendron yakushimanum* has long, shiny leaves with turned-down edges and furry underneath. In fact when they first emerge in the spring the whole leaf is covered in a fuzzy indumentum. It is worth growing just for the leafy dome it forms and a bonus is the pale pink and white apple-blossom flowers in spring.

This plant is extremely wind-hardy, which is unusual for any *Rhododendron* as they usually demand a sheltered site. It was found as recently as 1934 on the windswept hillsides of Yakushima Island in Japan. Height x width 3 ft (1 m). ZONE 5.

'Kochiro Wada' is considered the best form by many gardeners.

There are now hundreds of dwarf hybrids with *Rhododendron yakushimanum* blood in them. After the Second World War it was overly used as a parent in many breeding programs. Although there are many fine hybrids to be found, not many compare to the beauty of the original species.

Yakushimanum = from Yakushima Island, Japan.

Rhus

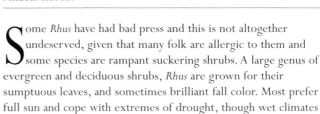

SUMACH
Anacardiaceae

Some *Rhus* have had bad press and this is not altogether undeserved, given that many folk are allergic to them and some species are rampant suckering shrubs. A large genus of evergreen and deciduous shrubs, *Rhus* are grown for their sumptuous leaves, and sometimes brilliant fall color. Most prefer full sun and cope with extremes of drought, though wet climates are no hindrance to them. They often have a quirky shape or unusual stems. No pests or diseases dare come near.

Rhus = from *rhodo* meaning red or rose (referring to the red fruits of *Cotinus*, which used to be a part of this genus).

Rhus glabra

SCARLET SUMAC, SMOOTH SUMAC
To me this plant is a treat, growing alongside American and Canadian highways, but the locals probably do not see it that way. It is especially beautiful in the fall. It suckers and is rampant, but it is still gorgeous.

The long, pinnate leaves are so appealing, I would forgive this plant any other sins. And when they color in fall in shades of peachy orange and red, you will think it is the best thing in the

Left: *Rhus succedanea*

Above: *Rhus typhina*

fluff. It is super cold-hardy. Height 15 ft (5 m) x width 20 ft (6 m). ZONE 3.

'**Laciniata**' is an unusual cut-leaf form of *Rhus typhina* with great leaves. It is still prone to suckering, unfortunately.

Typhina = like a bulrush (because the flowers resemble the bulrush or *Typha* genus).

Robinia

Fabaceae

*R*obinia is a genus of North American trees named for Jean Robin, a royal herbalist who first grew them in Paris about 1600. They are liked for their pinnate leaves, and hanging racemes of pea-like flowers. They make great specimen plants, the cultivars being especially suitable for a shrub border. Robinias are deciduous trees. Most of the species sucker prolifically and have vicious thorns.

Robinia pseudoacacia
BLACK LOCUST

This is a fast-growing, suckering, broadly columnar tree with dark green leaves and fragrant white flowers in late spring and early summer. A native of eastern U.S.A. Height 80 ft (25 m) x width 50 ft (15 m). ZONE 4.

Robinia pseudoacacia '**Frisia**'

The most popular of all the forms, 'Frisia' has fluorescent golden-green foliage all summer long, turning orange-yellow in the fall.

Above: *Robinia pseudoacacia* 'Frisia'

---

garden. You do need a big, rambling garden for this beauty, but perhaps there is a bit of waste ground where you could plant one.

The greenish yellow flowers are not startling, however, the plant is very hardy. Native to North America, including Mexico. Height x width 8 ft (2.5 m). ZONE 2.

'**Laciniata**', the beautiful divided leaf form, suckers too. Height 10 ft (3 m) x width 15 ft (5 m).

Glabra = smooth or bare (referring to the smooth stems that distinguish it from the furry-stemmed *R. typhina*).

Rhus succedanea
WAX TREE

Despite its name, the wax tree only succeeds in certain locations. It likes hot summer temperatures. For me, it is one of those rare gems providing fabulous fall color in a mild coastal climate. Plenty of plants color up well in cool inland climates, but few put on a display in warm coastal areas.

Pairs of small ash-like leaves look rather ordinary for most of the summer and then earn their keep in the fall with ravishing red leaves drawing you like a magnet. Some people are allergic to the sap. It is called the wax tree because the fruits were crushed and used for wax candles in its native China and Japan. Height x width 30 ft (10 m). ZONE 5.

Succedanea = supplying (wax).

Rhus typhina
STAG'S HORN

The sparse branches of stag's horn are covered in tactile, russet-brown fur looking just like stag's antlers. It is hard to resist touching the bare stems in winter. Luckily this plant is safe to touch, at least on the outside, though I cannot vouch for the sap of the bush should you ever prune one.

This super-hardy plant will grow in any soil, including alkaline, clay or dry banks. It prefers not to be in wet or shade but is otherwise indestructible.

Rhus typhina does sometimes sucker and needs room to roam. Sometimes it becomes rampant, and yet I have seen many a tidy single-stem specimen in English gardens looking the picture of decorum, and not even threatening the nearby border, let alone the neighbor's property.

It grows wild in eastern North America and can be seen on roadsides along the highways. The flowers are a bundle of green

It makes an ideal small-garden tree providing it is sheltered from strong winds. They love summer heat and seem to grow best in poor soil. Look out for suckers, as the plant will be grafted onto seedling rootstock. Height x width 30 ft (10 m).

Robinia pseudoacacia 'Pyramidalis'

This cultivar is free of thorns and tends to form a wide-spreading tree with lacy foliage made up of dainty pinnate leaves. The fall color is yellow to gold. White chains of fragrant pea flowers are followed by dangling pea pods. It eventually forms a tall tree, with dark, gnarled trunks. The branches are quite brittle and prone to breakage, especially when grown in lush conditions. It loves poor soil and drought and is less brittle when grown in hard conditions. It is quite tolerant of pollution and it has become naturalized in many countries. Height 50 ft (15 m) x width 10 ft (3 m).

Pseudoacacia = false acacia
(because of the similarity of the leaves to some *Acacia* species).

Sambucus

ELDERBERRY
Caprifoliaceae

Some plants we grow for beauty, others for a purpose, maybe shelter or wind hardiness, and then we grow some simply for the memories they hold. I grow elderberry because it reminds me of my childhood, wandering the country lanes in Somerset, England. Elderberry is one of the dominant plants of the region.

Sambucus is an upright shrub, eventually becoming a small tree, with rough, furrowed bark and brittle wood. The center of the branch is hollow and the wood is soft and pithy.

In a garden situation it can be given a regular light prune or an occasional drastic prune to keep it within bounds as it regenerates easily. In fact it is an easy plant in many ways. It will grow in extremely acidic or alkaline soil, very wet ground or heavy clay. If you have a wet spot in the garden where nothing seems to grow, try a *Sambucus* to give height and for the lacy foliage with an understory of *Hydrangea macrophylla*.

Although *Sambucus* are brittle, the plant will survive windy places, but in order to grow lush-looking leaves, choose a sheltered position. It is an extremely cold-hardy, deciduous shrub. The fall color is a combination of yellows and gold. The blooms are a flat layer of tiny white flowers on top of each stem. The resulting glossy black fruit are much appreciated by birds and by winemakers. In a tidy garden situation you are only likely to grow the cultivars.

Sambucus nigra

BLACK ELDER, ELDERBERRY, EUROPEAN ELDER
This forms an upright, bushy shrub. The pinnate leaves have mid-green leaflets. It bears panicles of musk-scented white flowers followed by glossy black fruit. A native of Europe, north Africa and southwest Asia. Height x width 20 ft (6 m). ZONES 6 TO 8.

Sambucus nigra 'Aurea'

'Aurea' forms a big, golden-yellow bush. It is easy to grow and easy to please in sun or light shade. Plant it as a backdrop to blue hydrangeas.

Sambucus nigra 'Guincho Purple'

I love it—the leaves start off dark green and acquire deeper purple colors as summer rolls on, and they even have red fall color. The flowers are pinkish white, contrasting with the gaudy purple foliage.

Sambucus nigra 'Laciniata'

This has dissected, ferny, feathery foliage. Try and plant it down a bank, somewhere you can look down on it to appreciate the foliage and the flowers.

Nigra = black.

Sambucus racemosa 'Plumosa Aurea'

A yellow version of *Sambucus racemosa* with serrated leaflets, it needs light shade to bring out the best colors and prevent sunburn. Height x width 10 ft (3 m). ZONES 3 TO 7.

Racemosa = flowers in racemes.

Sassafras UNIQUE

Lauraceae

This genus of generally deciduous trees offers a stately habit and glossy, aromatic foliage, with attractive fall colors. They grow in moist, well-drained, preferably acidic soil in full sun or partial shade.

Sassafras = a corruption of saxifraga, meaning stone breaker (early French settlers in North America used the bark to treat kidney and bladder stones).

Sassafras albidum, syn *S. officinale*

Sassafras albidum does not know whether it wants simple leaves, or a lobe to the left, or one lobe to the right or two lobes. So it usually ends up having all four: some of the leaves are simple, some have just one lobe and some have two. Not many plants have four different-shaped leaves all on the same tree.

Above: *Sambucus racemosa* 'Plumosa Aurea' with *Gunnera*.

Right: *Sassafras albidum* showing fall color.

Right: Sassafras albidum showing differently lobed leaves.

In a garden situation it is usually a small tree with a neat upright habit, but it is a large tree in the wild in eastern North America. It may need some training in the early years to develop a good shape. The outer branches tend to hang down in a neat, slightly pendulous, fashion. Often there is a gap between branches enhancing this effect, creating an Asian-style shrub.

Sometimes it has a tendency to sucker and at other times it is a single-trunk, non-suckering plant. Some regard it as a nuisance because of this suckering habit. It seems to depend on the source of the plant, as some clones appear to be non-suckering. One thing that everybody does agree on is that it has outstanding fall color, being one of the best plants in the world for this display. This array of brilliant golds, scarlets, reds and orange very rarely disappoints.

Plant in a sheltered site, preferably warm and sunny, to bring out the best fall colors. Grows in any soil except alkaline, and one possibility to prevent suckering is to plant it as a lawn specimen surrounded by mown grass. Your mower then deals with any emerging suckers. The tiny flowers are inconsequential. Because of its aromatic nature there are no pests and the timber is used to make insect-resistant furniture.

The roots and bark have been used for medicines, toothpaste, perfumes and soap. From eastern North America. Height 80 ft (25 m) x width 50 ft (15 m). ZONE 5.

Albidum = white or whitish.

Sassafras tzumu

This species is similar to *Sassafras albidum* but is more tender, needing a warmer climate. Like so many Chinese plants it was discovered by Augustine Henry (1857–1930) and introduced by E. H. Wilson (1876–1930). The species name is a native name. It is rare in cultivation. Height 30 ft (10 m) x width 10–15 ft (3–5 m). ZONES 8 OR 9.

Schinus

Anacardiaceae

*S*chinus make fabulous foliage trees for warmer areas. They must get enough heat to thrive, though they will take some frosts when established. Ideally they like a Mediterannean climate and are easy to grow in places near the sea. Hot, dry conditions suit them very well as they are exceptionally drought tolerant. The thick, waxy leaves resist wind and hot sun. Any well-drained soil is acceptable and it is almost a case of poor soil suiting them best. *Schinus* hate being shifted and should be grown in pots and left alone once planted. Transplanting at a later date rarely succeeds, so choose your site carefully.

They are most often seen as specimen trees and sometimes used as street trees. In some warm-climate areas (such as parts of California and Florida) *Schinus* have become invasive so check before you plant one.

Schinus molle
PEPPER TREE, PERUVIAN MASTIC
The more familiar of this South American genus comes from Peru. It usually has a small, rounded shape, with weeping foliage creating a very ornate tree. The tree has a light, airy feel about it and is often sparse enough to see through. The leaves have a central vein and shiny, sharp, pointed, thin leaflets. They would need to be thick and waxy to cope with drought, wind and hot sun. Tiny, insignificant flowers are followed by pepper-sized berries, giving the name pepper tree, though this is a much-overused common name and usually leads to confusion. The leaves have a pleasant smell if you brush past them. The tree makes an ideal lawn specimen tree and looks good in isolation rather than mixed in with other shrubs. It is a great shade tree in which to hang your hammock. The trunks have an old, gnarly appearance. A native of Mexico, Brazil, Bolivia, Chile, northern Argentina, Paraguay and Uruguay. Height 30–80 ft (10–25 m) x width 10–15 ft (3–5 m). ZONE 9.

Schinus = the Mastic tree, a type of *Pistacia*; *molle* = pliable or graceful.

Schinus terebinthifolius
BRAZILIAN PEPPER TREE, CHRISTMASBERRY TREE
This is usually seen as a small evergreen tree, though it has the potential to get very big. It tolerates wind but needs summer heat to prosper. The pinnate leaves are hard and waxy and each leaflet is much bigger than on *Schinus molle*. While the leaves are probably more impressive than those of *S. molle*, the overall appearance is not as graceful. Panicles of tiny white flowers are inconsequential and the resulting seeds can lead to a crop of nuisance plants. Originates from Venezuela to Argentina and southern Brazil. Height 15–22 ft (5–7 m) x width 10–15 ft (3–5 m). ZONE 9.

Terebinthifolius = foliage like a terebinth tree, *Pistacia terebinthus*.

Above: *Schinus molle*

Sciadopitys

Sciadopitys verticillata
UMBRELLA PINE
Taxodiaceae

*U*mbrella pine is a unique conifer from Japan. Somehow it looks Japanese, seemingly manicured to look the way it does. The thick, waxy leaves are arranged in whorls or circles, and look like the spokes of an umbrella, hence its common name.

In a garden it is very slow-growing, and makes an ideal focal point in a rockery or as a garden statement. It has a very neat pyramid shape, growing slowly to 6 ft (2 m) in 10 years.

Shiny red bark is revealed as the older layers peel away. However, one rarely sees the bark or trunks on this fine evergreen shrub as they are so slow-growing and the canopy is dense enough to hide the interior. It is very cold-hardy but grows well in warmer areas, too. It is generally happy in sun or shade, but really needs some isolation to show it off, which inevitably means growing it in the sun. It handles hot, dry summers and yet grows easily in wet, heavy rain districts. It is fairly tough in windy climates and seems untouched by pests and

Above: *Sciadopitys verticillata*

diseases. If you are an impatient gardener, large specimens can be moved if carefully root pruned in the winter. Any acidic or neutral soil will do, as long as the drainage is reasonable. Height 30–70 ft (10–20 m) x width 20–25 ft (6–8 m). ZONES 5 TO 9.

Sciadopitys = from Greek "skias," meaning parasol and "pitys," meaning fir tree; *verticillata* = whorls forming a ring (because the leaves are in whorls around the stem).

Sorbaria

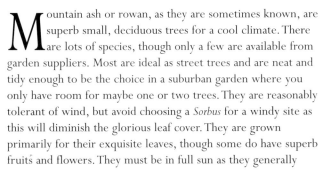

Sorbaria sorbifolia
URAL FALSE SPIREA
Rosaceae

This is a wonderful foliage plant with gorgeous plumes of white, fluffy flowers like candyfloss. Plant in full sun to get the maximum number of flowers because it is a highlight plant with its frothy summer blooms. It is a three-season show plant with neat spring and summer foliage, then summer blossoms, and finally in fall the leaves can turn to purple and bronzy colors. The compound ash-like leaves have beautiful corrugations, making them all the more appealing.

The plant needs room as it is slightly invasive, being a multi-stemmed shrub sending up suckers to gain more ground. It is not encroaching to the extent of pushing you out of house and home, but it does quietly acquire more territory. Dark, cane-like

stems seem to be more vigorous when they have come from below ground. The plant can be pruned drastically, even to ground level, to rejuvenate it.

It is not fussy about soil, being equally at ease with acidic or alkaline, clay or sandy soils. Okay in dry and hot climates as well as wet, moist, mild climates. It is an ideal shrub for planting near waterways and ponds, the body of water showing off the ferny foliage to good effect. From northern Asia and Japan. Height 6 ft (2 m) x width 10 ft (3 m). ZONE 5.

Sorbaria = leaf like a *Sorbus* or mountain ash.

Sorbus

MOUNTAIN ASH, ROWAN
Rosaceae

Mountain ash or rowan, as they are sometimes known, are superb small, deciduous trees for a cool climate. There are lots of species, though only a few are available from garden suppliers. Most are ideal as street trees and are neat and tidy enough to be the choice in a suburban garden where you only have room for maybe one or two trees. They are reasonably tolerant of wind, but avoid choosing a *Sorbus* for a windy site as this will diminish the glorious leaf cover. They are grown primarily for their exquisite leaves, though some do have superb fruits and flowers. They must be in full sun as they generally

Right: *Sorbaria sorbifolia*

Left: *Sorbus aria*

prefer their own space, and of course they look better when not crowded by other trees. They are not fussy about soil and grow on heavy clay as well as light soil, as long as it is acidic to neutral. *Sorbus aucuparia* is especially resentful of lime. *Sorbus* are equally happy in high rainfall or dry regions. It is essential they get a period of winter cold; they are not happy in warm climates where there is no winter chill.

Flowers appear on most species in early summer and usually consist of umbels of pretty creamy white blooms. The resulting berries are usually far more of a crowd-pleaser, varying from white to pink through to orange, yellows and reds.

Many species are used as avenue trees for their neat pompom habit. They can be transplanted at any age and size and are easy to establish if your climate is suitable.

Sorbus do seem prone to a host of pests and diseases ranging from stem borer and canker problems to fireblight and pear slug.

Sorbus = Latin for service tree chosen by Pliny
(derived from *sorbum*, the fruit of *S. domestica*).

Sorbus alnifolia
KOREAN MOUNTAIN ASH

This *sorbus* has great possibilities as a street or campus tree. The lovely leaves are somewhat like *Alnus glutinosa*, and have the same serrated edge but a more pronounced point or drip-tip. The fall color is bright yellow through to orange and scarlet, highlighting the clusters of pink to red berries. These berries, with a luster like grapes, are more exciting than the clusters of white flowers in late spring.

The plant seems to be resistant to fireblight and other *Sorbus* problems. It tolerates poor soil but is not happy with city pollution. A native of Korea and east Asia. Height 70 ft (20 m) x width 25 ft (8 m). ZONES 5 TO 8.

The Hillier cultivar **'Skyline'** is grown for its columnar, upright habit and yellow fall color. Height 40 ft (12 m) x width 15 ft (5 m). The cultivar **'Redbird'** has persistent rose red berries. Height 40 ft (12 m) x width 25 ft (18m).

Alnifolia = like *Alnus glutinosa* (the leaves are similar).

Sorbus aria
WHITEBEAM

The big, white, handkerchief-like leaves are far more robust than they first appear. The new leaves are covered in silver hairs, protecting them from strong winds and cold. They are bright green above and white beneath when mature. It has surprisingly good fall color in orange and golds and wonderful clusters of deep red berries.

This sorbus is happy in acidic or alkaline soil and, like the mountain ash, will grow in tough industrial sites. Native to Britain and Europe. Height 30–80 ft (10–25 m) x width 30 ft (10 m). ZONES 6 TO 8.

Aria = prop or beam.

Sorbus aucuparia
MOUNTAIN ASH, ROWAN

Mountain ash has a neat habit and round, mop-top shape. It looks like the shape children draw for trees. It has ash-like leaves, as you would expect, but they are more exciting than most with a pronounced valley between the arching leaflets. The clusters of white flowers are followed by a profusion of orange to red berries in late summer and fall. It is worth growing for the berries alone as they stay for a long time if the birds leave them alone. The fall color is not outstanding.

It tolerates poor and extremely acidic soil but is not happy with lime. It is often grown in industrial sites or reclaimed land where other trees would succumb to the harsh conditions. Native to Europe and Asia. Height 50 ft (15 m) x width 22 ft (7 m). ZONES 4 TO 8.

There are some excellent Dutch and English hybrids that are laden with berries. In particular, look out for **'Cardinal Royal'**, with bright red fruits. Height 30 ft (10 m) x width 10–15 ft (3–5 m). **'Sheerwater Seedling'** has an upright habit and orangey red fruits. Height 30 ft (10 m) x width 10–15 ft (3–5 m). **'Xanthocarpa'** has yellow fruit. Height 30 ft (10 m) x width 20 ft (6 m).

Aucuparia = useful for birds.

Sorbus commixta, syn S. discolor

With its compact nature this forms a small, upright tree ideal for small gardens. The very attractive and neat pinnate leaves with pointy leaflets often open with a bronzy hue, are shiny green through summer and turn to yellows, reds and purples in the fall. Clusters of bright red, shiny berries complete the picture. From Japan and Korea. Height 30 ft (10 m) x width 22 ft (7 m). ZONES 6 TO 8.

'Embley' is a form with consistently good red fall color.

Commixta = mixed together or mingled.

Sorbus decora

SHOWY MOUNTAIN ASH

Sorbus decora forms a large shrub or small tree with elegant pinnate leaves—each leaflet arching up and over to create a waved effect. These serrated-edged leaves are a bluish green through the summer, turning hot colors in the fall. The compact dense heads of fine, white, *Spiraea*-like flowers are followed by bright orange-red berries. This hardy cold-climate plant is not easy to grow in warmer zones. Found naturally from Newfoundland south into the northeastern U.S.A. Height 25 ft (8 m) x width 15 ft (5 m). ZONES 3 TO 8.

Decora = decorative.

Sorbus domestica

SERVICE TREE

Sorbus domestica forms a tall tree with rough, scaly bark. This beautiful tree is possibly too big for most gardens, but if you have room you will appreciate the clean pinnate leaves that turn yellow and red in the fall. The heads of white flowers are bigger than most others and are very imposing. The resulting fruits, looking like small pears, are eaten by the brave when half rotted. A native of central and southern Europe and north Africa. Height 70 ft (20 m) x width 40 ft (12 m). ZONES 6 TO 8.

Domestica = domesticated (a reference to the fruit being eaten).

Sorbus hupehensis

HUBEI MOUNTAIN ASH

A small upright tree with dark mahogany trunks and branches,

Right: *Sorbus aucuparia* 'Xanthocarpa'

Sorbus hupehensis has elegant pinnate leaves that are a blue-gray color and reminiscent of *Indigofera decora*. They surprise us by turning red in the fall. The creamy white berries take on a pinkish tinge about this time. From Hubei in China and the species name is derived from this region. Collected by E. H. Wilson (1876–1930) in 1910. Height x width 25 ft (8 m). ZONES 6 TO 8.

Sorbus x kewensis (S. pohuashanensis x S. aucuparia)

For years this was thought to be straight *Sorbus pohuashanensis*, but is now recognized as a hybrid and a very valuable one too for the mass of red fruits in fall. The branches sometimes bend with the weight of fruit. It has magnificent pinnate leaves up to 12 in (30 cm) long. Raised at Kew Gardens in England. Height x width 25 ft (8 m). ZONES 6 TO 8.

Sorbus pohuashanensis

This forms an upright tree, spreading with age. The dark green, pinnate leaves are gray and hairy beneath. The white spring flowers lead to heavy crops of red berries and are considered by connoisseurs the best of all the fruiting *Sorbus*. From North China, Pouashan is a regional name. Height 70 ft (20 m) x width 25 ft (8 m). ZONES 6 TO 8.

Sorbus sargentiana

A wide-spreading, cherry-sized tree with very long leaves up to 14 in (35 cm) long. The pinnate leaves turn blazing orange-reds in fall. Clusters of small orange-colored fruits merge into the background of the fall colors. Curiously, in winter the dormant buds are sticky. Discovered in western China by E. H. Wilson in 1907 and named for Charles Sargent (1841–1927) of Boston's Arnold Arboretum. Height x width 30 ft (10 m). ZONES 5 TO 7.

Sorbus thibetica

This forms a mopheaded tree with fabulous large, rounded leaves, green above and covered in tactile white felt beneath. It is worth growing for the simple leaves, contrasting with the usual ash-like leaves of most *Sorbus*. A native of southwest China and the Himalayas. The species name is from the old spelling of Tibet. Height 70 ft (20 m) x width 50 ft (15 m). ZONES 5 TO 7.

The form 'John Mitchell', with broadly rounded leaves, is considered the one to own. Height 50 ft (15 m) x width 30 ft (10 m).

Tetracentron

Tetracentron sinense

Tetracentraceae

Now here is an exotic-sounding name, laden with images of far-flung, mist-covered mountains in deepest western China. And it was in these hills that it was first discovered by Augustine Henry (1857–1930) and introduced to cultivation by Ernest Wilson (1876–1930). What a phenomenal combination these two were. Henry, an amateur botanist based in China sent

Above: *Tetracentron sinense*

Above: *Tetracentron sinense* showing the "drip-tip" leaves.

huge numbers of pressed plants to Kew Gardens in London. Wilson then tapped into Henry's knowledge of the country and gathered plants for the famous Veitch Nursery and later for the Arnold Arboretum in Boston.

This large, upright shrub or small tree is actually one of the world's largest trees in its wild state, though precious few remain because of deforestation. If you are lucky enough to own or purchase one, however, it is only going to be a large shrub in your lifetime.

The long, pointed drip-tip indicates that the plant grows in a very wet climate; the narrow, pointed leaf sheds water much faster than other shapes, preventing it from staying too wet for too long. It is deciduous, and the new spring foliage is a bronzy green, with a prominent red petiole and pretty serrated edges to each leaf. The base of each leaf is heart-shaped, and then it tapers down to the drip-tip. The tiny yellow flowers on a long thin pendulous catkin are easily missed.

Tetracentron sinense is best grown in a sheltered garden or woodland setting in sun or part shade. It prefers acidic soil and conditions which suit rhododendrons, though it will grow in neutral or limestone soil. It has no pests or diseases, and is quite cold-hardy.

The plant has been included with the *Magnolia* family at times but it now enjoys a family of its own. So it is not only rare but all alone in the plant world.

Grow it for the leaf shape and the tidy presentation of the leaves on the stems. Height 56–100 ft (17–30 m) x width 30 ft (10 m). ZONE 6.

Tetra = four; *centron* = a spur
(from the four spur-like appendages on the fruit); *sinense* = Chinese.

Tetrapanax

Tetrapanax papyrifer
RICE PAPER PLANT
Araliaceae

The huge leaves are straight out of a fairy tale. It is easy to imagine a sprite perched on one of these enormous leaves bringing a touch of the tropics right into your garden.

The leaves are covered in felty, cream hairs, especially on the stout, club-like stems and underside of the leaves. Creamy white flowers arise in large panicles in late spring to complete the picture.

It is best planted in full sun because in part shade the strong stems aim toward the sun, spoiling the shape of the plant by growing sideways. It is happy in sand, clay, dry and shade. Dry and heavy soils restrict the growth and reduce the plant's suckering ability. Frost will blacken the leaves and defoliate it, but if it is established it will come away again in the spring.

Left: *Tetrapanax papyrifer*

Right: *Thuja occidentalis* 'Pyramidalis' with a hedge of *Corokia cotoneaster* behind.

Probably better for a cool climate garden trying to look tropical rather than in a warmer, frost-free climate where it tends to take over. If you are worried about the suckers, then grow it in a restricted space such as a patio or raised bed. Not only will the plant be contained, but the whole bush will be smaller and more elegant. From southern China and Taiwan. Height x width 15 ft (5 m). ZONE 6.

Tetra = four; *panax* = ginseng; *papyrifer* = paper-making.

Thuja

Cupressaceae

Thujas have delightfully scented, soft, fan-like foliage. Just run your hand through the bush and the tangy scent wafts all around you.

Full sun is best and they are fine in cold or warm climates. They are not the best plants in windy places, but can be used for hedges and screens in less windy regions. They transplant easily and are not inclined to die out, which is essential for a hedge, as is the ability to put up with clipping. Some even have such a tidy habit they form a perfect hedge or screen without any pruning. If you need a replacement for that fast-growing, tired old hedge, then *Thuja* should be near the top of your list. Grow them in any reasonable, and even unreasonable, soil. We have some thujas growing in a stony parking lot with virtually no soil and they are a picture of health.

Thuja was a name given by the Greek botanist Theophrastus to a Moroccan tree now called tetraclinus. These were treasured resin-bearing trees. Some say the word is from "thyon," meaning sacrifice, as the resin was used as incense in Eastern sacrifices. It was also known as "Arbor-vitae," the tree of life, because the early seeds sent from Canada to France gained the name L'arb de Vie, referring to the lush evergreen nature of the plant.

Thuja occidentalis

AMERICAN ARBORVITAE, EASTERN ARBORVITAE, WHITE CEDAR

In its natural state this is a hardy column-like tree in eastern North America, where it is often found growing in swampy ground, though I would not recommend you plant it in such boggy soil. It often looks thin and jaded if grown in shade or dry places, and even temporary drought will do this. It has small, yellowish green leaves, pale or grayish beneath. Attractive red-brown, peeling bark is an additional feature. Height 30–60 ft (10–18 m) x width 10–15 ft (3–5 m). ZONES 2 TO 9.

There are many varieties of leaf form and color including the two below.

Occidentalis = Western.

Thuja occidentalis 'Pyramidalis', syn 'Fastigiata'

A perfect column-shaped bush, ideal for formal and informal situations. In ones and twos, they are the perfect statement or sentinel plant. Alternatively, use them in groups to add another dimension to your garden. It makes a fantastic garden hedge as it

Above: *Thuja occidentalis* 'Rheingold', the golden bush at left, with *Calluna* cultivars.

is such a perfect shape you will never need to trim or clip. Lush, dark green foliage is healthy all year except for the occasional attack of caterpillars. Height 12 ft (4 m) x width 3 ft (1 m).

Thuja occidentalis 'Rheingold'

One of the best golden conifers in the world and ideal for a position by steps or at a garden junction. It is one of those plants you need to lead you around corners. It forms a really dense pyramid of bright gold in summer and a bronzy hue in winter. It can be clipped if necessary. Height x width 3–6 ft (1–2 m).

Above: *Thuja plicata* (center).

Thuja plicata
WESTERN RED CEDAR

This tree likes a moist climate and is a very tough plant. It tolerates extremes of soil including chalk and clay and, more remarkably, extremely wet climates, even hot and wet regions. The tree seems free of disease and even the timber resists decay and pests. From western North America. Height 70–120 ft (20–35 m) x width 20–35 ft (6–11 m). ZONES 6 TO 9.

'Atrovirens' is an especially rich green form. Height 70 ft (20 m) x width 20 ft (6 m). **'Rogersii'** is a neat, conical bush in rich metallic golds and bronze. It stays very compact. Height x width 3 ft (1 m). **'Stoneham Gold'** is a slow-growing, gold conifer, ideal for colder regions where it produces wonderful orange-gold winter color, and is bright yellow in spring and summer. Best planted in full sun to get the full effect. It forms a dense, upright, conical bush that retains its modest proportions. Height x width 6 ft (2 m).

Plicata = folded together or double.

Tilia

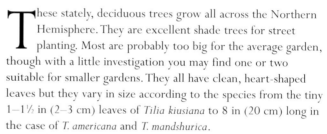

LIME, LINDEN TREE
Tiliaceae

These stately, deciduous trees grow all across the Northern Hemisphere. They are excellent shade trees for street planting. Most are probably too big for the average garden, though with a little investigation you may find one or two suitable for smaller gardens. They all have clean, heart-shaped leaves but they vary in size according to the species from the tiny 1–1½ in (2–3 cm) leaves of *Tilia kiusiana* to 8 in (20 cm) long in the case of *T. americana* and *T. mandshurica*.

Traditionally *Tilia* have been used for shade trees in the squares of European cities, though some have drawbacks. Aphids attacking the trees have the annoying habit of secreting a sticky honeydew, which drips onto cars and benches beneath the trees. It is essential to select the species resistant to attack from aphids, such as *T.* x *euchlora*. Some tilias have a tendency to throw up a mass of suckers around the base of the tree, spoiling the clean trunk effect we desire from large street trees. Again, choose the right species to have trees with clean trunks for planting. *T.* x *europaea* and *T. platyphyllos* are the worst culprits for having aphids and for suckering so choose some other species to avoid these problems. Limes have long been a favorite of woodworkers, as the pale, easily-worked timber is ideal for small, hard items such as clogs and statues.

Tilias like plenty of water, and a good, deep soil though they are not fussy about acidity or alkalinity. They are very hardy, coping with continental climates with extremely hot summers and equally crippling cold winters. A breezy climate is fine, but they do not like strong winds. They are often grown from seed; good forms need to be grown from layers, cuttings or by grafting onto a rootstock.

If you find yourself having lunch under a lime, try a leaf in your sandwiches. The edible leaves make a change from lettuce.

Most tilias have fragrant, creamy, cup-shaped flowers in summer. Each flower has a long, whitish bract that later acts as a wing to disperse the seeds. The scented flowers are a narcotic to bees and *Tilia tomentosa* is even toxic to them.

Tilia = an old Roman name for the tree.

Above: *Tilia americana* with *Liquidambar styraciflua*.

Tilia americana
AMERICAN LINDEN, BASSWOOD

The big, bold, coarsely toothed leaves are dark matt green above and glossy below. It becomes a broad-crowned tree in time. Yellowish green flowers arise in summer. Originates in central and eastern North America. Height 80 ft (25 m) x width 50 ft (15 m). ZONES 3 TO 9.

Americana = from America.

Tilia x euchlora
CRIMEAN LINDEN

A hybrid of doubtful origin, this makes a superb tree for street planting. Should be the first choice for city planting as no aphids attack it and therefore no honeydew occurs. Big, bright, shiny green leaves and a slightly pendulous habit add up to a magnificent tree. Height 70 ft (20 m) x width 50 ft (15 m). ZONES 3 TO 8.

Euchlora = dark green.

Tilia x europaea
EUROPEAN LINDEN

This is common in big cities in the Northern Hemisphere. It has dark green leaves, paler beneath. Cymes of pale yellow flowers arise in midsummer. The tree suffers from aphids and the suckering habit. Height 120 ft (35 m) x width 50 ft (15 m). ZONES 4 TO 8.

Europaea = from Europe.

Tilia henryana

A rare tree, slow-growing and therefore suited to smaller gardens. It has a unique and unforgettable leaf pattern. The bristly edged leaves are reminiscent of a Venus fly trap. The new foliage has a distinct bronzy tinge, adding to the appeal of this fine plant. The flowers are creamy white. It was found in central China by Augustine Henry in 1888 and introduced to Britain by E. H. Wilson in 1901. Height x width 80 ft (25 m). ZONES 6 TO 9.

Tilia kiusiana

Here is a *Tilia* that does not look like a *Tilia*. In fact it looks more like a pear tree, with its slender stems and small, ovate leaves. A native of Japan. Height 15 ft (5 m) x width 10 ft (3 m). ZONE 6.

Kiusiana = from Kyushu Island.

Tilia mandshurica

This is a wonderful tree with big, bold leaves like a grape, on slightly arching, pendulous stems. The heart-shaped leaves have large saw-tooth serrations and are up to 12 in (30 cm) long. They are smooth, dark green above and gray and slightly felty beneath. Obviously a plant for a sheltered site with such large leaves. Any soil will suffice.

The plant originates from northeast Asia, and, like so many plants from this region, it is often damaged by late frosts. Northeast China, Manchuria and Korea have very cold winters followed by a slow, gradual spring with no retreats and so the plants only have warmer weather ahead of them. In mild regions they are tempted into early growth, only to be damaged by a late frost. Height x width 15–25 ft (5–8 m). ZONE 5.

Mandshurica = Manchuria.

Tilia x moltkei (*T. americana* x *T. tomentosa*)

The most desirable of all the large lime trees. This noble tree has dense, dark green leaves with a slightly weeping outer canopy adding considerably to the appeal. It does not grow too fast or too big. Named after a German general who planted the first specimen at Späths Nursery in Berlin. Height 50 ft (15 m) x width 30 ft (10 m). ZONE 4.

Above: *Tilia henryana*

Tilia oliveri

An attractive tree with heart-shaped leaves, dark green above and silvery beneath. Free from aphids. Another Chinese plant in the Henry and Wilson team of introductions and named after Daniel Oliver, keeper of the herbarium at Kew Gardens during the time Augustine Henry was sending his vast collection of pressed specimens back home. Height 40 ft (12 m) x width 20 ft (6 m). ZONE 6.

Tilia tomentosa
EUROPEAN WHITE LINDEN, SILVER LIME

This is a beautiful big tree with a nice clean, broadly columnar outline and smooth-topped leaves, felted white below. In a breeze these white faces shimmer and thus give the name silver lime. The scented flowers are toxic to bees. From southern and eastern Europe and southwest Asia. Height 100 ft (30 m) x width 70 ft (20 m). ZONES 6 TO 9.

The clone **'Sterling'** is more resistant to any pests. Height 50 ft (15 m) x width 25 ft (8 m).

Tomentosa = hairy.

Toona

Toona sinensis, syn Cedrela sinensis
TOON TREE
Meliaceae

*T*oona sinensis forms a huge, fast-growing tree with smooth brown trunks and glorious ash-like leaves up to 24 in (60 cm) long. These enormous, pinnate leaves are like a huge tropical palm, and are bronze-red when young, turning yellow in fall. The tree has some unusual features. The leaves are edible and used in Chinese cooking. The bark contains an intoxicant as I found to my cost when pruning our tree. The pungent odor had me literally swooning and seeing stars. It seems the sap has potential for medicinal purposes—I am not surprised, it could be used as an anesthetic. With such toxins no pests dare attack it. On older trees the bark is peeling and flaky, though it is smooth on younger plants.

Tolerant of inland heat and cold, it seems to prefer a harsh, continental-style climate and is not very comfortable in soft, warm, moist conditions. It can be used as a park tree or a very tall street tree in big cities, coping well with pollution. Windy sites are less favorable, as the large, palm-like leaves get battered, so choose inland, windless sites if possible. It does sometimes send up suckers and this is far more likely if planted on a slope as the searching roots find light and send up another stem. Any soil seems to please it, although it suckers more in light soil. It transplants easily from suckers in winter if you want to make a new tree.

The pungent timber is insect-resistant and a related species, *Toona odorata*, is used for making cigar boxes.

The honey-scented, white flowers that arise in big, terminal panicles are an added bonus. Some clones have amazing spring foliage. Native to China. Height 50 ft (15 m) x width 30 ft (10 m). ZONES 6 TO 9.

Toona = a local name.

Toona sinensis 'Flamingo'

This Australian selection has stunning, eye-catching, bright-pink new growth in the spring. 'Flamingo' does not grow very tall and forms a suckering shrub with multiple stems. The pink new leaves turn cream and then green in midsummer. If the plant gets ragged or the spring color is not as spectacular as before, then a hard

Left: *Toona sinensis* 'Flamingo'

Above: *Trochodendron aralioides* with hydrangeas.

The clusters of strange, greenish yellow flowers are followed by green fruits. The tiny, plate-like flowers are similar to photos one sees of a splash of milk or water. The outer edge is surrounded by a ring of stamens, and there are no petals. It grows successfully in full sun or in shade and suffers no pests or diseases even when grown in dense shade. It tolerates wet climates and wettish soil, but not drought or alkaline soil. It is tough and hardy, having survived some of the coldest winters in the UK, and yet is equally at home in warmer climates. The plant was first discovered in the hills of Japan by Baron Philipp von Siebold in 1894 and later found also in the mountains of Korea and Taiwan. Height 30 ft (10 m) x width 25 ft (8 m). ZONE 6.

Trochodendron = wheel tree (for the way the stamens radiate like the spokes of a wheel); *aralioides* = like an *Aralia*.

Tsuga

HEMLOCK
Pinaceae

*T*suga is a genus of tall, elegant, evergreen conifers and one of the many link plants between China, Japan and America. Initially they are upright, conical trees and as the tree becomes more spreading the greenery tumbles and droops in pleasing fashion. We gardeners find it hard to resist any plant with a hint of pendulous foliage. The narrow, dark green leaves are not unlike a lighter version of yew trees with silver bands underneath. The spring combination of soft grass green and the darker older leaves is the most exciting phase of the year. Young plants are remarkably shade tolerant but the trees really need some isolation to show off their finery. They have small cones hanging beneath the branches and both sexes are found on the same tree. *Tsuga* like a cool, moist climate with well-drained soils, preferring neutral to acidic, though they will tolerate some alkalinity.

Tsuga = a Japanese name.

pruning close to ground level will encourage vigorous new growth with strong color.

The suckering habit can be a nuisance, though it is fairly easy to contain. It seems to need a reasonably cold winter climate or a distinct change of season. It hates the wind, so choose a sheltered site. Because of the strong coloration it is not an easy plant to blend in the garden. Height x width 9 ft (3 m). ZONE 6.

Trochodendron

Trochodendron aralioides
WHEEL TREE
Trochodendraceae

*H*ere is a plant that deserves much greater recognition and popularity. Although it looks like an *Aralia*, it is actually a very lonely plant, being the only one in the genus and in a plant family all of its own. Even the name conjures up exotic images. It sounds more like a dinosaur than a plant.

This large shrub fits easily into most gardens, being a slow-growing evergreen. It deserves a place in any collection by virtue of the magnificent hand-shaped leaves. Each leaf is made up of five glossy leaflets in olive green, looking almost like plastic, with neat scalloped edges. The new spring growth is bright green and contrasts wonderfully with the older, darker foliage. Typically, it is a multi-trunked bush, 9 ft (3 m) high and wide (though it achieves a larger size in the wild) and it blends well with rhododendrons. Somehow it has a woodland garden look to it, though it does not have to be in that setting.

The branches are highly sought after by florists for the unique leaf patterns. You will have to be patient if you grow a plant for floral art work because the growth rate is slow. It might pay to plant two of them; one to enjoy and one to cut for the vase.

Tsuga canadensis
EASTERN HEMLOCK, CANADA HEMLOCK
Tsuga canadensis forms a large, often multi-trunked tree with finely toothed, mid-green leaves. It has a unique structure with upside

Above: *Tsuga canadensis* 'Pendula'

Above and top: *Tsuga heterophylla*

down leaves sitting in a linear fashion on the topside of the twigs between the more obvious horizontal leaves. It has pretty little terminal cones with scales like roofing shingles. Although the trees grow naturally on acidic soils, this species does cope with alkaline soils better than most. The plant grows naturally from Canada down through the Appalachians. Height 80 ft (25 m) x width 30 ft (10 m). ZONES 4 TO 8.

There are numerous fine cultivars for gardens of all sizes and persuasions. **'Aurea'** is a slow-growing form with golden yellow new leaves gradually greening in the summer. Height 25 ft (8 m)

x width 12 ft (4 m). **'Cole'** (syn **'Cole's Prostrate'**) is a ground-hugging plant ideal for rockeries. Height 12 in (30 cm) x width 3 ft (1 m). **'Jeddeloh'** is a peculiar form with a crab-like shape, being lower in the center with branches arching out and over, and bright green leaves. Height 5 ft (1.5 m) x width 6 ft (2 m). **'Pendula'** (Sargent's weeping hemlock) is a big, dense mound of a plant with more obvious pendulous growth. Height 12 ft (4 m) x width 25 ft (8 m).

Canadensis = from Canada.

Tsuga caroliniana
CAROLINE HEMLOCK

This species has larger, longer, shinier leaves and they seem to go in every direction rather than in a flat plane like *Tsuga canadensis*. It is a more compact tree and useful for city planting, as it copes with pollution. It also handles wind and dry conditions far better than most of the genus. It is hardy enough to be used for hedges. It grows naturally in a more restricted range in the southern part of the Appalachians, from Virginia to Georgia. Height 50–70 ft (15–20 m) x width 25 ft (8 m). ZONES 5 TO 7.

Caroliniana = from Carolina.

Tsuga chinensis
CHINESE HEMLOCK

Tsuga chinensis forms a domed or rounded-top small tree with large, glossy, dark green leaves. It tolerates lime and poor soils. It was discovered in central China by Paul Farges (1844–1912) and introduced by E. H. Wilson in 1903. Height 140 ft (45 m) x width 80–100 ft (25–30 m). ZONES 5 TO 9.

Chinensis = from China.

Tsuga diversifolia
NORTHERN JAPANESE HEMLOCK

This is regarded by many as the most frost-hardy and wind tolerant of all the species. It forms a relatively small, rounded tree with horizontal branches and dark green, glossy leaves. The shoots are hairy or downy. The plant was collected in Japan by John Gould Veitch (1839–1870) in 1861. Height 50 ft (15 m) x width 25 ft (8 m). ZONES 6 TO 8.

Diversifolia = diverse or variable foliage.

Tsuga heterophylla
WESTERN HEMLOCK

An attractive, tall, fast-growing tree, with the outer branches drooping. The long, shiny dark green leaves have two white bands on the underside. It needs a moist climate and acidic soil to perform well, along with shelter from winds. It is very shade tolerant. A native of North America, from Alaska to California, the plant was discovered by David Douglas in 1826 and introduced to Europe by John Jeffrey in 1851. Height 70–130 ft (20–40 m) x width 20–30 ft (6–10 m). ZONES 6 TO 8.

Heterophylla = variable leaves.

Tsuga sieboldii
SOUTHERN JAPANESE HEMLOCK

The southern Japanese version has horizontal branches and glossy green leaves with white stripes beneath. The ends of the branches fold over, creating a lively tree worthy of a space in gardens because it is slow-growing. It needs a moister, milder climate than most. The plant was named after Philipp von Siebold, a Dutch eye surgeon and botanist who lived in Japan for many years. Height 50 ft (15 m) x width 25 ft (8 m). ZONES 6 TO 8.

Ulmus

ELM
Ulmaceae

Elms are tough plants, coping with very wet or dusty, dry climates, and extremes of acidity or alkalinity. Wind is no threat and neither is city pollution. It has just one drawback—the deadly Dutch Elm disease, which devastated the elms of Europe and America in the 1970s.

The English elm was the dominant tree in my native Somerset, and now none are left because of the disease. Dutch elm disease attacks only adult plants, but as soon as the juveniles grow big, they die. Part of the reason they all succumbed is they were grown from suckers, rather than seeds. Being all the same clone, they were all equally prone to the disease. This is a good lesson about plant diversity and how we need genetic variation instead of everybody growing the same clone.

Elms have rough, textured leaves with serrated or toothed edges. The small flowers without petals turn into round, winged seeds in pale green to white, later changing to brown. Most trees have attractive, furrowed trunks. Some species have a thicket of stems at the base of the trunk while others will send up suckers further out from the roots.

Ulmus glabra
WYCH ELM, DUTCH ELM
The wych elm's big, hairy, dark green leaves are rough and bristly to touch. Prone to Dutch elm disease. From Europe and south-west Asia. Height 120–130 ft (35–40 m) x width 80 ft (25 m). ZONE 5. For small gardens the best choice is the weeping version, **'Horizontalis**, which makes a round dome of foliage. Height x width 15–20 ft (5–6 m).

Glabra = smooth.

Ulmus minor
EUROPEAN FIELD ELM, SMOOTH-LEAF ELM
This forms a broadly columnar tree with arching branches, bearing glossy, mid-green leaves, which turn yellow in fall. A native of Europe, north Africa and southwest Asia. Height 100 ft (30 m) x width 70 ft (20 m). ZONES 5 TO 8.

Above and right:
Ulmus glabra
'Horizontalis'

Left: *Ulmus minor* 'Louis van Houtte' with *Agapanthus.*

Ulmus minor 'Jacqueline Hillier'

Perhaps you do not have room for a big elm tree in your garden, but you could surely find a spot for this bush. It is a small, upright shrub with distinctive angular stems creating fans of foliage like coy ladies at a 19th-century ball. The plant is ideal for small hedges and bonsai. Height 6 ft (2 m) x width 3 ft (1 m). ZONE 6.

Ulmus minor 'Louis van Houtte'

This has to be one of the best garden or avenue trees in the world. It is dazzling, it is bright and, better still, it is tough. The plant copes with very windy climates, much better than most deciduous trees. It is happy in very acidic or very alkaline soil, increasing its possible range. Poor soil and heavy clay are no problem, and it grows easily and fast, does not get too big and has no significant pests or diseases. The foliage is bright yellow in the spring, fading to a mellow yellow through summer, and even by fall does not look too jaded. Height x width 30 ft (10 m). ZONE 4.

Ulmus minor 'Variegata'

'Variegata' looks ghastly at close quarters, but once it gets up a bit, too high in fact to see the detail of the leaf, it takes on a new charm. Seen with late afternoon sunlight filtering through the leaves it really is quite beautiful. Height 40 ft (12 m) x width 20 ft (6 m). ZONE 5.

Minor = small.

Ulmus parvifolia

CHINESE ELM, LACEBARK ELM

Landscapers take note, this one is for you. This tree deserves to be used much more. It is tidy, not too big and reasonably wind-tolerant. A small-leafed, deciduous tree, it has inconsistent fall color, sometimes yellow and sometimes not. It is likely to become more popular as it appears to be resistant to Dutch elm disease, and grows slowly into a tidy mop-top tree, ideally suited as a street

Left: *Ulmus minor* 'Frosty'

tree. Some forms have lovely hammered bark of gray and soft orange. It often keeps its leaves late into winter, making up for the variable fall color, though named forms for color will alleviate this problem. It has a slightly drooping or weeping habit on mature trees. It tolerates most soil, including heavy clay and alkaline, and seemingly any climate. A native of China, Korea and Japan. Height 60 ft (18 m) x width 25–40 ft (8–12 m). ZONES 5 TO 9.

'Allee' is the best clone for bark color with hammered orange-toned bark. Height 60 ft (18 m) x width 30 ft (10 m). **'Frosty'** is a shrubby form with white frosting on the teeth of the leaf, giving the appearance of permanent frost. Height x width 8 ft (2.5 m).

Parvifolia = small leaf.

Ulmus pumila

DWARF ELM, SIBERIAN ELM

This tree has two major claims to fame. It will grow in areas of extreme drought and cold, such as the American Midwest, and it

Above: *Ulmus minor* 'Variegata'

Below: *Ulmus minor* 'Jacqueline Hillier'

is resistant to Dutch elm disease. However, it is not the most exciting species and if your climate is kinder, there are better options than *Ulmus pumila*.

It has dark, almost black, rugged bark and small, dark green, coarsely toothed leaves. They are even and rounded at the base, while all other elms have uneven bases. The plant was introduced by that gatherer of useful plants, Frank Meyer (1875–1918). He is often forgotten because he concentrated on edible and useful economic plants. But, no less devoted than other more famous collectors, he spent years collecting in China, Manchuria and Korea. Native to eastern Siberia, Kazakhstan and northern China. Height 70–100 ft (20–30 m) x width 40 ft (12 m). ZONES 3 TO 9.

Pumila = small.

Viburnum

Caprifoliaceae

Viburnums are a diverse and interesting genus. Many of them are grown for their fragrant flowers. Some have rounded, pompom-type flowers while many of the species have lacecap flowers similar to hydrangeas. As regards the foliage, they range from soft, deciduous leaves to corrugated evergreen and deciduous types, right through to glossy, near indestructible, evergreen leaves. Most are content in any soil and they are supremely hardy.

Viburnum davidii

A marvelous shrub for suppressing weeds and for its ability to "ground" an area near steps. Dense, wide-spreading evergreen shrubs like this are ideal for adding stability to a garden scene.

The long, elliptical leaves have prominent veins and the mottled flowers are worthwhile because they are the source of the beautiful turquoise berries. You will need male and female plants to ensure a crop of these translucent gems. Grows in part shade and poor soil. The one fault is devastating attacks of thrips in a warm climate. Named after Père Armand David (1826–1900), a French missionary in China, and introduced by E. H. Wilson (1876–1930). Height x width 3–5 ft (1–1.5 m). ZONES 8 OR 9.

There is a very good fruiting clone called **'Femina'**. Height x width 3–5 ft (1–1.5 m).

Above: *Viburnum japonicum*

Viburnum japonicum

Viburnum japonicum has shiny, evergreen leaves in rich, dark green, topped with fragrant white flowers followed by red fruits. The leaves are better than the flowers, and it is usually grown just as a dense, wind-hardy evergreen where you need a shrub as a backdrop. The name tells you it is from Japan, collected by Charles Maries (1851–1902) for the Veitch Nursery in England. Height 6 ft (2 m) x width 8 ft (2.5 m). ZONES 8 OR 9.

Japoncium = from Japan.

Above: *Viburnum rhytidophylloides*

Viburnum odoratissimum
SWEET VIBURNUM

Here is a surprise, a reasonably hardy evergreen from Asia. It also shows how diverse the *Viburnum* genus really is, growing all across the Northern Hemisphere. This one is not immediately recognizable as a *Viburnum*. For a start, the leaves are waxy and polished and very tough. You can assume from the shiny leaf that it is very wind-hardy. It forms a shrub grown solely for its brilliant leaves and tough disposition. The leaves are similar to those of *V. japonicum*. The umbels of tiny whitish flowers appear in summer and are fragrant. Native to India, China, Burma, the Philippines and Japan. Height x width 15 ft (5 m). ZONES 8 OR 9.

'Emerald Lustre' is a sterile clone with even bigger leaves, but not quite as wind-hardy. Height x width 15 ft (5 m).

Odoratissimum = fragrant.

Viburnum rhytidophyllum
LEATHERLEAF VIBURNUM

This is an undervalued evergreen shrub. Like so many viburnums, it is very tough and perhaps that is why it is not rated more highly. It grows easily in sun or shade, hot or cold, wet or dry and is equally happy in extremely acidic or alkaline soil. So few shrubs relish growing on lime soil, it is a treat when one so good is happy with lime. The glossy, dark green to grayish leaves are about the size of a typical rhododendron leaf and the corrugated surface is like a contour map with hills and valleys. Creamy white umbels of flowers arise in summer.

The plant can be attacked by thrips in warm climates and especially when grown in shade. If you have room for more than one, be sure to get a male and female plant and have the added joy of the red and black berries. The red berries turn black, but for a while you will have both at once. Introduced from China by E. H. Wilson (1876–1930). Height 15 ft (5 m) x width 12 ft (4 m). ZONES 6 TO 8.

Viburnum rhytidophylloides, a cross between *V. lantana* and *V. rhytidophyllum*, has even better foliage, with a rougher, more contured leaf. Height x width 6 ft (2 m).

Rhytidophyllum = wrinkled leaf.

Right: *Viburnum rhytidophyllum* (center).

Viburnum tinus
LAURUSTINUS

This is very common but nonetheless lovely. It was much used, perhaps overused, in the Victorian era and is only just emerging from that stigma. A useful shrub for shady, dry and traffic-polluted sites.

The glossy, green, oval leaves of this evergreen *Viburnum* have made a worthwhile addition to our gardens since Tudor times. It grows well in coastal regions, but is perfectly hardy inland. It is a Mediterranean plant, which explains the coastal hardiness.

Heads of pink buds open to white throughout winter and spring followed by shiny blue berries. It makes a very good hedge for small gardens. Height x width 10 ft (3 m). ZONE 6.

The variegated form, **'Variegatum'**, is gaudy with splashes of creamy yellow, but is not as hardy as the type. Height x width 10 ft (3 m). ZONE 7.

Tinus = obscure Latin name, meaning unclear.

Vitis

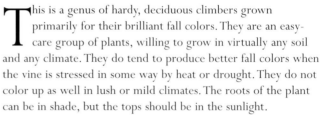

Vitaceae

This is a genus of hardy, deciduous climbers grown primarily for their brilliant fall colors. They are an easy-care group of plants, willing to grow in virtually any soil and any climate. They do tend to produce better fall colors when the vine is stressed in some way by heat or drought. They do not color up as well in lush or mild climates. The roots of the plant can be in shade, but the tops should be in the sunlight.

The vines hang tendrils, clinging onto twigs and wires.

Vitis amurensis
AMUR GRAPE

The big, bold leaves turn rich reds and purple in the fall. They are sometimes lobed like a maple and have serrated edges. The tiny

Above left and right:
Vitus amurensis

flowers are insignificant. This vine is named for the Amur River area of Manchuria, and is also found native in China, Korea and Japan. Height 50 ft (15 m). ZONES 4 TO 9.

Vitis coignetiae
CRIMSON GLORY VINE

The huge, dark green leaves, up to 12 in (30 cm) long, are spectacular in the fall in burnished reds and crimsons. Named after Madame Coignet who introduced the plant from Japan in 1875. Also native to Korea. Height 50 ft (15 m). ZONES 5 TO 9.

Xanthorhiza

Xanthorhiza simplicissima, syn X. apiifolia
YELLOWROOT
Ranunculaceae

Above: *Xanthorhiza simplicissima*

This is a shrubby plant in a genus of its own and related to the buttercup. The low, dense plant is deciduous and can cover quite a large area by suckering underground. Although it is constantly gaining more ground, it does so in orderly fashion in a rounded circle shape. In keeping with this tidy habit it remains dense and does not die out in the center as some creeping plants can. So if you have a large garden it is a superb ground cover or it could be used in a smaller garden if you are willing to restrict or maintain it a little. The celery-like leaves are pinnate, with three to five jagged-edged, pointed leaflets. They tend to be clustered around the tip of the stem with bare wood beneath, but the overall leaf cover is dense,

145

making it a good weed suppressor. These leaves turn rich purple-reds and bronzes in fall, leaving lots of little upright, pale stems. Tiny, insignificant, purple flowers appear in early spring as drooping, arching panicles similar to *Epimedium*, but nowhere near as pretty. It will grow in very moist or dry climates and puts up with heavy soils, preferably neutral or acidic. The plant is happy in full sun or part shade, though the fall color is improved by more sunlight. Being a very easy-care plant, if you fancy a drift of ground cover, this would be just the plant you need. Native to eastern U.S.A. Height 24 in (60 cm) x width 5 ft (1.5 m). ZONES 3 TO 9.

Xantho = yellow; *rhiza* = rhizome or roots (roots are yellow);
simplicissima = single or whole.

Zanthoxylum

Rutaceae

Y ou have all heard the term "last before least," well this plant will indeed make you sit up and take notice. It is one of the best foliage plants in the book. Even the smaller species have nice dark green, waxy leaves. Pests seem to make no impact on these plants, perhaps the thorns put them off, but more likely it is because of the strong peppery taste and smell of the bark. Most of the zanthoxylums are rather tough, nuggety shrubs with spiny stems and hard, shiny, pinnate leaves. Some species have aromatic leaves and others have small, hot-to-taste fruits used as a pepper substitute. They all have tiny yellow flowers. Where most gardens would accommodate the smaller zanthoxylums, once you have seen the family giant you will not settle for second best. The first time I saw *Zanthoxylum ailanthoides* I was enchanted, and I have loved it ever since.

Zanthoxylum = yellow wood (for the tree's yellow timber).

Zanthoxylum ailanthoides

The "big daddy" of the genus, this incredible plant grows rapidly in its early years. The trunks are covered in fierce black spines on a bluish stem. As the plant ages the trunks become dark brown with primitive rough bumps with sharp points, almost like the skin of some prehistoric creature. The opposite leaves of a juvenile plant can be up to 3 ft (1 m) long and have opposite pairs of glaucous, blue-green leaflets. The tree needs shelter for its big, bold leaves in the young stage of growth. In time the leaves take on more modest proportions. It can get to be a mighty tree—I have seen huge old trees in Korea. It transplants easily and its best use is as a dramatic impact plant for large gardens and lawns.

As regards climate, it is easy to please. Plant it in full sun, on any soil, in a wet or dry region; it just grows three times as fast in a wet climate. It is difficult to know how hardy it is. It seems to be very hardy if given hot summers to ripen the wood in readiness for the winter cold. Originates from Korea. Height 20–60 ft (6–20 m) x width 15–50 ft (5–15 m). ZONE 7.

Ailanthoides = leaf like an *Ailanthus*, or tree of heaven.

Zanthoxylum piperitum
JAPAN PEPPER

This is a tough-looking bush with attractive pinnate leaves made up of a dozen or more leaflets. These rich dark leaves turn a stunning yellow in the fall. The trunks have sharp spines so plant it away from paths or where children play. The small, yellowish flowers produce red fruits containing black seeds used as a pepper substitute (thus the species name). A native of Japan, Korea, Taiwan and China. Height x width 8 ft (2.5 m). ZONES 6 TO 9.

Piper = pepper, the seeds are used as a pepper subsitute.

Zanthoxylum planispinum

A big, open shrub or small tree, *Zanthoxylum planispinum* has glossy leaves made up of three or five leaflets with spines attached underneath, so take care when you handle this plant. The attractive leaves are all the more unusual as they have wings like strips of leaf along the petiole or leaf stalk. Crush a leaf for a heady, spicy smell.

Small, yellowish flowers arise in spring followed by red fruits. Native to Japan, Korea, China and Taiwan. Height x width 8–12 ft (3–4 m). ZONE 6.

Plani = flat or smooth; *spinum* = spines (not as vicious as they look).

Zelkova

Ulmaceae

Zelkova are glorious hardy, deciduous trees from the eastern Mediterranean across to China, Korea and Japan. Eventually they become huge, wide-spreading trees but in a gardener's lifetime are more modestly proportioned. They are related to elms and have similar rough leaves with serrated or toothed edges, but the gray fruit lacks the wings of an elm seed. The flowers are insignificant but the tree is worth growing for its stately habit and fine leaf cover. The trunks are also divine, being smooth like a beech, though the older bark does peel off. They like deep, moist, heavy soil but put up with less than perfect conditions including acidic and alkaline soils and windy sites. They are happy in cold to hot conditions as long as they keep their roots moist. Like the elm they are prone to Dutch elm disease.

Zelkova = is a local name for this plant.

Zelkova carpinifolia, syn *Z. crenata*
CAUCASIAN ELM

Zelkova carpinifolia forms a big, tall tree with a crowded head of branches that are ever more dividing and getting more and more crowded at the tips and outer extremities. The trunk is a smooth, beech-like bole. The young shoots are very hairy and the rough-surfaced, dark green leaves are coarsely toothed and turn warm and orange-brown fall colors. From Turkey and Iran. Height 100 ft (30 m) x width 80 ft (25 m). ZONES 5 TO 9.

Carpinifolia = leaf like *Carpinus* or hornbeam.

Zelkova serrata
JAPANESE ZELKOVA

This magnificent wide-spreading tree can reach huge proportions. It forms a big, rounded crown with a dense mass of branches and smooth trunks. It has smooth twigs and dark green, toothed, elm-like leaves and although the top surface is very rough the under-side is surprisingly smooth. Lovely reds, bronze yellow and orange colors occur in the fall. A native of Korea, Japan and Taiwan and first collected by John Gould Veitch (1839–1870) in Japan in 1861. Height 100 ft (30 m) x width 60 ft (18 m). ZONES 5 TO 9.

'Goblin', as the name suggests, is a dwarf form, remaining small enough for any garden. Height x width 3 ft (1 m). 'Village Green' is prized for being resistant to Dutch elm diseases. It has good red fall colors. Height x width 30 ft (10 m).

Serrata = serrated leaves.

Left: *Zelkova serrata*

Ready-reference table

Species or cultivar	page reference	hardiness zones	evergreen	fall color	native to North America	height x width
Abies alba	10	5-8	●			80-100 x 12-20 ft (25-45 x 4-6 m)
Abies balsamea	10	3-9	●		*	50 x 15 ft (15 x 5 m)
'Nana'	11	3-9	●			2 x 3 ft (60 x 90 cm)
'Hudsonia'	11	3-9	●			2 x 3 ft (60 x 90 cm)
Abies concolor	11	3-8	●		*	80-130 x 15-22 ft (25-40 x 5-7 m)
Abies concolor lowiana	11	3-8	●		*	80-130 x 15-22 ft (25-40 x 5-7 m)
Abies fargesii	11	5	●			30-50 x 10-12 ft (10-15 x 3-4 m)
Abies firma	11	7	●			30-50 x 10-12 ft (10-15 x 3-4 m)
Abies grandis	11	5	●		*	80-200 x 15-25 ft (25-60 x 5-8 m)
Abies holophylla	11	5	●			30-60 x 15-20 ft (10-20 x 5-6 m)
Abies koreana	12	5	●			30 x 20 ft (10 x 6 m)
Abies lasiocarpa	12	5-6	●		*	90 x 10-12 ft (25 x 3-4 m)
Abies lasiocarpa var arizonica 'Compacta'	12	5	●			10-15 x 6-10 ft (3-5 x 2-3 m)
Abies magnifica	12	6-8	●		*	80-120 x 15-20 ft (25-35 x 5-6 m)
Abies nordmanniana	12	4-8	●			130 x 20 ft (40 x 6 m)
Abies procera	12	5	●		*	80-150 x 20-28 ft (25-45 x 6-9 m)
'Glauca'	12	5	●			50 x 20 ft (15 x 6 m)
Abies veitchii	13	3-8	●			50-70 x 12-20 ft (15-20 x 4-6 m)
Abies vejari	13	7	●			30-70 x 10-15 ft (10-20 x 3-5 m)
Acer buergerianum	14	5-9		●		30 x 25 ft (10 x 8 m)
Acer davidii	15	5-7		●		50 x 50 ft (15 x 15 m)
'Ernest Wilson'	15	5-7		●		25 x 30 ft (8 x 10 m)
'George Forrest'	15	5-7		●		40 x 15 ft (12 x 5 m)
Acer griseum	15	4-9		●		30 x 30 ft (10 x 10 m)
Acer henryi	15	4		●		25 x 30 ft (8 x 10 m)
Acer negundo	16	5			*	50 x 30 ft (15 x 10 m)
'Flamingo'	16	5				50 x 30 ft (15 x 10 m)
'Kelly's Gold'	16	5				50 x 30 ft (15 x 10 m)
Acer negundo var violaceum	16	5		●		50 x 30 ft (15 x 10 m)
Acer palmatum	16	6-9		●		25 x 30 ft (8 x 10 m)
'Bloodgood'	16	6-9		●		15 x 15 ft (5 x 5 m)
'Butterfly'	16	6-9		●		10 x 5 ft (3 x 1.5 m)
'Crimson Queen'	17	6-9		●		10 x 12 ft (3 x 4 m)
'Dissectum'	17	6-9		●		6 x 10 ft (2x 3 m)
'Seiryu'	17	6-9		●		9-15 x 6-10 ft (3-5 x 2-3 m)
'Senkaki'	17	6-9		●		20 x 15 ft (6 x 5 m)
'Shishigashira'	17	6-9		●		12 x 10 ft (4x 3 m)
'Trompenburg'	18	6-9		●		6 x 10 ft (2x 3 m)
'Villa Taranto'	18	6-9		●		10 x 10 ft (3 x 3 m)
Acer pentaphyllum	18	7		●		30 x 25 ft (10 x 8 m)
Acer platanoides	18	3-7		●		80 x 50 ft (25 x 15 m)
'Crimson King'	18	3-7		●		50 x 50 ft (15 x 15 m)
'Drummondii'	18	3-7		●		30-40 x 30-40 ft (10-12 x 10-12 m)
Acer pseudoplatanus	18	4-8				100 x 80 ft (30 x 25 m)
'Brilliantissimum'	19	4-8		●		6-12 x 6-10 ft (2-4 x 2-3 m)
'Esk Sunset'	19	4-8		●		6-12 x 6-10 ft (2-4 x 2-3 m)
'Prinz Handjery'	19	4-8		●		6-12 x 6-10 ft (2-4 x 2-3 m)
Acer rubrum	19	3-9		●	*	70 x 30 ft (20 x 10 m)
'October Glory'	19	3-9		●		40 x 20 ft (12 x 6 m)
'Red Sunset'	19	3-9		●		40 x 20 ft (12 x 6 m)
'Scanlon'	19	3-9		●		50 x 15 ft (15 x 5 m)
Acer saccharinum	19	4-9		●	*	80 x 50 ft (25 x 15 m)
Acer saccharum	20	4-9		●	*	70 x 40 ft (20 x 12 m)
'Newton Sentry'	20	4-9		●		30 x 8 ft (10 x 2.5 m)
'Temple's Upright'	20	4-9		●		70 x 15 ft (20 x 5 m)
Acer shirasawanum	20	5-9		●		20 x 20 ft (6 x 6 m)
'Aureum'	20	5-9		●		20 x 20 ft (6 x 6 m)
'Vitifolium'	20	5-9		●		20 x 20 ft (6 x 6 m)
Actinidia kolomikta	20	5-8				15 ft (5 m) (climber)
Alangium platanifolium	21	6-9		●		10 x 6 ft (3 x 2 m)
Albizia julibrissin	21	6				20 x 12-20 ft (6 x 4-6 m)
'Rosea'	22	6				20 x 12-20 ft (6 x 4-6 m)
Albizia lophantha	22	8	●			6-30 x 3-10 ft (2-10 x 1-3 m)
Alniphyllum fortunei	22	6		●		30 x 20 ft (10 x 6 m)
Alniphyllum fortunei var macrophyllum	23	7		●		30 x 20 ft (10 x 6 m)
Amelanchier alnifolia	23	4		●	*	12 x 12 ft (4 x 4 m)
'Regent'	23	4		●		4-6 x 4-6 ft (1.2-2 x 1.2-2 m)
Amelanchier arborea	24	4-9		●	*	25 x 30 ft (8 x 10 m)
Amelanchier asiatica	24	5-9		●		25 x 30 ft (8 x 10 m)
Amelanchier canadensis	24	3-9		●	*	20 x 10 ft (6 x 3 m)
Amelanchier x grandiflora	24	5-8		●		25 x 30 ft (8 x 10 m)
'Ballerina'	24	5-8		●		25 x 30 ft (8 x 10 m)
'Fall Brilliance'	24	5-8		●		25 x 30 ft (8 x 10 m)
'Robin Hill'	24	5-8		●		25 x 15 ft (8 x 5 m)
'Rubescens'	24	5-8		●		25 x 30 ft (8 x 10 m)
Amelanchier laevis	24	5-9		●	*	25 x 25 ft (8 x 8 m)
'Cumulus'	24	5-9		●		25 x 25 ft (8 x 8 m)
Amelanchier lamarckii	24	5-9		●	*	30 x 40 ft (10 x 12 m)
Ampelopsis brevipedunculata 'Elegans'	25	5-8				15 ft (5 m) (climber)
Ampelopsis megalophylla	25	5-8		●		30 ft (10 m) (climber)
Aphananthe aspera	26	5				60 x 60 ft (18 x 18 m)
Aralia chinensis	26	4-9		●		30 x 30 ft (10 x 10 m)
Aralia continentalis	26	6		●		10 x 10 ft (3 x 3 m)
Aralia elata	26	4-9		●		6-10 x 6-10 ft (2-3 x 2-3 m)
'Aureovariegata'	27	4-9		●		15 x 15 ft (5 x 5 m)
'Variegata'	27	4-9		●		15 x 15 ft (5 x 5 m)
Aralia spinosa	27	4-9			*	30 x 15 ft (10 x 5 m)
Araucaria araucana	27	7	●			50-80 x 22-30 ft (15-25 x 7-10 m)
Aronia arbutifolia	28	5-9		●	*	10 x 5 ft (3 x 1.5 m)
'Brilliantissima'	28	5-9		●		6-8 x 4-6 ft (2-2.5 x 1.2-2 m)
Aronia melanocarpa	28	4-9		●	*	6 x 10 ft (2 x 3 m)
'Fall Magic'	28	4-9		●		6 x 10 ft (2 x 3 m)
Aucuba japonica	28	6	●			10 x 10 ft (3 x 3 m)
'Crotonifolia'	28	6	●			10 x 10 ft (3 x 3 m)
'Gold Dust'	28	6	●			10 x 10 ft (3 x 3 m)
'Mr Goldstrike'	28	6	●			4-6 x 4-6 ft (1.2-2 x 1.2-2 m)
'Picturata'	28	6	●			10 x 10 ft (3 x 3 m)
'Sulfurea Marginata'	28	6	●			10 x 10 ft (3 x 3 m)
Aucuba omeiensis	29	9	●			15 x 10 ft (5 x 3 m)
Berberis darwinii	29	7-9	●			6-10 x 6-10 ft (2-3 x 2-3 m)
Berberis thunbergii	30	5-8		●		3 x 8 ft (1 x 2.5 m)
'Aurea'	30	5-8		●		3-4 x 3-4 ft (1-1.2 x 1-1.2 m)
'Rose Glow'	30	5-8		●		3 x 8 ft (1 x 2.5 m)
Betula albo-sinensis	31	5-8		●		80 x 30 ft (25 x 10 m)
Betula albo-sinensis var septentrionalis	31	5-8				80 x 30 ft (25 x 10 m)
Betula alleghaniensis	31	4-9		●	*	80 x 30 ft (25 x 10 m)
Betula ermanii	31	5-9		●		70 x 40 ft (20 x 12 m)
'Grayswood Hill'	31	5-9		●		70 x 40 ft (20 x 12 m)
Betula lenta	31	3-9		●	*	50 x 40 ft (15 x 12 m)

Species or cultivar	page reference	hardiness zones	evergreen	fall color	native to North America	height x width
Betula maximowicziana	31	6-9		●		80 x 40 ft (25 x 12 m)
Betula nigra	31	4-9		●	*	60 x 40 ft (18 x 12 m)
'Heritage'	32	4-9		●		60 x 40 ft (18 x 12 m)
Betula papyrifera	32	2-9		●	*	70 x 30 ft (20 x 10 m)
Betula pendula	32	2-8				80 x 30 ft (25 x 10 m)
'Dalecarlica'	32	2-8				70 x 20 ft (20 x 6 m)
'Laciniata'	32	2-8				70 x 20 ft (20 x 6 m)
'Tristis'	32	2-8				70 x 20 ft (20 x 6 m)
'Youngii'	32	2-8				25 x 25 ft (8 x 8 m)
Betula platyphylla var *japonica*	33	4-9				70 x 40 ft (20 x 12 m)
'Whitespire'	33	4-9				70 x 40 ft (20 x 12 m)
Betula utilis	33	5-9				60 x 30 ft (18 x 10 m)
Betula utilis jacquemontii	33	5-9				60 x 30 ft (18 x 10 m)
Betula utilis var *prattii*	33	5-9				60 x 30 ft (18 x 10 m)
Buxus microphylla	34	6-9	●			30 in x 5 ft (75 x 150 cm)
Buxus microphylla var *japonica*	34	6	●			5 x 4 ft (1.5 x 1.2 m)
Buxus microphylla var *koreana*	34	5	●			24 x 30 in (60 x 75 cm)
Buxus sempervirens	34	6-8				15 x 15 ft (5 x 5 m)
'Aureomarginata'	34	6	●			8 x 10 ft (2.5 x 3 m)
'Suffruticosa'	34	6	●			6 x 9 ft (2 x 2.5 m)
Camptotheca acuminata	34	7				60 x 40 ft (20 x 12 m)
Carpinus betulus	35	4-8		●		80 x 70 ft (25 x 20 m)
Carpinus caroliniana	36	3-9		●	*	40 x 50 ft (12 x 15 m)
Carpinus turczaninowii	36	6-9		●		20-40 x 30 ft (6-12 x 10 m)
Carya aquatica	37	6		●	*	80 x 30 ft (25 x 10 m)
Carya cordiformis	37	5-8		●	*	80 x 50 ft (25 x 15 m)
Carya illinoinensis	37	5-9		●	*	100 x 70 ft (30 x 20 m)
Carya ovata	37	4-8		●	*	80 x 50 ft (25 x 15 m)
Carya tomentosa	37	5		●	*	80 x 30 ft (25 x 10 m)
Cedrus atlantica	38	6-9	●			130 x 30 ft (40 x 10 m)
'Glauca'	38	6-9	●			130 x 30 ft (40 x 10 m)
'Glauca Pendula'	38	6-9	●			30 x 30 ft (10 x 10 m)
Cedrus deodara	38	7-9	●			130 x 30 ft (40 x 10 m)
'Aurea'	38	7-9	●			50 x 25 ft (15 x 8 m)
'Pendula'	38	7-9	●			3 x 10 ft (1 x 3 m)
'Prostrata'	38	7-9	●			4 in x 3 ft (10 cm x 1 m)
'Vink's Golden'	38	7-9	●			50 x 25 ft (15 x 8 m)
Cedrus libani 'Golden Dwarf'	39	7-9	●			4 x 5 ft (1.2 x 1.5 m)
'Nana'	39	7-9	●			4 x 5 ft (1.2 x 1.5 m)
'Sargentii'	39	7-9	●			3-6 x 3-6 ft (1-2 x 1-2 m)
Cercidiphyllum japonicum	39	4-8		●		70 x 50 ft (20 x 15 m)
'Pendulum'	39	4-8		●		20 x 25 ft (6 x 8 m)
Cercidiphyllum japonicum var *sinense*	39	4-8		●		70 x 50 ft (21 x 15 m)
Cercidiphyllum japonicum var *magnificum*	39	6		●		30 x 25 ft (10 x 8 m)
Cercis canadensis	40	5-9			*	30 x 30 ft (10 x 10 m)
'Forest Pansy'	40	6		●		15 x 15 ft (5 x 5 m)
'Oklahoma'	40	6-9				15 x 15 ft (5 x 5 m)
Cercis chinensis	40	6-9				20 x 15-30 ft (6 x 5-10 m)
'Avondale'	41	6-9				10 x 10 ft (3 x 3 m)
Cercis siliquastrum	41	6-9				30 x 30 ft (10 x 10 m)
Chamaecyparis lawsoniana	42	5-9	●		*	50-130 x 6-15 ft (15-40 x 2-5 m)
'Columnaris'	42	5-9	●			30 x 3 ft (10 x 1 m)
'Lane'	43	5-9	●			9 x 9 ft (3 x 3 m)
'Pembury Blue'	43	5-9	●			50 x 25 ft (15 x 8 m)
'Triomphe de Boskoop'	43	5-9	●			30 x 20 ft (10 x 6 m)
Chamaecyparis obtusa	43	4-8	●			70 x 20 ft (20 x 6 m)
'Caespitosa'	43	4-8	●			6-12 in (15-30 cm)
'Crippsii'	43	4-8	●			50 x 25 ft (15 x 8 m)
'Minima'	43	4-8	●			16 x 16 in (40 x 40 cm)
'Nana Aurea'	43	4-8	●			6 x 4-6 ft (2 x 2-3 m)
'Nana Gracilis'	43	4-8	●			10 x 6 ft (3 x 2 m)
'Nana Lutea'	43	5-8	●			12 x 10 in (30 x 25 cm)
Chamaecyparis pisifera	43	4-8	●			70 x 15 ft (20 x 5 m)
'Boulevard'	43	4-8	●			3-30 x 3-15 ft (1-10 x 1-5 m)
'Filifera Aurea'	43	4-8	●			40 x 30 ft (12 x 10 m)
'Gold Spangle'	43	4-8	●			10 x 6 ft (3 x 2 m)
Cornus alternifolia	44	4-8			*	20 x 20 ft (6 x 6 m)
'Argentea'	44	4-8				10 x 8 ft (3 x 2.5 m)
Cornus capitata	44	8	●			40 x 40 ft (12 x 12 m)
Cornus controversa	44	6-9		●		50 x 50 ft (15 x 15 m)
'Variegata'	45	6				25 x 25 ft (8 x 8 m)
Cornus 'Eddie's White Wonder'	45	5-8		●		20 x 15 ft (6 x 5 m)
Cornus florida	45	5-8		●	*	20 x 25 ft (6 x 8 m)
'Rainbow'	46	5-8		●		10 x 8 ft (3 x 2.5 m)
Cornus kousa var *chinensis*	46	5-8		●		8 x 6 ft ((2.5 x 2 m
Cornus nuttallii	46	7		●	*	40 x 25 ft (12 x 8 m)
Cornus walteri	46	6				20-30 x 10-15 ft (6-10 x 3-5 m)
Cotinus coggygria	47	5		●		15 x 15 ft (5 x 5 m)
'Daydream'	47	5		●		15 x 15 ft (5 x 5 m)
'Nordine Red'	47	4		●		15 x 15 ft (5 x 5 m)
'Royal Purple'	47	4		●		15 x 15 ft (5 x 5 m)
Cotinus x 'Grace'	47	4-9		●		15 x 15 ft (5 x 5 m)
Cotinus x 'Flame'	48	5-9		●		20 x 15 ft (6 x 5 m)
Cotinus obovatus	47	4-9		●	*	30 x 25 ft (10 x 8 m)
Cotoneaster bullatus	48	6-8		●		9 x 9 ft (3 x 3 m)
Cotoneaster congestus	48	7	●			28 x 36 in (70 x 90 cm)
Cotoneaster franchetii	48	7-9	●			10 x 10 ft (3 x 3 m)
Cotoneaster horizontalis	48	5-9		●		3 x 5 ft (1 x 1.5 m)
Cotoneaster x *watereri* 'John Waterer'	48	6-8	●			15 x 15 ft (5 x 5 m)
Cryptomeria japonica	49	6-9	●			80 x 20 ft (25 x 6 m)
'Araucarioides'	50	6-9	●			6 x 6 ft (2 x 2 m)
'Bandai-sugi'	50	6-9	●			6 x 6 ft (2 x 2 m)
'Elegans'	50	6-9	●			20-30 x 20 ft (6-10 x 6 m)
'Elegans Compacta'	50	6-9	●			6-12 x 6-12 ft (2-4 x 2-4 m)
Cunninghamia konishii	51	7	●			50 x 15 ft (15 x 5 m)
Cunninghamia lanceolata	51	6	●			70 x 20 ft (20 x 6 m)
'Chason's Gift'	51	6	●			50 x 15 ft (15 x 5 m)
'Glauca'	51	6	●			50 x 15 ft (15 x 5 m)
Cupressus arizonica var *glabra*	52	7	●		*	30-50 x 12-15 ft (10-15 x 4-5 m)
Cupressus macrocarpa	52	8	●		*	100 x 12-40 ft (30 x 4-12 m)
'Aurea Saligna'	52	8	●			30 x 15 ft (10 x 5 m)
'Greenstead Magnificent'	52	8	●			2 x 4-5 ft (60 cm x 1.5 m)
'Horizontalis Aurea'	52	8	●			2 x 6 ft (60 cm x 2 m)
'Lutea'	52	8	●			30 x 20 ft (10 x 6 m)
Cupressus sempervirens	52	8	●			70 x 3-20 ft (20 x 1-6 m)
'Green Pencil'	53	8	●			10 x 2 ft (3 m x 60 cm)
'Horizontalis'	53	8	●			70 x 20 ft (20 x 6 m)
'Stricta'	52	8	●			70 x 10 ft (20 x 3 m)
'Swane's Golden'	53	8	●			20 x 3 ft (6 x 1 m)
Cupressus torulosa	53	7	●			100 x 30 ft (30 x 10 m)
'Cashmeriana'	53	8	●			100 x 30 ft (30 x 10 m)
Daphniphyllum humile	54	8	●			3 x 3-6 ft (1 x 1-2 m)
Daphniphyllum macropodum	54	7	●			20 x 15 ft (6 x 5 m)

Species or cultivar	page reference	hardiness zones	evergreen	fall color	native to North America	height x width
Decaisnea fargesii	54	6		●		6-20 x 6-20 ft (2-6 x 2-6 m)
Dipteronia sinensis	55	7				30 x 30 ft (10 x 10 m)
Disanthus cercidifolius	56	4-8		●		6-10 x 6-10 ft (2-3 x 2-3 m)
Eleagnus angustifolia	56	3				20 x 20 ft (6 x 6 m)
'Quicksilver'	56	3				12 x 12 ft (4 x 4 m)
Elaeagnus x ebbingei	56	7	●			12 x 12 ft (4 x 4 m)
'Gilt Edge'	56	7	●			10 x 10 ft (3 x 3 m)
Limelight'	56	7	●			10 x 10 ft (3 x 3 m)
Elaeagnus pungens	56	7	●			12 x 15 ft (4 x 5 m)
Elaeagnus umbellata	57	4				15 x 15 ft (5 x 5 m)
'Titan'	57	4				12 x 6 ft (4 x 2 m)
Enkianthus campanulatus	58	5		●		12-15 x 12-15 ft (4-5 x 4-5 m)
Enkianthus perulatus	58	6		●		6 x 6 ft (2 x 2 m)
Enkianthus quinqueflorus	58	8	●			10 x 3-4 ft (3 x 1 m)
Eucalyptus ficifolia	59	9	●			20-50 x 15-70 ft (6-15 x 5-20 m)
Eucalyptus globulus	59	8	●			50-160 x 30-80 ft (15-50 x 10-25 m)
Eucalyptus gunnii	59	7	●			30-80 x 20-50 ft (10-25 x 6-15 m)
Eucalyptus nicholii	59	8	●			40-52 x 15-40 ft (12-16 x 5-12 m)
Euodia daniellii	60	5		●		12-18 x 30 ft (4-6 x 10 m)
Euodia henryi	60	5		●		15-20 x 15-20 ft (5-6 x 5-6 m)
Euonymus alatus	61	4-9		●		15-20 x 10 ft (5-6 x 3 m)
'Compactus'	61	4-9		●		10 x 10-15 ft (3 x 3-5 m)
Euonymus europaeus	61	4-8		●		10 x 8 ft (3 x 2.5 m)
Euonymus fortunei	61	5-9	●			24 in or 15 ft (60 cm or 5 m)
'Emerald Cushion'	61	5-9	●			12 x 18 in (30 x 45 cm)
'Emerald Gaiety'	61	5-9	●			3 x 5 ft (1 x 1.5 m)
'Emerald n'Gold'	61	5-9	●			24 x 36 in (60 x 90 cm)
Euonymus japonicus	61	6-9	●			12 x 6 ft (4 x 2 m)
Euonymus myrianthus	62	7-9	●			10 x 12 ft (3 x 4 m)
Euptelea pleiosperma	62	6-9		●		25 x 20 ft (8 x 6 m)
Fagus sylvatica	63	5-9		●		80 x 50 ft (25 x 15 m)
'Dawyck'	64	5-9		●		60 x 22 ft (18 x 7 m)
'Dawyck Gold'	64	5-9		●		60 x 22 ft (18 x 7 m)
'Dawyck Purple'	64	5-9		●		70 x 15 ft (20 x 5 m)
'Pendula'	64	5-9		●		50 x 50 ft (15 x 15 m)
'Riversii'	64	5-9		●		80 x 50 ft (25 x 15 m)
'Rohanii'	65	5-9		●		6 x 6 ft (2 x 2 m)
'Swat Magret'	65	5-9		●		80 x 50 ft (25 x 15 m)
'Zlatia'	65	5-9		●		60 x 50 ft (18 x 15 m)
x *Fatshedera lizei*	65	8	●			4-6 x 10 ft (1.2-2 x 3 m)
Fatsia japonica	66	8	●			5-12 x 5-12 ft (1.5-4 x 1.5-4 m)
Firmiana simplex	66	7				50 x 30 ft (15 x 10 m)
Fraxinus americana	68	6-9		●	*	80 x 50 ft (25 x 15 m)
'Fall Purple'	68	6-9		●		60 x 40 ft (18 x 12 m)
'Rose Hill'	68	6-9		●		50 x 30 ft (15 x 10 m)
Fraxinus angustifolia 'Raywood'	68	5		●		70 x 50 ft (20 x 15 m)
Fraxinus chinensis rhyncophylla	68	6		●		12-15 x 12-15 ft (4-5 x 4-5 m)
Fraxinus dipetala	68	9			*	12-15 x 10 ft (4-5 x 3 m)
Fraxinus excelsior	68	5-9		●		100 x 70 ft (30 x 20 m)
'Jaspidea'	68	5		●		20 x 20 ft (6 x 6 m)
Fraxinus ornus	69	6-9				50 x 50 ft (15 x 15 m)
Fraxinus pennsylvanica 'Summit'	69	4		●		45 x 25 ft (14 x 8 m)
Fraxinus spaethiana	69	6		●		12-15 x 12-15 ft (4-5 x 4-5 m)
Fraxinus velutina	69	6			*	30 x 30 ft (10 x 10 m)
'Fan-Tex'	69	6				30 x 30 ft (10 x 10 m)
Ginkgo biloba	70	5-9		●		100 x 25 ft (30 x 8 m)
'Fairmount'	71	5-9		●		50 x 20 ft (15 x 6 m)
'Fall Gold'	71	5-9		●		50 x 30 ft (15 x 10 m)
'Fastigiata'	71	5-9		●		50 x 15 ft (15 x 5 m)
'Pendula'	71	5-9		●		30 x 30 ft (10 x 10 m)
'Princeton Sentry'	71	5-9		●		50 x 15 ft (15 x 5 m)
'Variegata'	71	5-9				30 x 20 ft (10 x 6 m)
Gleditsia triacanthos inermis	71	3		●	*	30-80 x 25-35 ft (10-25 x 8-11 m)
'Bujotii'	72	3		●		15-25 x 15 ft (5-8 x 5 m)
'Elegantissima'	72	3		●		15-25 x 15 ft (5-8 x 5 m)
'Majestic'	72	3		●		40 x 30 ft (12 x 10 m)
'Moraine'	72	3		●		40 x 30 ft (12 x 10 m)
'Ruby Lace'	72	3		●		40 x 30 ft (12 x 10 m)
'Shademaster'	72	3		●		45 x 30 ft (12 x 10 m)
'Skyline'	72	3		●		50 x 30 ft (12 x 10 m)
'Sunburst'	72	3		●		40 x 30 ft (12 x 10 m)
Hedera canariensis	72	8	●			30 ft (10 m) (climber)
Hedera helix	72	5	●			30 ft (10 m) (climber)
Hydrangea macrophylla	73	6-9				6 x 8 ft (2 x 2.5 m)
Hydrangea quercifolia	73	5-9		●	*	6 x 8 ft (2 x 2.5 m)
Idesia polycarpa	74	6-9		●		40 x 40 ft (12 x 12 m)
Ilex x altaclerensis	76	7-9	●			70 x 40-50 ft (20 x 12-15 m)
'Golden King'	76	7-9	●			15 x 15 ft (5 x 5 m)
'Lawsoniana'	76	7-9	●			20 x 15 ft (6 x 5 m)
'Wilsonii'	76	7-9	●			25 x 15 ft (8 x 5 m)
Ilex aquifolium	76	7-9	●			80 x 25 ft (25 x 8 m)
'Argeneamarginata'	76	7-9	●			12 x 12 ft (4 x 4 m)
'Ferox'	76	7-9	●			9 x 6 ft (3 x 2 m)
'Golden Milkboy'	76	7-9	●			20 x 12 ft (5 x 4 m)
'Silver Queen'	76	7-9	●			12 x 12 ft (4 x 4 m)
Ilex cornuta	76	7-9	●			15 x 15 ft (5 x 5 m)
'Burfordii'	76	7-9	●			12-15 x 12-15 ft (4-5 x 4-5 m)
'D'Or'	76	7-9	●			3-4 x 3-4 ft (1 x 1 m)
'O'Spring'	76	7-9	●			3-4 x 3-4 ft (1 x 1 m)
Ilex crenata	76	5-9	●			15 x 12 ft (5 x 4 m)
'Convexa'	76	5-9	●			8 x 6 ft (2.5 x 2 m)
'Golden Gem'	76	5-9	●			3.5 x 4-5 ft (1.1 x 1.2-1.5 m)
'Mariesii'	77	5-9	●			24-36 x 18-24 in (60-90 x 45-60 cm)
Ilex x meserveae						
'Blue Angel'	77	5-9	●			12 x 6 ft (4 x 2 m)
'Blue Boy'	77	5-9	●			10 x 12 ft (3 x 4 m)
'Blue Girl'	77	5-9	●			10 x 12 ft (3 x 4 m)
'Blue Prince'	77	5-9	●			10 x 12 ft (3 x 4 m)
'Blue Princess'	77	5-9	●			10 x 12 ft (3 x 4 m)
Ilex 'Nellie R. Stevens'	77	7-9	●			22 x 12 ft (7 x 4 m)
Ilex perado	77	7-9	●			20-30 x 22 ft (6-10 x 7 m)
Ilex pernyi	78	6-9	●			28 x 10 ft (9 x 3 m)
Ilex verticillata	78	5-8		●	*	15 x 15 ft (5 x 5 m)
Juniperus chinensis	78	3-9	●			70 x 20 ft (20 x 6 m)
'Aurea'	78	3-9	●			35 x 15 ft (11 x 5 m)
'Blue Vase'	78	3-9	●			2-3 x 2-3 ft (60-90 x 60-90 cm)
'Kaizuka'	78	3-9	●			20 x 10-12 ft (6 x 3-4 m)
Juniperus x pfitzeriana	79	4-9	●			4 x 10 ft (1.2 x 3 m)
'Dandelight'	79	4-9	●			2 x 6 ft (60 cm x 2 m)
Juniperus scopulorum	79	4-7	●		*	50 x 20 ft (15 x 6 m)
'Skyrocket'	79	4-7	●			20 ft x 20-24 in (6 m x 50-60 cm)
Juniperus squamata	80	5-8	●			30 x 3-25 ft (10 x 1-8 m)
'Blue Star'	80	5-8	●			16 in x 3 ft (40 cm x 1 m)
'Meyeri'	80	4	●			12-30 x 20 -25 ft (4-10 x 6-8 m)
Juniperus taxifolia var *lutchuensis*	80	9	●			1-2 x 10 ft (30-60 cm x 3 m)

Species or cultivar	page reference	hardiness zones	evergreen	fall color	native to North America	height x width
Juniperus virginiana	80	3-9	●		*	50-100 x 15-25 ft (15-30 x 5-8 m)
Kalopanax pictus	80	5-9		●		30 x 30 ft (10 x 10 m)
Kalopanax pictus var maximowiczii	81	5-9		●		6 x 6 ft (2 x 2 m)
Larix decidua	81	3-8		●		100 x 12-20 ft (30 x 4-6 m)
Larix kaempferi	81	5-8		●		100 x 12-20 ft (30 x 4-6 m)
Larix occidentalis	81	4-8		●	*	80 x 15 ft (25 x 5 m)
Leucothoe fontanesiana	82	5-9	●		*	3-6 x 10 ft (1.2 x 3 m)
'Nana'	82	5-9	●			2-3 4-5 ft (60-90 cm x 1.2-1.5 m)
'Rainbow'	82	5-9	●			5 x 6 ft (1.5 x 2 m)
'Scarletta'	82	5-9	●			5 x 6 ft (1.5 x 2 m)
Leucothoe grayana	82	6	●			3 x 5 ft (1 x 1.5 m)
Leucothoe keiskei	82	6-8	●			24 x 24 in (60 x 60 cm)
Lindera benzoin	82	5-9		●	*	10 x 10 ft (3 x 3 m)
Lindera erythrocarpa	83	6		●		15-20 x 15-20 ft (5-6 x 5-6 m)
Lindera obtusiloba	83	6-9		●		20 x 20 ft (6 x 6 m)
Liquidambar formosana	85	7-9		●		40 x 30 ft (12 x 10 m)
Liquidambar orientalis	85	7-9		●		20 x 12 ft (6 x 4 m)
Liquidambar styraciflua	85	6		●	*	80 x 40 ft (25 x 12 m)
'Burgundy'	85	6		●		60 x 60 ft (18 x 18 m)
'Festeri'	85	6		●		60 x 60 ft (18 x 18 m)
'Festival'	85	6		●		60 x 60 ft (18 x 18 m)
'Golden Treasure'	85	6		●		30 x 20 ft (10 x 6 m)
'Lane Roberts'	85	6		●		60 x 60 ft (18 x 18 m)
'Palo Alto'	85	6		●		60 x 60 ft (18 x 18 m)
'Rotundiloba'	85	6		●		40 x 20 ft (12 x 6 m)
'Variegata'	85	6		●		50 x 25 ft (15 x 8 m)
'Worplesdon'	85	6		●		50 x 25 ft (15 x 8 m)
Liriodendron chinense	86	7-9		●		80 x 40 ft (25 x 12 m)
Liriodendron tulipifera	86	5-9		●	*	100 x 50 ft (30 x 15 m)
'Arnold'	86	5-9		●		70 x 25 ft (20 x 8 m)
'Aureomarginatum'	86	5-9		●		70 x 30 ft (20 x 10 m)
'Compactum'	86	5-9		●		40 x 25 ft (12 x 8 m)
'Fastigiatum'	86	5-9		●		70 x 25 ft (20 x 8 m)
Lonicera korolkowii	87	5-9				10 x 15 ft (3 x 5 m)
Lonicera nitida	87	6-9	●			11 x 10 ft (3.5 x 3 m)
'Baggessens Gold'	87	6-9	●			5 x 5 ft (1.5 x 1.5 m)
Lyonia ligustrina	88	5			*	3-4 x 6 ft (1 x 2 m)
Lyonia lucida	88	7	●		*	3-4 x 6 ft (1 x 2 m)
Lyonia mariana	88	5-9			*	6 x 4 ft (2 x 1.2 m)
Lyonia ovalifolia	88	6				15 x 15 ft (5 x 5 m)
Lyonothamnus floribundus var aspleniifolius	88	9	●		*	40 x 20 ft (12 x 6 m)
Maackia amurensis	89	5-8		●		50 x 30 ft (15 x 10 m)
Magnolia delavayi	90	7-9	●			30 x 30 ft (10 x 10 m)
Magnolia grandiflora	90	6	●		*	20-60 x 50 ft (6-18 x 15 m)
Magnolia hypoleuca	91	5-9				50 x 30 ft (15 x 10 m)
Magnolia macrophylla	91	6-9			*	30 x 30 ft (10 x 10 m)
Magnolia macrophylla ashei	91	6-9			*	10-15 x 10-15 ft (3-5 x 3-5 m)
Magnolia x soulangeana	91	5-9				20 x 20 ft (6 x 6 m)
'Alexandrina'	91	5-9				20 x 20 ft (6 x 6 m)
'Lennei'	91	5-9				20 x 20 ft (6 x 6 m)
'Rustica Rubra'	92	5-9				20 x 20 ft (6 x 6 m)
Magnolia virginiana	92	5-9	●		*	15 x 15 ft (5 x 5 m)
Mahonia aquifolium	92	6-9	●		*	3 x 5 ft (1 x 1.5 m)
Mahonia fortunei	92	8-9	●			4 x 3 ft (1.2 x 1 m)

Species or cultivar	page reference	hardiness zones	evergreen	fall color	native to North America	height x width
Mahonia japonica	92	7	●			6 x 10 ft (2 x 3 m)
'Bealei'	93	7	●			6 x 10 ft (2 x 3 m)
Mahonia lomariifolia	93	8	●			10 x 6 ft (3 x 2 m)
Mahonia mairei	93	8	●			10-12 x 6 ft (3-4 x 2 m)
Mahonia x media	93	8	●			12-15 x 12 ft (4-5 x 4 m)
Melia azedarach	93	7		●		30-50 x 15-25 ft (10-15 x 5-8 m)
'Umbraculiformis'	94	7				30 x 30 ft (10 x 10 m)
Melianthus major	94	8	●			6-10 x 3-10 ft (2-3 x 1-3 m)
Nandina domestica	95	6-9	●			6 x 5 ft (2 x 1.5 m)
'Firepower'	95	6-9	●			18 x 24 in (45 x 60 cm)
'Gulf Stream'	95	6-9	●			3 x 4 ft (1 x 1.2 m)
'Harbor Dwarf'	95	6-9	●			3 x 4 ft (1 x 1.2 m)
'Nana'	95	6-9	●			2-4 x 2-4 ft (60-120 x 60-120 cm)
'San Gabriel'	96	6-9	●			3 x 4 ft (1 m x 1.2 m)
Neolitsea sericea	96	9	●			20 x 10 ft (6 x 3 m)
Nothofagus menziesii	97	8-9	●			50 x 25 ft (15 x 8 m)
Nothofagus obliqua	97	8-9				70 x 50 ft (20 x 15 m)
Nothofagus procera	97	8-9				80 x 50 ft (25 x 15 m)
Nothofagus solandri	98	8-9	●			50 x 30 ft (15 x 10 m)
Nyssa aquatica	98	5			*	30-50 x 20-30 ft (10-15 x 6-10 m)
Nyssa sinensis	98	7-9		●		30 x 30 ft (10 x 10 m)
Nyssa sylvatica	98	5-9		●	*	70 x 30 ft (20 x 10 m)
'Dirr's Selection'	99	5-9		●		70 x 30 ft (20 x 10 m)
'Jermyns Flame'	99	5-9		●		70 x 30 ft (20 x 10 m)
'Pendula'	99	5-9		●	*	15 x 15 ft (5 x 5 m)
'Sheffield Park'	99	5-9		●		70 x 30 ft (20 x 10 m)
Osteomeles schweriniae	99	7	●			10 x 10 ft (3 x 3 m)
Oxydendrum arboreum	100	5-9		●	*	30-50 x 25 ft (10-15 x 8 m)
Parrotia persica	101	4-9		●		25 x 30 ft (8 x 10 m)
'Pendula'	102	4-9		●		5 x 10 ft (1.5 x 3 m)
Parrotiopsis jacquemontiana	102	6-9		●		20 x 12 ft (6 x 4 m)
Parthenocissus henryana	102	7		●		30 ft (10 m) (climber)
Parthenocissus quinquefolia	102	3-9		●	*	50 ft (15 m) (climber)
Parthenocissus tricuspidata	103	4-8		●		70 ft (20 m) (climber)
Paulownia fargesii	103	6				25 x 20 ft (8 x 6 m)
Paulownia fortunei	103	6-9				25 x 25 ft (8 x 8 m)
Paulownia tomentosa	103	5-8				40 x 30 ft (12 x 10 m)
Phellodendron amurense	104	3-9		●		46 x 50 ft (14 x 15 m)
Photinia x fraseri	104	8	●			15 x 15 ft (5 x 5 m)
'Birmingham'	104	8	●			15 x 15 ft (5 x 5 m)
'Red Robin'	105	7	●			10-15 x 10-15 ft (3-5 x 3-5 m)
'Robusta'	105	7	●			30 x 20 ft (10 x 6 m)
Photinia glabra	105	7	●			10 x 10 ft (3 x 3 m)
'Rubens'	105	7	●			10 x 10 ft (3 x 3 m)
Photinia serratifolia	105	7	●			30-40 x 25 ft (10-12 x 8 m)
Photinia villosa	105	4-9		●		15 x 15 ft (5 x 5 m)
'Village Shade'	105	4-9		●		15 x 15 ft (5 x 5 m)
Physocarpus opulifolius	105	3		●	*	10 x 15 ft (3 x 5 m)
Picea abies	107	3-8	●			70-130 x 20 ft (20-40 x 6 m)
'Aurea'	107	3-8	●			50 x 15-20 ft (15 x 5-6 m)
'Pyramidalis'	107	3-8	●			50 x 15-20 ft (15 x 5-6 m)
Picea breweriana	107	6-8	●		*	30-50 x 10-12 ft (10-15 x 3-4 m)
Picea engelmannii	107	3-8	●		*	70-130 x 15 ft (20-40 x 5 m)
Picea glauca var albertiana	107	3-8	●		*	3-6 x 2-4 ft (1-2 x 1 m)
Picea glauca 'Echiniformis'	107	3-8	●			3x 3 ft (1 x 1 m)

Species or cultivar	page reference	hardiness zones	evergreen	fall color	native to North America	height x width
Picea likiangensis purpurea	108	6-8	●			100 x 20-28 ft (30 x 6-9 m)
Picea omorika	108	5-8	●			70 x 6-10 ft (20 x 2-3 m)
Picea orientalis	108	5-8	●			100 x 20-25 ft (30 x 6-8 m)
Picea pungens 'Koster'	108	3-8	●			50 x 3 ft (15 x 1 m)
Picea sitchensis	108	7-8	●		*	80-160 x 20-40 ft (25-50 6-12 m)
Picea smithiana	109	8	●			70-100 x 20-28 ft (28-30 6-9 m)
Picrasma quassioides	109	6-9		●		25 x 25 ft (8 x 8 m)
Pieris floribunda	110	5-9	●		*	6 x 10 ft (2 x 3 m)
Pieris formosa	110	7-9	●			15 x 12 ft (5 x 4 m)
Pieris formosa var forrestii	111	8	●			8 x 8 ft (2.5 x 2.5 m)
'Charles Michael'	111	8	●			8 x 8 ft (2.5 x 2.5 m)
'Henry Price'	111	8	●			8 x 8 ft (2.5 x 2.5 m)
'Jermyns'	111	8	●			8 x 8 ft (2.5 x 2.5 m)
'Wakehurst'	111	8	●			8 x 8 ft (2.5 x 2.5 m)
Pieris japonica	111	6-9	●			12 x 10 ft (4 x 3 m)
Pieris taiwanensis	111	7	●			3-5 x 5 ft (1-1.4 x 1.4 m)
Pileostegia viburnoides	111	7	●			20 ft (6 m) (climber)
Pinus elliotii	112	9	●		*	30 x 30 ft (10 x 10 m)
Pinus flexilis var reflexa	112	3-8	●		*	50-70 x 20-28 ft (15-20 x 6-9 m)
Pinus koraiensis	112	4-9	●			70 x 25 ft (20 x 8 m)
'Compacta Glauca'	112	4-9	●			10-20 x 6-10 ft (3-6 x 2-3 m)
Pinus mugo	112	3-8	●			11 x 15 ft (3.5 x 5 m)
Pinus parviflora	112	6-9	●			30-70 x 20-25 ft (10-20 x 6-8 m)
Pinus wallichiana	112	6-9	●			70-120 x 20-40 ft (20-35 x 6-12 m)
Pinus yunnanensis	113	9	●			20-30 x 20-30 ft (6-10 x 6-10 m)
Pistacia chinensis	113	7-9		●		50-80 x 22-30 ft (15-25 x 7-10 m)
Pittosporum eugenoides	114	9	●			15-40 x 6-15 ft (5-12 x 2-5 m)
Pittosporum tenuifolium	114	9	●			12-30 x 6-15 ft (4-10 x 2-5 m)
Pittosporum tobira	114	9	●			6-30 x 5-10 ft (2-10 x 1.5-3 m)
Platanus x acerifolia	115	5				100 x 70 ft (30 x 20 m)
Platanus occidentalis	115	5			*	80 x 70 ft (25 x 20 m)
Platanus orientalis	115	7				100 x 100 ft (30 x 30 m)
Platanus racemosa	116	8			*	80 x 70 ft (25 x 20 m)
Podocarpus alpinus	116	7	●			6 x 6 ft (2 x 2 m)
Podocarpus gracilior	116	8	●			9 x 6 ft (3 x 2 m)
Podocarpus henkelii	116	9	●			6-9 x 6 ft (2-3 x 2 m)
Podocarpus macrophyllus	116	7	●			50 x 20-25 ft (15 x 6-8 m)
'Maki'	117	7	●			10-15 x 6 ft (3-5 x 2 m)
Podocarpus salignus	117	8	●			70 x 20-28 ft (20 x 6-9 m)
Podocarpus totara	117	8	●			30 x 15 ft (10 x 5 m)
Populus balsamifera	117	5-9			*	100 x 25 ft (30 x 8 m)
Populus deltoides	117	3-9		●	*	100 x 70 ft (30 x 20 m)
Populus lasiocarpa	117	6-9				70 x 40 ft (20 x 12 m)
Populus maximowiczii	118	4-8		●		100 x 30 ft (30 x 10 m)
Populus nigra var italica	118	3-9		●		100 x 15 ft (30 x 5 m)
Populus szechuanica	118	4-9				130 x 30 ft (40 x 10 m)
Prunus cerasifera 'Nigra'	118	5-9		●		30 x 30 ft (10 x 10 m)
Prunus laurocerasus	119	6-9	●			25 x 30 ft (8 x 10 m)
'Castlewellan'	119	6-9	●			6 x 6 ft (2 x 2 m)
'Magnoliifolia'	120	6-9	●			6 x 6 ft (2 x 2 m)
'Otto Luyken'	120	6-9	●			3 x 5 ft (1 x 1.5 m)
'Rotundifolia'	120	6-9	●			6 x 6 ft (2 x 2 m)
'Zabeliana'	120	6-9	●			3 x 6 ft (1 x 2 m)

Species or cultivar	page reference	hardiness zones	evergreen	fall color	native to North America	height x width
Prunus lusitanica	120	7-9	●			70 x 70 ft (20 x 20 m)
Prunus sargentii	120	5-9		●		70 x 50 ft (20 x 15 m)
Prunus serrulata	120	6-9		●		30 x 30 ft (10 x 10 m)
'Kanzan'	120	6-8		●		30 x 30 ft (10 x 10 m)
Prunus subhirtella	120	6-9		●		25 x 25 ft (8 x 8 m)
'Autumnalis'	120	6-9		●		25 x 25 ft (8 x 8 m)
'Pendula'	121	6-9		●		25 x 25 ft (8 x 8 m)
Pyrus calleryana	121	5		●		50 x 30 ft (15 x 10 m)
'Aristocrat'	121	5		●		40 x 20 ft (12 x 6 m)
'Bradford'	121	5		●		40 x 20 ft (12 x 6 m)
'Chanticleer'	121	5		●		40 x 20 ft (2 x 6 m)
Pyrus salicifolia 'Pendula'	121	5-9		●		15 x 12 ft (5 x 4 m)
Quercus coccinea	122	5-9		●	*	70 x 50 ft (20 x 15 m)
Quercus marilandica	122	6-9		●	*	40 x 50 ft (12 x 15 m)
Quercus palustris	122	4		●	*	70 x 40 ft (20 x 12 m)
Quercus robur	123	5-8				120 x 80 ft (35 x 25 m)
Quercus rubra	123	3		●	*	80 x 70 ft (25 x 20 m)
Rhododendron arboreum 'Sir Charles Lemon'	123	7-9	●			40 x 12 ft (12 x 4 m)
Rhododendron cinnabarinum	124	8-9	●			20 x 6 ft (6 x 2 m)
Rhododendron forrestii	124	7-9	●			8 in x 5 ft (20 cm x 1.5 m)
Rhododendron fortunei series	124	6-9	●			30 x 8 ft (10 x 2.5 m)
Rhododendron grande	124	8	●			30 x 30 ft (10 x 10 m)
Rhododendron macabeanum	124	8	●			30 x 30 ft (10 x 10 m)
Rhododendron magnificum	124	8	●			30 x 30 ft (10 x 10 m)
Rhododendron pachysanthum	125	7-9	●			5-8 x 8 ft (1.5-2.5 x 2.5 m)
Rhododendron sinogrande	124	8	●			30 x 30 ft (10 x 10 m)
Rhododendron wardii	125	7-9	●			20 x 15 ft (6 x 5 m)
Rhododendron williamsianum	125	7-9	●			5 x 4 ft (1.5 x 1.2 m)
Rhododendron yakushimanum	126	5	●			3 x 3 ft (1 x 1 m)
Rhus glabra	126	2		●	*	8 x 8 ft (2.5 x 2.5 m)
'Laciniata'	127	2		●		10 x 15 ft (3 x 5 m)
Rhus succedanea	127	5		●		30 x 30 ft (10 x 10 m)
Rhus typhina	127	3		●	*	15 x 20 ft (5 x 6 m)
Robinia pseudoacacia	127	4		●	*	80 x 50 ft (25 x 15 m)
'Frisia'	127	4		●		30 x 30 ft (10 x 10 m)
'Pyramidalis'	128	4		●		50 x 10 ft (15 x 3 m)
Sambucus nigra	128	6-8		●		20 x 20 ft (6 x 6 m)
'Aurea'	128	6-8		●		20 x 20 ft (6 x 6 m)
'Guincho Purple'	128	6-8		●		20 x 20 ft (6 x 6 m)
'Laciniata'	128	6-8		●		20 x 20 ft (6 x 6 m)
Sambucus racemosa 'Plumosa Aurea'	128	3-7		●		10 x 10 ft (3 x 3 m)
Sassafras albidum	128	5		●	*	80 x 50 ft (25 x 15 m)
Sassafras tzumu	129	8		●		30 x 10-15 ft (10 x 3-5 m)
Schinus molle	130	9	●			30-80 x 10-15 ft (10-25 x 3-5 m)
Schinus terebinthifolius	130	9	●			15-22 x 10-15 ft (5-7 3-5 m)
Sciadopitys verticillata	130	5-9	●			30-70 x 20-25 ft (10-20 x 6-8 m)
Sorbaria sorbifolia	131	5				6 x 10 ft (2 x 3 m)
Sorbus alnifolia	132	5-8		●		70 x 25 ft (20 x 8 m)
'Redbird'	132	5-8		●		40 x 25 ft (12 x 18 m)
'Skyline'	132	5-8		●		40 x 15 ft (12 x 5 m)
Sorbus aria	132	6-8		●		30-80 x 30 ft (10-25 x 10 m)

Species or cultivar	page reference	hardiness zones	evergreen	fall color	native to North America	height x width
Sorbus aucuparia	132	4-8				50 x 22 ft (15 x 7 m)
'Cardinal Royal'	132	4-8				30 x 10-15 ft (10 x 3-5 m)
'Sheerwater Seedling'	132	4-8				30 x 10-15 ft (10 x 3-5 m)
'Xanthocarpa'	132	4-8				30 x 20 ft (10 x 6 m)
Sorbus commixta	133	6-8		●		30 x 22 ft (10 x 7 m)
Sorbus decora	133	3-8		●	*	25 x 15 ft (8 x 5 m)
Sorbus domestica	133	6-8		●		70 x 40 ft (20 x 12 m)
Sorbus hupehensis	133	6-8		●		25 x 25 ft (8 x 8 m)
Sorbus x kewensis	133	6-8		●		25 x 25 ft (8 x 8 m)
Sorbus pohuashanensis	133	6-8				70 x 25 ft (20 x 8 m)
Sorbus sargentiana	133	5-7		●		30 x 30 ft (10 x 10 m)
Sorbus thibetica	133	5-7				70 x 50 ft (20 x 15 m)
'John Mitchell'	133	5-7				50 x 30 ft (15 x 10 m)
Tetracentron sinense	133	6				56-100 x 30 ft (17-30 x 10 m)
Tetrapanax papyrifer	134	6	●			15 x 15 ft (5 x 5 m)
Thuja occidentalis	135	2-9	●		*	30-60 x 10-15 ft (10-18 x 3-5 m)
'Pyramidalis'	135	2-9	●			12 x 3 ft (4 x 1 m)
'Rheingold'	136	2-9	●			3-6 x 3-6 ft (1-2 x 1-2 m)
Thuja plicata	136	6-9	●		*	70-120 x 20-35 ft (20-35 x 6-9 m)
'Atrovirens'	136	6-9	●			70 x 20 ft (20 x 6 m)
'Rogersii'	136	6-9	●			3 x 3 ft (1 x 1 m)
'Stoneham Gold'	136	6-9	●			6 x 6 ft (2 x 2 m)
Tilia americana	137	3-9			*	80 x 50 ft (25 x 15 m)
Tilia x euchlora	137	3-8				70 x 50 ft (20 x 15 m)
Tilai x europaea	137	4-8				120 x 50 ft (35 x 15 m)
Tilia henryana	137	6-9				80 x 80 ft (25 x 25 m)
Tilia kiusiana	137	6				15 x 10 ft (5 x 3 m)
Tilia mandshurica	137	5				15-25 x 15-25 ft (5-8 x 5-8 m)
Tilia x moltkei	137	4				50 x 30 ft (15 x 10 m)
Tilia oliveri	138	6				40 x 20 ft (12 x 6 m)
Tilia tomentosa	138	6-9				100 x 70 ft (30 x 20 m)
'Sterling'	138	6-9				50 x 25 ft (15 x 8 m)
Toona sinensis	138	6-9				50 x 30 ft (15 x 10 m)
'Flamingo'	138	6				9 x 9 ft (3 x 3 m)
Trochodendron aralioides	139	6	●			30 x 25 ft (10 x 8 m)
Tsuga canadensis	139	4-8	●		*	80 x 30 ft (25 x 10 m)
'Aurea'	140	4-8	●			25 x 12 ft (8 x 4 m)
'Cole'	140	4-8	●			12 in x 3 ft (30 cm x 1 m)
'Jeddeloh'	140	4-8	●			5 x 6 ft (1.5 x 2 m)
'Pendula'	140	4-8	●			12 x 25 ft (4 x 8 m)
Tsuga caroliniana	140	5-7	●		*	50-70 x 25 ft (15-20 x 8 m)
Tsuga chinensis	140	5-9	●			140 x 80-100 ft (45 x 25-30 m)
Tsuga diversifolia	140	6-8	●			50 x 25 ft (15 x 8 m)
Tsuga heterophylla	140	6-8	●		*	70-130 x 20-30 ft (20-40 x 6-10 m)
Tsuga sieboldii	140	6-8	●			50 x 25 ft (15 x 8 m)
Ulmus glabra	141	5				120-130 x 80 ft (35-40 x 25 m)
'Horizontalis'	141	5				15-20 x 15-20 ft (5-6 x 5-6 m)
Ulmus minor	141	5-8				100 x 70 ft (30 x 20 m)
'Jacqueline Hillier'	142	6				6 x 3 ft (2 x 1 m)
'Louis van Houtte'	142	4		●		30 x 30 ft (10 x 10 m)
'Variegata'	142	5				40 x 20 ft (12 x 6 m)
Ulmus parvifolia	142	5-9		●		60 x 25-40 ft (18 x 8-12 m)
'Allee'	142	5-9		●		60 x 30 ft (18 x 10 m)
'Frosty'	142	5-9				8 x 8 ft (2.5 x 2.5 m)
Ulmus pumila	142	3-9				70-100 x 40 ft (20-30 x 12 m)
Viburnum davidii	143	8-9	●			3-5 x 3-5 ft (1-1.5 x 1-1.5 m)
'Femina'	143	8-9	●			3-5 x 3-5 ft (1-1.5 x 1.1-5 m)
Viburnum japonicum	143	8-9	●			6 x 8 ft (2 x 2.5 m)
Viburnum odoratissimum	144	8-9	●			15 x 15 ft (5 x 5 m)
'Emerald Lustre'	144	8-9	●			15 x 15 ft (5 x 5 m)
Viburnum rhytidophyllum	144	6-8	●			15 x 12 ft (5 x 4 m)
Viburnum rhytidophylloides	144	6-8	●			6 x 6 ft (2 x 2 m)
Viburnum tinus	111	6	●			10 x 10 ft (3 x 3 m)
'Variegatum'	144	7	●			10 x 10 ft (3 x 3 m)
Vitis amurensis	144	4-9		●		50 ft (15 m) (climber)
Vitis coignetiae	145	5-9		●		50 ft (15 m) (climber)
Xanthorhiza simplicissima	145	3-9		●	*	24 in x 5 ft (60 cm x 1.5 m)
Zanthoxylum ailanthoides	146	7				20-60 x 15-50 ft (6-20 x 5-15 m)
Zanthoxylum piperitum	146	6-9				8 x 8 ft (2.5 x 2.5 m)
Zanthoxylum planispinum	146	6				8-12 x 8-12 ft (3-4 x 3-4 m)
Zelkova carpinifolia	147	5-9				100 x 80 ft (30 x 25 m)
Zelkova serrata	147	5-9		●		100 x 60 ft (30 x 18 m)
'Goblin'	147	5-9		●		3 x 3 ft (1 x 1 m)
'Village Green'	147	5-9		●		30 x 30 ft (10 x 10 m)

Mail-order sources for trees and shrubs

The importation of live plants and plant materials across state and country borders may require special arrangements, which will be detailed in suppliers' catalogs.

American regulations vary according to the country of origin and type of plant. Every order requires a phytosanitary certificate and may require a CITES (Convention on International Trade in Endangered Species of Wild Fauna and Flora) certificate. For more information contact:
USDA-APHIS-PPQ
Permit Unit
4700 River Road, Unit 136
Riverdale, Maryland 20727-1236
Tel: (301) 734-8645/Fax: (301) 734-5786
Website: www.aphis.udsda.gov

Canadians importing plant material must pay a fee and complete an "application for permit to import." Contact:
Plant Health and Production Division
Canadian Food Inspection Agency
2nd Floor West, Permit Office
59 Camelot Drive
Nepean, Ontario K1A 0Y9
Tel: (613) 225-2342/Fax: (613) 228-6605
Website: www.cfia-agr.ca

Angelgrove Tree Seed Company
P.O. Box 74, Riverhead
Harbour Grace, Newfoundland A0A 3P0
Website: www.tree-seeds.com
Mail order supplier of seeds for hardy trees and shrubs.

ArborVillage
PO Box 227
Holt, Missouri 64048
Tel: (816) 264-3911/Fax: (816) 264-3760
Email: Arborvillage@aol.com
Wide variety of common and unusual trees and shrubs. Catalog available.

Camellia Forest Nursery
125 Carolina Forest Road
Chapel Hill, North Carolina 27516
Tel: (919) 968-0504/Fax: (919) 960-7690
Website: www.camforest.com
Flowering shrubs and trees from China and Japan.

Collins Lilac Hill Nursery
2366 Turk Hill Road
Victor, New York 14564
Tel: (716) 223-1669
More than 200 lilacs from Ted "Doc Lilac" Collins.

Eastern Plant Specialties
P.O. Box 226W
Georgetown, Maine 04548
Tel: (732) 382-2508
Website: www.easternplant.com
Catalog available.

Forestfarm
990 Tetherow Road
Williams, Oregon 97544-9599
Tel: (541) 846-7269/Fax: (541) 846-6963
Website: www.forestfarm.com
E-Mail: forestfarm@rvi.com
Good selection of trees and shrubs. Ships to Canada.

Fraser's Thimble Farms
175 Arbutus Road
Salt Spring Island, British Columbia V8K 1A3
Tel/Fax: (250) 537-5788
Website: www.thimblefarms.com
E-mail: thimble@saltspring.com
Order by fax or e-mail. Ships to U.S.

Great Plant Company
Tel: (415) 362 5430/Fax: (415) 362 5431
Website: www.greatplants.com
E-mail: plants@greatplants.com
Catalog available. Does not ship to Canada.

Greer Gardens
1280 Goodpasture Island Road
Eugene, Oregon 97401-1794
Tel: (541) 686-8266/Toll-free Tel: (800) 548-0111
Fax: (905) 686-0910
Website: www.greergardens.com
Catalog available. Ships to Canada.

Heronswood Nursery, Ltd.
7530 NE 288th Street
Kingston, Washington 98346
Tel: (360) 297-4172/Fax: (360) 297-8321
Website: www.heronswood.com
Excellent catalog.

Hortico Inc.
723 Robson Road, R.R. 1
Waterdown, Ontario L0R 2H1
Tel: (905) 689-6984/Fax: (905) 689-6566
Website: www.hortico.com
Catalog available. Ships to the U.S.

Louisiana Nursery
5853 Highway 182
Opelousas, Louisiana 70570
Tel: (337) 948-3696/Fax: (337) 942-6404
Website: www.louisiananursery.org
Wide selection including over 600 different varieties of magnolias. Full-color catalog. Ships to Canada.

Molbaks's
13625 N.E. 175 Street
Woodinville, Washington 98072
Tel: (425) 483-5000
Wide range of plants and seeds.

Select Plus International Nursery
1510 Pine
Mascouche, Quebec J7L 2M4
Tel: (450) 477-3797
Website: www.spi.8m.com
Informative website. Ships to the U.S.

Wayside Gardens
1 Garden Lane
Hodges, South Carolina 29695
Toll-free: 1 (800) 213-0379
Website: www.waysidegardens.com
Wide selection. Free catalog.

Glossary

Acidic Any substance with a low pH. See also pH.

Acuminate Tapering to a point.

Acute Sharp pointed, without tapering.

Adventitious Occurring away from the usual place, e.g. aerial roots on stems.

Alkaline Any substance with a high pH. See also pH.

Alternate With leaves arranged singly on different sides of the stem and at different levels.

Apex The tip of a leaf or organ.

Attenuate Very gradually tapering.

Axil The upper angle between the stem and a leaf.

Bare rooted Trees and shrubs that are lifted from the open ground and sold with their roots wrapped in damp shredded newspaper, sphagnum moss, etc.

Bipinnate A leaf that is doubly pinnate, the primary leaflets being again divided into secondary leaflets, e.g. *Jacaranda*.

Bract A modified leaf or sepal at the base of a flower, often the most colorful part, e.g. *Cornus* and *Bougainvillea*.

Bullate A puckered leaf surface.

Calyx (pl. calyxes) The outer, often decorative, covering of a flower bud, usually consisting of united sepals.

Chlorophyll The green pigment in plants essential for the process of photosynthesis.

Clone An exact replica of an individual plant. Any plant propagated by vegetative means.

Cone The seed-bearing organs of conifers, composed of over-lapping scales on a central axis.

Conifer A plant that bears its seeds in cones.

Container-grown Plants raised entirely in containers, as opposed to open ground or field grown.

Cordate Heart-shaped.

Corymb A more or less flat-topped inflorescence, the outer flowers opening first.

Crenate Having shallow, rounded teeth or scalloped edges.

Crenulate Finely crenate.

Cultivar A botanical term for a variety that has arisen or is maintained in cultivation.

Cuneate Wedge-shaped with a gradual, even taper to the base.

Cyme A type of broad, flat-topped inflorescence in which the central flowers open first.

Dead heading The removal of faded flower heads to prevent the production of seed or to encourage heavier flowering.

Deciduous A plant that sheds all its leaves for part of the year.

Dentate With a serrated or toothed edge.

Denticulate Very finely toothed.

Digitate A leaf shape that resembles the arrangement of the fingers on a hand, e.g. *Aesculus*.

Dioecious Having male and female reproductive organs on separate plants.

Dissected Deeply cut into numerous segments.

Divaricate Spreading widely.

Drip line The circle around the outermost branch tips of a shrub or tree, the limit to which rainwater drips fall from the plant.

Drip tip The tapering, pointed end of a leaf, usually indicating an origin in a wet climate as the drip tip of the leaf helps to shed water.

Endemic Native to a particular restricted area.

Evergreen Retaining foliage throughout the year.

Exotic A plant originating in a foreign country and which is not native or endemic.

Family A group of related genera.

Fastigiate Narrow and upright with branches or stems erect and more or less parallel.

Floret One of many small flowers in a compound head.

Genus (pl. genera) A grouping of closely related species.

Glabrous Without hairs of any kind.

Glaucous A distinct blue or gray tint, especially leaves.

Globose Globe-shaped.

Gymnosperm A plant in which the seeds are not enclosed in an ovary, e.g. conifers and podocarps.

Honeydew The sticky secretion of many sap-sucking insects.

Hybrid The result of cross-fertilization of different parent plants.

Indigenous Native to a particular country or area. See also endemic and exotic.

Indumentum See tomentum.

Inflorescence The flower-bearing part of a plant, irrespective of arrangement.

Internode The length of stem between two nodes.

Invasive Said of a plant that grows quickly and spreads to occupy more than its allotted space, usually to the detriment of surrounding plants.

Juvenile A young or immature plant. Many plants display distinct differences between juvenile and adult foliage and growth habit.

Laciniate Having fine lobes, giving the impression of being cut by hand.

Lanceolate Lance-shaped, long and gradually tapering.

Leader The plant's dominant central shoot or one of several lateral shoots trained to produce a particular growth form.

Leaflet One of the smaller leaf-like parts of a compound leaf.

Leaf scar The mark left after a leaf falls. Very noticeable on some plants, e.g. *Aesculus*.

Legume A plant that produces pea-type seeds attached alternately to both sides of the pod and has root nodules that fix atmospheric nitrogen, e.g. peas, beans and lupins.

Lenticel Breathing hole on a stem or trunk, usually seen as a raised bump.

Lepidote Covered in small scales.

Linear Narrow and short with sides almost parallel.

Monoecious Having male and female reproductive organs in separate flowers on the one plant.

Monotypic A genus containing only one species.

Mucronate With a sharply pointed tip.

Mutant A spontaneous variant differing genetically and often visibly from its parent.

Mycorrhiza A beneficial association between a fungus and plant roots. Some plants, such as *Pinus*, rely on mycorrhizae for proper development.

Native A plant that occurs naturally in the area in which it is growing.

Natural cross A hybrid that occurs between two distinct, but usually related, plant species without human help.

Node A point on a stem on which leaves, buds or branches are borne.

Obovate Egg-shaped, with the broadest end at the top.

Open ground Plants raised in fields and lifted prior to sale, as opposed to container-grown plants.

Opposite Leaves on both sides of the stem at the same node.

Ovate Egg-shaped, with the broadest end at the base.

Palmate Roughly hand-shaped, with three or more lobes radiating fan-like from the petiole.

Panicle A branching cluster of flowers.

Parasite A plant that lives off another plant and which is usually unable to survive without the host plant.

Pathogen An organism, especially a bacterium or fungus, capable of causing disease.

Pedicel The stalk of an individual floret within a compound head.

Peduncle The main stalk of an inflorescence or of a flower borne singly.

Peltate Shield-shaped.

Petiole The stalk of a leaf.

pH The degree of acidity or alkalinity of the soil as measured on a scale from 0 (acidic) to 14 (alkaline), with 7 as the neutral point.

Photosynthesis The process whereby plants use solar energy, through the catalytic action of chlorophyll, to convert water and carbon dioxide into carbohydrates.

Pinnate A leaf form with leaflets arranged on both sides of the stalk, like a feather.

Pubescent Covered, often sparsely, in short hairs.

Raceme A stalk with flowers along its length, the individual blossoms with short stems.

Recurved Bent backward and/or downward.

Reflexed Sharply recurved.

Reticulate A net-like structure or markings.

Rootstock A rooted section of plant used as the base onto which a scion from another plant is grafted.

Russet A rough, brownish marking on leaves, fruits or tubers.

Scandent Having a climbing habit.

Scion A bud or shoot that is grafted onto the stock of another plant.

Sepal The individual segment of a calyx.

Serrate Having a saw-toothed or serrated edge.

Species The basic or minor unit in binomial nomenclature.

Specific name A plant's second name, e.g. *Pinus* **radiata.**

Spike A series of stalkless flowers on a single stem. The lower flowers are the first to open.

Sport A mutation showing distinct variations from the norm, e.g. a different foliage form or flower color.

Stellate Star-like or star-shaped.

Sub-shrub A permanently woody plant with soft pliable stems. Often green barked but woody at the base.

Sucker An adventitious stem arising from the roots of a woody plant, often from the stock rather than the scion of a grafted plant.

Systemic Any substance capable of permeating through the entire plant. Often said of insecticides and fungicides.

Taxonomy The science of plant classification.

Tepal The petal-like structures of a flower that does not have clearly defined sepals and petals, e.g. *Magnolia.*

Terminal bud The bud at the tip of the stem. Usually the first to burst into growth at bud break.

Tomentum The furry coating found on some leaves and stems, e.g. many rhododendrons. Also known as indumentum.

Topiary Trimming shrubs and trees to predetermined shapes for aesthetic appeal rather than growth restriction or function.

Trifoliate A leaf that is divided into three leaflets, e.g. clover.

Triploid A plant with three complete sets of chromosomes.

Truncate Ending or cut off abruptly or at right angles.

Truss A compound terminal cluster of flowers borne on one stalk.

Umbel A group of flower heads growing from a common point on a stem, hence umbellate.

Undulate Having a wavy edge.

Varietal name see Cultivar.

Variety Strictly a subdivision of a species, but often refers to a recognizably different member of a plant species worthy of cultivation.

Whorl A circle of three or more flowers or branches on a stem at the same level.

Bibliography

American Horticultural Society. *A-Z Encyclopedia of Garden Plants.* C. Brickell and J. Zuk (Editors-in-Chief). New York: Dorling Kindersley, 1997.

Bean, W. J. *Trees and Shrubs Hardy in the British Isles.* London: John Murray, 1986.

Benvie, S. *The Encyclopedia of North American Trees.* Toronto: Firefly, 2000.

Bryant, G. (Chief Editor). *Botanica: The illustrated A-Z of over 10,000 garden plants.* Auckland: David Bateman Ltd, 1997.

Callaway, D. *The World of Magnolias.* Oregon: Timber Press, 1994.

Chicheley Plowden, C. *A Manual of Plant Names.* Sydney: Allen & Unwin, 1968.

Coates, A. M. *The Quest for Plants.* Studio Vista, 1969.

Harrison, R. E. *Handbook of Trees and Shrubs.* Auckland: Reed, 1981.

Haworth-Booth, M. *Effective Flowering Shrubs.* London: Collins, 1965.

Hillier, H. G. *The Hillier Manual of Trees and Shrubs.* Newton Abbot: David & Charles, 1992.

Johnson, A. T. and Smith, H. A. *Plant Names Simplified.* London: W. H. & L. Collingridge, 1931.

Kim, Tae-Wook. *The Woody Plants of Korea.* Seoul: Kyo-Hak, 1994.

Krussmann, G. *A Manual of Cultivated Broad Leaved Trees and Shrubs.* Oregon: Timber Press, 1984.

Krussmann, G. *A Manual of Cultivated Conifers.* Oregon: Timber Press, 1984.

Lancaster, R. *Travels in China.* Woodbridge: Antique Collectors Club, 1989.

Lance, R. *Woody Plants of the Blue Ridge.* Self-published, 1994.

Little, E. *National Audubon Society Field Guide to North American Trees.* New York: Alfred Knopf, 1980.

Petrides, G. *Eastern Trees.* Boston: Houghton & Mifflin, 1988.

Petrides, G. *Trees and Shrubs.* Boston: Houghton & Mifflin, 1986.

Pizzetti, I. and Cocker, H. *Flowers: A Guide for your Garden.* New York: Abrams, 1975.

Tripp, K.E. and Raulston, J.C. *The Year in Trees.* Oregon: Timber Press, 1995.

van Gelderen, D.M., de Jong P.C., Oterdoom H.J., van Hoey Smith J.R.P. *Maples of the World.* Oregon: Timber Press, 1994.

Whittle, T. *The Plant Hunters.* Oxford: Heinemann, 1970.

Index

Page numbers in italics indicate that the plant is illustrated.

Acknowledgements

I would like to thank everyone who helped in any way with the making of this book. Most especially, I would like to thank Pat Greenfield for the fantastic photographs; Gail Church for help, advice and support; Theresa Greally for running my nursery and garden during my absence at the computer; Michael Hudson, the most knowledgable plantsman I know, for being my botanical dictionary; and Graham Smith for leading me onto this book-writing trail.

I would also like to thank Tracey Borgfeldt, Jennifer Mair, Errol McLeary, Brian O'Flaherty and Paul Bateman for editing and producing the book, and for frequent advice.

Thank you to the people who hosted us during research trips and who helped with photographs, especially Garry Clapperton, Michael and Carola Hudson, Bob and Lady Anne Berry, John and Fiona Wills, David and Noeline Sampson, Mr Min Pyong-gal (Mr Ferris-Miller), Peter Cave, Graham Smith, Andrew Brooker, Greg Rine, Gwyn Masters, Mark and Abbie Jury, Ian McDowell, Ian and Sheryl Swan, Tony Barnes and John Sole, Margaret and Richard Hodges, Margaret Bunn, Les Taylor, Alan Jellyman, Frédéric Tournay and Geoff Bryant.

And my thanks to Joni Mitchell, for the music to write to.

Picture credits

All photographs by Pat Greenfield except for the following:
Geoff Bryant p. 15 *Acer griseum*; p. 65 x *Fatshedera lizei*; p. 81 *Larix decidua*; p. 127 *Rhus typhina*; p. 132 *Sorbus aria*; p. 133 *Sorbus aucuparia*.
Glyn Church p. 20 *Actinidia kolomikta*; p. 61 *Euonymous fortunei*; p. 74 (bottom right) *Buxus sempervirens*; p. 84 *Liquidambar formosana*; Frédéric Tournay p. 83 *Lindera benzoin*.